# REGULATING BUSINESS BY INDEPENDENT COMMISSION

By Marver H. Bernstein

GREENWOOD PRESS, PUBLISHERS
WESTPORT, CONNECTICUT

Library of Congress Cataloging in Publication Data

Bernstein, Marver H
    Regulating business by independent commission.

    Reprint of the ed. published by Princeton University
Press, Princeton, N. J.
    Includes bibliographical references and index.
    1.  Industry and state--United States.  2.  Indepen-
dent regulatory commissions--United States.  I.  Title.
[HD3616.U47B5  1977]    322'.3'0973        77-2985
ISBN 0-8371-9563-2

Grateful acknowledgment is made for use of quotations
by permission from
*Public Administration and the Public Interest,*
by E. P. Herring. Copyright, 1936.
McGraw-Hill Book Co., Inc.

Originally published in 1955 by Princeton University Press,
Princeton, N.J.

Reprinted with the permission of Princeton University Press

Reprinted in 1977 by Greenwood Press
A division of Congressional Information Service, Inc.
88 Post Road West, Westport, Connecticut 06881

Library of Congress catalog card number 77-2985
ISBN 0-8371-9563-2

Printed in the United States of America

*TO SHEVA*

# ACKNOWLEDGMENTS

Much of the research and writing connected with publication of this volume has been financed by grants from the Research Committee of Princeton University and from research funds made available to me by Princeton University as a bicentennial preceptor during the period 1951-1954. The study was stimulated by Elmer B. Staats, who, as executive assistant to the director of the budget and later as assistant director of the Bureau of the Budget, encouraged me to undertake a series of studies for the Bureau of the activities of the various independent regulatory commissions. In this work I was closely associated with William D. Carey, then budget examiner in charge of the Bureau's activities concerning the independent commissions, who directed my studies and provided wise and perceptive counsel.

Colleagues at Princeton University have been extremely generous with their time and helpful in their comments and advice. I am especially grateful to William Beaney, Harold W. Chase, William Ebenstein, George A. Graham, and Paul J. Strayer. Helen Fairbanks, librarian of the Public Administration Collection of the Princeton University library, has been helpful far beyond the call of duty. I appreciate the willingness of the editors of *The Journal of Politics* to publish Chapter 7 as an article in the May 1954 issue in substantially the form in which it appears in this book. I am deeply grateful to Sheva Bernstein for aid and advice for which mention here can be merely a token acknowledgment. Finally, I wish to record my gratitude to the Research Committee of Princeton University for financial aid that made publication possible and to the editors of Princeton University Press for their help in clarifying the text and eliminating errors.

# CONTENTS

*ix*

# CONTENTS

Regulating Business
by
Independent Commission

# INTRODUCTION

ONE of the most significant phenomena in the evolution of American political institutions in the last 100 years has been the growth of public regulation of economic life. Exercising controls over certain industrial practices and over particular industries has become a normal activity of government in an industrialized, urbanized society. Since the birth of the Interstate Commerce Commission in 1887, the independent regulatory commission has become a major institution of public regulation of economic affairs. It is now commonly regarded as an adequate, satisfactory, and even ideal instrument of governmental control. Political progressives have relied upon it as an agent of reform, and the regulated interests have accepted it as the appropriate governmental instrument of regulation.

Despite this general acceptance, the theory and practice of the independent commission have been subject to criticism.[1] Commissions, it is charged, are influenced excessively by the groups subject to regulation and are too easily

[1] Criticism of commissions is not a recent development. One of the early attacks on government commissions in England was published by Joshua Toulmin Smith in 1849, in a book suggestively titled *Government by Commissions Illegal and Pernicious*. Smith identified the government commission with current trends which he deplored, especially the general expansion of governmental activities at the national level. A commission, he said, "is had recourse to whenever anything is wanted to be done which ought not to be done at all; whenever any crotchet or new experiment is sought to be enforced on the land by which that shall be done in an irregular and jobbing way which there are recognized and legal means of doing in a regular and open way; whenever a false expression on public opinion is desired to be vamped up on any matter; whenever it is desired effectually to *shelve* any important question to which attention has been called; whenever it is desired to conceal any flagrant job or blunder; whenever it is desired to shift off responsibility from those to whom it properly belongs; whenever there are any needy men, hangers-on of the Whig party, who happen to be out of a situation, and who are in want of a comfortable *plant* in the breeches-pocket of the people" (p. 22; italics his). Smith denounced all types of commissions and committees as agents of centralization of government and therefore as subverters of local self-government. He regarded administrative commissions as "always the chosen instruments of schemers and of the enemies of public liberty" (p. 157), and as destructive of responsibility (p. 254).

3

molded into instruments to protect private interests. Some observers have suggested that they are ineffective and will remain so as long as they are caught in the political cross fire between the president and Congress. Other critics assert that commissions have failed to develop a reasonable regard for the public interest in their area of jurisdiction and, therefore, do not operate satisfactorily as democratic instruments of economic regulation. These critics suggest that the political facts of life have been largely ignored in relying upon commissions as policy-making bodies in highly controversial areas of public policy.

Some elements of current dissatisfaction with commissions can be identified readily. First of all, the controversial nature of the commission highlights the wide differences of opinion concerning the political advantages and disadvantages of specific types of governmental regulation. The bitterness and invective that characterize public discussion in this field, especially in connection with legal aspects of the treatment accorded private parties subject to public regulation, stem from personal beliefs and convictions about the desirability and practicability of certain regulatory policies. Arguments over the procedures of regulatory commissions are frequently symptomatic of conflicting views about the substantive policies of regulation.

Over and above differences of opinion on substantive policy, advocacy of and opposition to the independent regulatory commission as an organizational vehicle for governmental control of the economy reflect varying approaches to the process of administrative regulation. In general, the commission form has been championed by those who believe that administrative regulation requires a high degree of expertness, a mastery of technical detail, and continuity and stability of policy. These requirements, it is alleged, can only be met by a board of commissioners functioning in a neutral environment, free from partisan political considerations. Congress tends to regard the commission as a bulwark against excessive centralization of power in the executive branch. Industries generally prefer

4

regulation by commission rather than by executive departments of the government in the belief that commissions will treat them more favorably.

Critics of independent commissions have emphasized their administrative deficiencies. It is claimed that commissions do not plan their operations satisfactorily and do not coordinate their regulatory policies with the major economic policies of executive departments. These critics minimize the organizational advantages of the commission form of regulation and stress the importance of executive integration of regulatory policies in the framework of national economic policy.

Many ideas about the independent commission are based, implicitly or explicitly, upon general political and administrative considerations. For example, thinking about commissions is influenced by attitudes concerning the proper relationship between the legislative and executive branches, the desirability or undesirability of regulatory policies, the general nature of the political process, and administration of government agencies. Current opinions and judgments with respect to the independent commissions usually imply certain ideas about the nature of regulation by government, but these ideas are rarely developed and applied in a systematic way to the work of the commissions.

## Focus of the Study

The literature of economics and political science in the United States deals extensively with certain aspects of governmental regulation. For example, there has been ample study of the development of regulatory policies and the legislative history of various commissions. Their constitutional status has been analyzed thoroughly. Economists have discussed policies and techniques of regulation, while political scientists have described the administrative operations of independent commissions. Legal periodicals and texts abound with studies of legal problems of governmental regulation, especially the administrative procedures of adjudication and judicial review of administrative decisions.

Studies of independent commissions by students and practitioners of public administration deal usually with the organizational characteristics of commissions and their advantages and disadvantages as compared with those of executive departments. This study disavows a concern with the alleged virtues of structural neatness or organizational clarity in commissions. Considerations relating to span of control and policy coordination are important and sometimes crucial, but commissions cannot be dismissed merely because they do not fit neatly into a symmetrical organizational pattern of the executive branch of the government. Commissions cannot be rejected just because they may offend certain organizational principles, nor can modifications in organization, in themselves, produce certain desirable changes in administrative regulation.

Until 1940 the independent commissions remained the most important instrument of national regulation of business. With the end of the Great Depression, and the beginning of World War II, their impact on economic affairs began to decline. Nevertheless, most students of commissions assume that they still play a highly strategic role in the process of governmental control of economic life. Recovery from depression, promotion of agriculture and labor, economic mobilization for defense and war, governmental underwriting of a minimum standard of living for all Americans, and a growing reliance upon fiscal and monetary policies have lessened the significance of commissions. Increasingly, key economic controls are being administered by single-headed agencies responsible to the president. Moreover, Congress does not hesitate, on occasion, to assign regulatory tasks to the executive departments. On the whole, the attention given to the commissions has been out of proportion to their increasingly marginal role in the regulation of economic affairs. Regulation by commission no longer encompasses the most central and critical economic activities of the national government.

The objective of the present study is threefold: (1) to evaluate critically the role of the independent regulatory commissions, (2) to develop a more realistic concept of the process of governmental regulation, and (3) to appraise the independent commission as an agent of governmental regulation at the national level.

In this analysis governmental regulation of economic life is viewed as a highly political process embracing some of the most controversial areas of public policy. Administrative regulation is conceived as a public activity that raises fundamental questions concerning the role of government in modern society. Regulatory agencies are shown to be affected directly and indirectly by well-organized private groups seeking to identify their interests with the general welfare. Because the stakes of regulation are high, the achievement and maintenance of effective control require great political skill, dynamic political leadership, and widespread public support.

In order to evaluate the independent regulatory commissions as instruments of governmental regulation of business, one must examine the environment in which they have developed and matured as well as the objectives and ideas of their promoters. The rise and decline of commissions should be analyzed in the light of major developments in the institutional process of government and the adjustments made by regulated industries to the regulatory process. In the following chapters an attempt will be made to show that regulation by commission is ideally suited to the slow development of regulatory policies at best and to annulment of legislative policies of regulation at worst. The study examines the charge that regulation by commission encourages a showing of favoritism to the regulated groups, a narrow view of the public interest, an unrealistic concept of the democratic political process, and the maintenance of localism and particularism in Congress.

This work appraises the independent regulatory commission in terms of its capacity to develop political responsibility, act in the public interest, generate administrative vitality and initiative, and maintain independence from regulated groups. It focuses attention on the relations of commissions to Congress and the Presidency. It analyzes the factors of expertness and continuity of policy in commission operation. It outlines the problems facing commissions in developing public support for and compliance with their programs.

In this study seven agencies are regarded as independent regulatory commissions.[2] They include: *two which regulate transportation carriers*, the Interstate Commerce Commission,[3] which regulates rail, motor, and water carriers in interstate commerce, and also pipelines and freight forwarders, and the Civil Aeronautics Board, which regulates air carriers;[4] *two which regulate other utilities*, the Federal Power Commission, which regulates the interstate transmission of electricity and manufactured and natural gas, and the Federal Communications Commission, which regulates the telephone, telegraph, and radio and television

[2] The United States Maritime Commission, established in 1936, remained an independent regulatory commission until 1950, when it was transferred to the Department of Commerce and renamed the Federal Maritime Board. It is subject to some but not full departmental control by the Secretary of Commerce. Although the Board of Governors of the Federal Reserve System is usually considered to be an independent regulatory commission, it is excluded from this classification in the present study. Its members are appointed for staggered terms of fourteen years at a salary of $16,000. It is not required to abide by Civil Service rules in employing its staff but does so voluntarily. It is financed not by appropriations made available by Congress, but by a special system of contributions from member banks of the Federal Reserve System. The close relation between the management of the public debt and the maintenance of economic stability through monetary controls has placed a special burden of policy integration upon the Federal Reserve System. The rather unique position of the Federal Reserve System as a governmental institution suggests that little is gained and much may be lost by retaining the classification of the Board of Governors as an independent regulatory commission.

[3] From 1887 to 1889 the Interstate Commerce Commission was located in the Department of the Interior, and the annual reports for 1887 and 1888 were transmitted to Congress through the Secretary of the Interior.

[4] Since 1940 the Department of Commerce has provided certain administrative services for the CAB.

broadcasting industries; and *three which regulate practices in special fields,* the Federal Trade Commission, which seeks to prevent monopolistic and unfair trade practices and false and misleading advertising, the National Labor Relations Board, which regulates the labor practices of employers and unions, and the collective bargaining process, and the Securities and Exchange Commission, which regulates security exchanges, the issuance of securities, and public utility holding companies.

Members of the seven commissions are appointed for staggered terms by the president with the consent of the Senate. Terms of office range from five to seven years, and the salary of commissioners is $15,000.[5] The president designates the chairmen of all independent commissions except the Interstate Commerce Commission. Administrative responsibility is vested by law in the chairmen of the SEC, FPC, CAB, and FTC. The requirement of bipartisan membership of the commissions applies to all except the NLRB. The power of the president to remove members of commissions is limited to removal for cause[6] in the case of the ICC, NLRB, CAB, and FTC. Annual appropriations for individual commissions for the 1955 fiscal year ranged

[5] The typical commissioner's salary of $15,000 compares with the following prevailing salaries for government officials:

| | |
|---|---:|
| Head of a Cabinet department | $22,500 |
| White House aides | 15,000-20,000 |
| Under secretaries of Cabinet departments, Comptroller-General, Director of the Budget, heads of the General Services Administration and Housing and Home Finance Agency | 17,500 |
| Director of the CIA, director of the Export-Import Bank, members of the Council of Economic Advisers, directors of the FDIC, members of the Board of Governors of the FRS, director of the FBI, director of the Federal Mediation and Conciliation Service, Assistant Director of the Budget, Assistant Comptroller-General, chairman of the Civil Service Commission | 16,000 |
| Members of the National Mediation Board, Railroad Retirement Board, TVA, Civil Service Commission, U.S. Tariff Commission | 15,000 |

[6] Removal for cause usually means removal because of neglect of duty, inefficiency, or malfeasance in office.

from $3.8 to 11.7 million. Total personnel employed by the seven commissions on August 31, 1954 was 6,645. In terms of costs of operation and personnel employed, the independent regulatory commissions have a negligible effect on total federal employment and appropriations for administrative agencies. The information above is broken down by commissions in Table 1.

## TABLE 1. *Data on Independent Regulatory Commissions*

| Commission | Number of Members | Salary ($) | Term of Office (Years) | Bipartisan | Designation of Chairman by Law | Administrative Responsibility Vested in Chairman by President | Removal by President | 1954 Estimated Obligations ($Million) | 1955 Appropriations ($Million) | Number of Employees, August 31, 1954 |
|---|---|---|---|---|---|---|---|---|---|---|
| CAB | 5 | 15,000 | 6 | Yes | By president | Yes | Removal for cause only | 3.8 | 3.8 | 541 |
| FCC | 7 | 15,000 | 7 | Yes | Since 1950, by president | No | Removal power discretionary | 7.6 | 6.5 | 1,110 |
| FPC | 5 | 15,000 | 5 | Yes | Since 1950, by president | Yes | Removal power discretionary | 4.3 | 4.1 | 653 |
| FTC | 5 | 15,000 | 7 | Yes | Since 1950, by president | Yes | Removal for cause only | 4.1 | 4.0 | 588 |
| ICC | 11 | 15,000 | 7 | Yes | Selected annually by the Commission | No | Removal for cause only | 11.3 | 11.7 | 1,868 |
| NLRB | 5 | 15,000 | 5 | No | By president | No | Removal for cause only | 9.0 | 8.4 | 1,183 |
| SEC | 5 | 15,000 | 5 | Yes | Since 1950, by president | Yes | Removal power discretionary | 5.0 | 4.7 | 702 |

Source: U.S. Statutes, Civil Service Commission reports of monthly employment, *The United States Budget for the Fiscal Year Ending June 30, 1955*, and Appropriation Acts for 1955.

# CHAPTER 1

# The Intellectual Development of the Regulatory Movement: 1887-1920

## *Commissions as Reflectors of American Political Institutions*

ALTHOUGH regulatory commissions have usually been treated as isolated or independent governmental phenomena, they illustrate remarkably well some basic trends in the development of American economic and political institutions. For example, the laissez-faire bias in popular American thinking has placed the commission on the defensive. Popular preference for a self-regulating economy operating according to natural economic law rather than governmental direction challenges one of the premises upon which the idea of the commission is based, namely, that government commissions are needed to help save capitalism from destroying itself through its own abuses. Even though the laissez-faire notion scarcely offers a reasoned and plausible explanation of the way in which the economy operates, it still forms the basis of much popular thinking about economic affairs.[1] Herein lies part of the explanation for the existence of the obstacles to modification of the statutory powers of commissions and for the lack of flexibility and adaptability in their operating methods. The commissions are a reminder that the economy is not self-regulating, but evidently a price of their survival is minimal interference with the operation of the private sectors of the economy.

The laissez-faire approach in popular economics is supported by the political view that the scope of governmental power should be limited to the protection of life and property and the maintenance of certain essential services. The

[1] The most lucid statement of traditional laissez-faire thinking in economics is found in the first half of J. Kenneth Galbraith, *American Capitalism*, Houghton Mifflin Co., Boston, 1952.

notion that the least government is the best has had much the same effect on the commissions as laissez-faire economic thinking. Operating in an environment frequently hostile to the expansion of government services and activities, commissions tend to define their goals in extremely limited terms and to be hesitant in upsetting traditional ways of doing business. The timidity displayed by commissions in developing their policies and programs probably reflects the ambivalence of public thinking about the legitimacy of substituting public for private decision in economic matters.

The American tradition of political opportunism and a high regard for performance have led occasionally to piece-meal extensions of governmental activity despite deeply felt notions about the inherent evilness or efficiency of government. The acceptance of governmental expansion has frequently been called "pragmatic." Our refusal to take political ideas more seriously and to formulate programs of public action consistent with basic political ideas suggests an anti-theoretical and anti-intellectual approach in American politics. Therefore, it should not be surprising that independent commissions, which did not develop in accordance with any firm convictions about the proper scope of governmental activity, should turn out to be the product of very hazy and perhaps naïve notions about the democratic political process.

In the absence of a systematic political theory of the democratic state, the mainstay of public debate about the regulatory commissions has been slogans and catchwords. The Supreme Court, the bar, Congress, and the executive branch have contributed to public confusion by using slogans to describe and analyze the work of the independent regulatory commissions. The labeling of independent commissions as quasi-judicial and/or quasi-legislative to distinguish them from executive or administrative agencies has produced unworkable and undefinable concepts. These labels have proved meaningless for purposes of analysis but not for purposes of political persuasion. For example, descriptions of commissions by analogies to the separation-of-powers doctrine have bolstered the position of those anxious to insulate the regulatory commissions from the influence and political strength of the president.

The reluctance of the businessman to stand for elective political office and his willingness to participate in the political process through brokers of one kind or another have been important characteristics of the business community since the latter part of the nineteenth century. Up to 1950 the political field was left open for the only professional group interested and equipped for political responsibility, namely, the lawyers. Lawyers became residuary legatees of the political process and imposed a strong legal bias on our political institutions and discussions of public issues. In *The Promise of American Life*, published in 1909, Herbert Croly discussed the dominance of lawyers in American politics in these words: "The American would claim, of course, that the unprecedented prominence of the lawyer in American politics is to be explained on the ground that the American government is a government by law."[2] "When they talk about a government by law, they really mean a government by lawyers; and they are by way of believing that government by anybody but lawyers is really unsafe." Croly concluded that government by law is not only government by lawyers, but "is a government in the interest of litigation. It makes legal advice more constantly essential to the corporation and the individual than any European political system."[3]

Whether or not Croly overemphasized or overstated his case, the influence of the lawyer in the field of governmental regulation of business has been pervasive and in some respects possibly decisive.[4] Lawyers have preempted the term

[2] Herbert Croly, *The Promise of American Life*, The Macmillan Co., New York, 1909, pp. 132-133.

[3] *ibid.*, p. 136. For an essay on the historic meaning of "government of laws," see Jerome Frank, *If Men Were Angels*, Harper and Brothers, New York, 1942, pp. 190-211.

[4] For the pungent comments of Senator Paul H. Douglas on lawyers in the governmental process, see U.S. Congress, Senate, Committee on Labor

"administration" to refer to the adjudication of cases by government agencies. They have been far more inventive in devising ways of protecting individual interests than in promoting the public interest without violating individual rights. The American Bar Association from time to time has taken the position that the regulatory agencies cannot be trusted because they are prone to "administrative absolutism" and incapable of dealing justly in matters involving rights of private parties. Prevailing legal opinion has been in favor of prescribing a fixed code of procedure that the regulatory agencies must follow, widening opportunities for judicial review of administrative decisions, and giving parties affected by regulations all possible opportunity to participate in the making of regulatory decisions. In terms of research and study, more attention has been devoted to the legal aspects of regulation by commission than the political, administrative, and economic aspects. The concentration on legal problems of regulation reflects the general American preoccupation with legal matters in discussions of controversial political questions.

## The Growth of Regulation

Public regulation of business affairs developed as a reaction to the process of industrial and economic change that has drastically altered the shape of American society. Technological advances increased the rate of industrialization, as well as the urbanization of the population. While heavy immigration in the latter part of the nineteenth century was absorbed throughout the country, the cities and the new industrial areas were the principal points of immigrant settlement.

The forces of industrialization and urbanization set in motion a chain of trends and events that made the United States a dominant world power within a few decades. A national railroad system helped to create regional and

---

and Public Welfare, *Hearings on the Establishment of a Commission on Ethics in Government*, June-July 1951, 82nd Congress, 1st session, p. 221.

national markets, and the population became increasingly mobile. Industrial cities became safety valves for discontented rural populations, and steady streams of immigrants provided a source of cheap labor for factories and trades. The corporation, with the privilege of limited liability, became the principal vehicle of economic expansion together with its progeny, the trust, the pool, and the holding company.

In the 1870's and 1880's groups that were dissatisfied with their share in the profits of industrial development found little comfort or pride in rapid economic growth. Farmers, small businessmen, and workingmen organized to protect and promote their respective interests. New labor organizations attempted to unionize the workingman and to lower his working hours and increase his wages. In an effort to relieve discontent caused by a decline in agricultural prices from 1870 to 1896, farmers established protest organizations for the protection of rural interests. Small businessmen and farmers joined forces in demanding governmental action to outlaw discriminatory abuses practiced by the railroads. When state railroad legislation proved inadequate, farm and small business groups that were dependent on railroads to carry their goods to market turned for help to the national government. Their prolonged agitation for public protection resulted in the passage in 1887 of the Interstate Commerce Act, which established the first national commission for the regulation of economic affairs.

Characteristics of the growth of regulation of business in the United States have been set forth clearly by Fainsod and Gordon.[5] First, the growth of regulation "has not been the product of any farsighted plan or design or the result of any thoroughly worked out rationale or theory. Step by step, whether in state or nation, it has represented a series of empirical adjustments to felt abuses. It has been initiated

[5] Merle Fainsod and Lincoln Gordon, *Government and the American Economy*, rev. edn., W. W. Norton and Co., Inc., New York, 1948, esp. pp. 3-80 and 221-236.

by particular groups to deal with specific evils as they arose, rather than inspired by any general philosophy of governmental control."[6] Second, groups demanding governmental regulation of certain industrial practices turned first to local governments. As it became clear that these governments could not provide satisfactory public protection against economic abuses, demands for regulation were shifted to the states and then to the national government. To a considerable extent, national regulation has been symptomatic of the inability of state and local governments to meet the insistent demands of politically effective groups for public regulation of business. Third, although the New Deal did expand significantly the scope of public regulation, it did not originate the movement to regulate economic life. Fourth, the expansion of governmental regulation of the economy in the United States has been accompanied by similar developments in other industrialized countries. While regulation by commission has tended to be a unique American experience, governmental control of economic affairs in one form or another has been a universal trend in modern times. And fifth, regulation is largely a product of the clash of organized private economic interests seeking to utilize governmental powers for the enhancement of private interests.[7]

The history of national regulatory commissions can be divided conveniently into six chronological periods: (1) 1837-1887: experiments in regulation of business by state governments. (2) 1887-1906: agrarian reform and the ICC. (3) 1906-1917: the Progressive reform movement that led to the establishment of the Federal Trade Commission in 1914. (4) 1920-1929: postwar normalcy, during which were established the original Federal Power Commission (in 1920) and the Federal Radio Commission, the predecessor

[6] *ibid.*, p. 226.

[7] This point is developed particularly in Merle Fainsod, "Some Reflections on the Nature of the Regulatory Process," in C. J. Friedrich and E. S. Mason, eds., *Public Policy, 1940*, Harvard University Press, Cambridge, 1940, pp. 297-323.

of the Federal Communications Commission (in 1927). (5) The 1930's: depression and economic recovery, and the creation of the Securities and Exchange Commission, the Federal Communications Commission, the National Labor Relations Board, the U.S. Maritime Commission, and the Civil Aeronautics Board. (6) Since 1940: mobilization for war and defense.

Each of these periods will be discussed in order that we may understand more fully the context and environment in which the national regulatory commission developed.

### State Experimentation in Regulation

Recent research has shown clearly that governmental control of economic life originated before the Civil War. Studies of the attempts of selected states, including Pennsylvania, Massachusetts, New Jersey, and Virginia, to promote, guide, and regulate their economies in the period from 1790 to 1860 demonstrate conclusively that relations between the states and economic life have always been close and intimate.[8] Hartz, who analyzed the effort of the state of Pennsylvania to promote and regulate industrial development within its boundaries, concluded that the "objectives of economic policy cherished by the state from the Revolution to the Civil War . . . ramified into virtually every phase of business activity, were the constant preoccupations of politicians and entrepreneurs, and they evoked interest struggles of the first magnitude. Government assumed the job of shaping decisively the contours of economic life."[9]

This effort of states to regulate, guide, and promote economic activity within their boundaries subsided after the

[8] See Louis Hartz, *Economic Policy and Democratic Thought*, Harvard University Press, Cambridge, 1948; John William Cadman, *The Corporation in New Jersey*, Harvard University Press, Cambridge, 1949; Oscar and Mary Handlin, *Commonwealth*, New York University Press, New York, 1947; Carter Goodrich, "The Virginia System of Mixed Enterprise: A Study of State Planning of Internal Improvements," *Political Science Quarterly*, vol. 64, September 1949, pp. 355-387.

[9] Hartz, *op.cit.*, p. 289.

beginning of the Civil War. Technically, the use by state legislatures of the charter of incorporation as a regulatory device was inherently sound and effective. After the Civil War the major regulatory development was the formation of the Granger movement to fight the political battles of discontented farmers. The Granger movement opposed the railroads, denounced monopoly in general, deplored the existence of the middleman, and advocated cheap money and easy credit to relieve economic distress. In midwestern states like Iowa, Minnesota, Illinois, and Wisconsin, state legislatures enacted statutes prohibiting abusive railroad practices and establishing maximum rates for freight and passenger transportation. Solon Buck, the historian of the Granger movement, commented that "on the whole, it is not too much to say that the fundamental principles upon which American regulation of railroads by legislation has developed were first worked out in the Granger states of the Northwest during the decade of the Seventies."[10] The Granger movement, for a time, succeeded in several states in establishing and maintaining a commission with power to fix maximum rates for railroads, prevent discriminatory short-haul clauses, maintain competition on the railroads, and outlaw free passes to public officials. And more significantly, the movement supported the agitation for national regulation of railroad rates.

Despite the close association of government and economic life in the period both before and after 1860, the post-Civil War era, except in the case of the temporary successes of Granger legislation, was nurtured on the myth of *laissez faire*. Although the doctrine of *laissez faire* in its original formulation allowed considerable scope for governmental action, its nineteenth century popularization held that government should have nothing to do with economic affairs except that it should safeguard the rights of private property. The great expansion of American industry after the Civil War strengthened a limited concept

[10] Solon J. Buck, *The Granger Movement*, Harvard University Press, Cambridge, 1913, p. 205.

of the state and a narrow view of the proper scope of governmental activities. In popular thinking, business existed independent of government, and government remained an independent entity in American society. The implication was that business existed first and was then subjected to unwarranted control by the government. Although the facts of economic life and governmental practice cried out against this interpretation, the view persisted that government and business lived in two separate spheres and would coexist in peace and prosperity so long as government made no attempt to usurp the functions of private business. Paradoxically, *laissez faire*, as a doctrine of limited state intervention in economic affairs, became the central dogma of American conservatism during the period in which individualism was gradually disappearing as the basis of business organization. While the role of the entrepreneur remained crucial, economic enterprise was becoming more and more collectivist in character.

### *1887-1906: Establishment of the Interstate Commerce Commission*

The independent regulatory commission was a product of post-Civil War industrial development. Although the Interstate Commerce Act of 1887 marked the first significant effort of the national government to regulate economic affairs since the expiration of the charter of the second Bank of the United States in 1836, the advocates of national railroad legislation did not feel that they were violating the principles of political *laissez faire*. They offered no countertheory of the relationship between government and the economy. National regulation of railroad transportation was supported primarily by economic groups that were more individualistic in outlook than the large corporations that opposed the commission idea. Furthermore, since one of the main objectives of the Act was the elimination of monopolistic abuses, the Interstate Commerce Commission was hailed by agrarian and middle-class groups as the protector of individual private enterprise. The economic groups that turned "pragmatically" to the government for protection still maintained the general view that government should interfere as little as possible with economic affairs. In the struggle to use governmental power to promote their private economic interests, these groups were guided more by short-run, "common sense" considerations than basic notions about the relation of government to economic life. They found no embarrassment in maintaining a verbal allegiance to a doctrine of limited government that did not quite square with their efforts to bend public power to private ends.

As Cushman records in his definitive legislative history of the national commissions, the Act of 1887 was the culmination of a twenty-year struggle for legislation during which more than 150 bills were introduced in Congress providing for some variety of federal control over railroads.[11] The Act placed the new Commission in the De-

11 Robert E. Cushman, *The Independent Regulatory Commissions*, Oxford University Press, New York, 1941, pp. 40-41. The leader in the drive to enact railroad legislation was Judge Reagan, who represented Texas in the House from 1857 to 1861 and from 1875 to 1887, and in the Senate from 1887 to 1891. Reagan succeeded in getting the support of the House for a bill which contained rather drastic regulatory provisions that relied on the ordinary courts for enforcement. The Senate tended to take a more conservative view of the railroad problem. In 1883 Senator Cullom of Illinois introduced a bill providing for a federal railroad commission but without the more stringent prohibitions of discriminatory and monopolistic practices of the Reagan bill. Despite an adverse report on the Cullom bill from the Senate Commerce Committee, the Senate passed the bill in January 1885. In order to break the deadlock between the House and Senate bills, the Senate followed Cullom's proposal to establish a select committee of five to study the problem of railroad legislation. Cullom's views about the need for a regulatory commission with limited powers prevailed in the Senate Commerce Committee, and the Cullom bill was passed in 1886 and sent to the House. Judge Reagan, as chairman of the House Committee on Interstate and Foreign Commerce, substituted the Reagan bill, which the House passed. Congress adjourned in the summer of 1886 before the conference committee could arrive at a compromise measure.

In October 1886 the Supreme Court decided the Wabash case (Wabash, St. Louis, and P.R. v. Illinois, 118 U.S. 557 [1886]), holding that the states, even in the absence of federal regulation, could not regulate interstate railroad transportation. This decision, together with the decision in the Railroad Commission cases (116 U.S. 307 [1886]), which upheld the legality of the state regulatory commission, "exerted a profound influence upon

partment of the Interior and gave the Secretary of the Interior general supervision over the housekeeping activities of the Commission, its budget and supplies, and the appointment and compensation of its employees. The Commission's annual report was transmitted to Congress by the Secretary of the Interior. Twice the Secretary requested that Congress take the Commission out of the Department. Finally, in 1889, Congress abolished the Secretary's powers of supervision, and the Commission became completely independent.[12]

According to Louis Brownlow, the Commission achieved full independence because of a historical accident, the antipathy of Senator Reagan of Texas for President Benjamin Harrison, who was elected in 1889: ". . . Mr. Reagan of Texas, the author of the interstate commerce bill, said that since a railroad lawyer named Ben Harrison had been elected President, he did not trust the President any more with this matter, so he invented the . . . independent commission. Thereafter any bill or regulatory matter that came to the Interstate and Foreign Commerce Committee resulted in the appointment of a commission."[13]

The first full-scale discussion of the advantages and disadvantages of the regulatory commission at the national

---

the conferees struggling to effect a legislative compromise between the Senate and House bills" (Cushman, *op.cit.*, p. 44). The conference committee reported a compromise bill in December 1886 which accepted the Senate demand for an interstate commerce commission together with some of the more drastic regulatory provisions of the Reagan bill. Despite the opposition of the railroads, both houses passed the measure, which was signed by President Cleveland in February 1887.

[12] 25 Stat. at L. 855, Act of March 2, 1889.

[13] U.S. Congress, Senate, Committee on Labor and Public Welfare, *Hearings on the Establishment of a Commission on Ethics in Government*, June-July 1951, 82nd Congress, 1st session, Mr. Brownlow's testimony at p. 213. Brownlow's story is somewhat misleading, although it apparently reflects Reagan's views accurately.

The Secretary of the Interior exercised only nominal control over the Commission. In addition, Cushman states that there was no suggestion in the debate on the Interstate Commerce Act that location in the Department of the Interior was incompatible with the idea of independence. See Cushman, *op.cit.*, p. 62.

level is contained in the hearings and debates on the Inter-state Commerce bills and on the final compromise bill worked out in conference committee. Cushman has summarized these arguments about the commission as a technique for regulation.[14]

ARGUMENTS IN FAVOR OF A COMMISSION

1. A commission would provide flexible and expert administration of railroad regulation. Since railroad problems were complex and intricate, the traditional mechanism of enforcing inflexible laws through court processes would not work here.

2. The commission, as an expert body, would aid Congress in the planning of regulatory policy. As a continuing administrative body, it "could accumulate experience and ideas which could be passed along in the form of legislative recommendations."

3. The commission would defend the public and shippers against the railroads and "protect the rights of those whose resources left them otherwise defenseless." The commission would serve as "the poor man's court."

4. The commission would serve as a tribunal to adjust the conflicting interests of the railroads and save the railroads from the effects of cutthroat competition.

5. The commission would render a valuable service to the courts, which would make final decisions in particular matters.

6. The experience of the states and of Great Britain was cited to support the concept of a strong commission.

MAJOR ARGUMENTS AGAINST A COMMISSION

1. Through the exercise of its discretion, the commission could soften the force of the regulatory statute. As the Grange testified, "We want an absolute law, if you can consistently give it to us, and we do not want our justice strained through a commission, because our experience

14 Cushman, *op.cit.*, pp. 45-61.

with a commission . . . is that they are not only worthless, but worse than worthless."

2. Appointments to the commission would be influenced by the railroads, and the commission would represent railroad interests. Judge Reagan said in 1886 in the House debate: ". . . I shall fear that the railroad interests will combine their power to control the appointment of the commissioners in their own interest. We all understand how easy it is for a few persons controlling larger interests to unite their influence to carry out their wishes. . . . The notorious facts as to how railroad managers have corruptly controlled Legislatures, courts, governors, and Congress in the past give us sufficient warning as to what may be expected of them in the future. It is not to be supposed that they would directly approach any President of the United States and corruptly propose to secure the appointment of commissioners in their own interests; but the vast resources which they control, with the power of levying any tribute they please on the commerce of the country to secure means for the employment of men, enables them to control the best legal and business talent of the country, and would enable them to procure influential men in their interest to appeal to the President in the name of justice and on account of capacity to appoint such men as would serve their purposes."

3. The commission would become "the football of politics." The bipartisan requirement would impose political bias upon the commission.

4. The job of railroad regulation was too vast for one commission or agency of the government to handle.

5. The establishment of the commission would create delays and obstructions to effective regulation.

6. State commissions had fallen short of their promise and had failed to provide effective regulation in the public interest.

As Cushman points out, the hearings and debates did not discuss the question of the independence of the commission. "The word independence does not appear in the legislative debates and the problem itself escaped any direct consideration." However the requirement of bipartisan membership was regarded as an important guarantor of impartiality.

CHARACTERISTICS OF COMMISSION REGULATION: 1887-1906

Other forces were at work in the evolution of the commission as a major device of governmental regulation of industry. During the nineteenth century the character of economic regulation shifted gradually. At first it was essentially legislative. State legislatures granted charters to railroad promoters and passed general and special laws defining the legal position of railroads. *Ad hoc* legislative committees from time to time investigated railroad operations and proposed new legislation to protect the community and the shippers from discriminatory railroad practices. For the enforcement of railroad laws, individuals and the government relied upon the judicial process. As the courts proved their inability to deal with complex economic relationships in railroad management, attention was centered on the possibility of devising an administrative mechanism which would be more flexible than the legislature and more competent than the judiciary in dealing with complicated economic matters. The transition from legislative and judicial control to administrative control was marked by the search for new techniques to take the place of older ones that no longer satisfied the demand for regulation.

Second, the commission developed partly in response to the felt need for a new type of administrative agency to handle a new type of problem. Older executive departments were regarded as unsuitable for the rapid development of new regulatory techniques. Moreover, at the time the commission was established at the national level of government, there was almost no comparable activity carried out by an executive department. The Civil Service system had been established only four years before the creation of the ICC, and the merit principle had been extended only to a small number of government employees. The departments did not appear to offer a creative environment for regulatory administration. Faith was placed rather in the new commission, which would presumably be unhampered by fixed operating precedents and, therefore, might have a greater opportunity to rise above the average level of administrative competence of the executive departments.

Third, the commission seemed more promising than the executive departments with respect to the development of a high degree of expertness and the capacity to handle difficult and technical regulatory problems. The nature of railroad regulation was sufficiently different from the ordinary work of administrative agencies to require a degree of specialization. It was felt that executive departments could not provide the expertness and specialization that the regulatory process required. The commission, it was argued, would give continuing attention to problems of regulation and remain relatively free from partisan political considerations. It would be able to act more expeditiously and with a more comprehensive grasp of the regulatory problem than the courts. It offered some hope of achieving, in a complex economic field, an expertness that would enable both Congress and the courts to function more effectively.

Fourth, after the Fourteenth Amendment became effective, the courts used the commerce and due process clauses of the Constitution to invalidate most of the efforts of the states to regulate the economy and promote the public welfare. Demands for public protection against business abuses appeared to be blocked by the judiciary. As a result, agrarian and other protest groups experienced a certain amount of disenchantment and frustration with respect to the courts and the bar. The courts were accused of extraordinary delays in handling problems growing out of regulatory legislation, lack of sympathy with regulatory objectives, and lack of the specialized knowledge required to deal intelligently with complex economic data. The judicial process itself was regarded as deficient for purposes of regulation. Courts dealt only with cases brought before them and could not initiate cases on their own motion. Their procedures were slow and costly. Courts, moreover, depended on the parties to a proceeding to develop the facts in a controversy. They had no independent means of investigation and could exercise little initiative in discovering relevant facts.

Distrust of the judiciary played an important role in strengthening the case for transferring regulatory responsibilities to an administrative agency. As it turned out, however, the judiciary maintained its pivotal position in the determination of regulatory policies by reviewing administrative decisions. Courts were not reluctant to substitute their opinion of regulatory policy for the judgment of a commission. The railroads employed highly paid lawyers to discover the most effective means of hampering and obstructing the work of the ICC. Justice Harlan, in his dissent in the Alabama Midland case in 1897, asserted: "Taken in connection with other decisions defining the powers of the Interstate Commerce Commission, the present decision, it seems to me, goes far to make that Commission a useless body for all practical purposes, and to defeat many of the important objects designed to be accomplished by the various enactments of Congress relating to interstate commerce. The Commission was established to protect the public against the improper practices of transportation companies engaged in commerce among the several states. It has been left, it is true, with power to make reports, and to issue protests. But it has been shorn, by judicial interpretation, of authority to do anything of an effective character."[15]

Fifth, despite the success of the courts, both before and immediately after the creation of the ICC, in maintaining their key position in the determination of regulatory policy, the judicial pattern of procedure carried a considerable

[15] Interstate Commerce Commission v. Alabama Midland Ry. Co., 168 U.S. 144, 176 (1897).

appeal for the new commissioners. The first chairman of the ICC, Judge Thomas M. Cooley, not only gave the new agency great prestige but also established a pattern of operations closely resembling that of a court of law. The ICC embarked on a case-by-case consideration of regulatory matters from which it has scarcely deviated since 1887. Although administrative regulation was devised in part to overcome the disadvantages of the legislative and judicial processes, the ICC failed to develop techniques required for administering novel, experimental, and complex regulatory policies. It regarded itself as a tribunal for the adjudication of disputes between private parties, rather than an aggressive promoter of the public interest in railroad transportation.

The obstacles to the development of a more aggressive and forthright approach by the ICC were formidable. It was widely believed that the judicial approach would aid the Commission to establish itself in the controversial area of regulatory policy. The courts presumably would look more favorably upon the decisions of the Commission if it operated more like a court than an administrative agency. Members of the Commission seemed to prefer the known virtues of the judicial model to the untried advantages of the administrative process. Legal actions by the railroads held up the activities of the Commission and forced it to fight its regulatory battles in the courts. Moreover, the very novelty and controversial character of administrative regulation and the strong opposition of the railroads to regulation provided a strong case for a conservative and cautious approach.

The period from 1872 to 1896 was marked by political discontent. The two major political parties were almost evenly matched in terms of popular votes in presidential elections, although the Republican party managed to capture the Presidency throughout these years with the exception of Cleveland's two terms. The period was also one of the richest in the literature of American political reform. Agrarian and labor unrest influenced the popular radicalism of Henry George and Edward Bellamy and led to the formulation of the Omaha platform of the Populist party of 1892. Christian Socialism added a deeply religious and emotional basis to political reform. Henry Demarest Lloyd stirred thinking citizens with the publication of *Wealth against Commonwealth* in 1894. Simple-minded panaceas for economic and political problems vied with serious analyses for popular approval.

## JUSTICE BREWER'S VIEWS

The liberal currents of political and economic thought moved the defenders of the *status quo*, especially lawyers and judges, to impassioned justification of the going state of affairs. One of the major spokesmen for the rights of private property against interference by government, state or federal, was Justice J. David Brewer of the United States Supreme Court. In a speech before the New York State Bar Association in January 1893, Brewer stated the conservative position on the rights of property and the evils of governmental regulation of the economy. Brewer denounced the "movement of coercion" that was destroying the rights of private property. The attack on private property, according to Brewer, took two forms: "the improper use of labor organization to destroy the freedom of the laborer, and control the uses of capital," and the "regulation of the charges for the use of property subjected, or supposed to be, to a public use."[16]

Brewer regarded regulation of the economy as an attack upon private property and as an effort to undermine "that long self-denial and saving which makes accumulation possible" and "the business tact and sagacity which bring about large combinations and great financial results." According to Brewer, "that government is best which protects to the fullest extent each individual, rich or poor, high or

[16] Justice J. David Brewer, "The Movement of Coercion," in Alpheus T. Mason, ed., *Free Government in the Making*, Oxford University Press, New York, 1949, pp. 615-616. Other quotations from Brewer are taken from this source.

low, in the possession of his property and the pursuit of his happiness." He opposed the view that judges cannot handle regulatory matters through the regular judicial process and asserted the unique capacity of the judiciary to dispense justice. The proponents of regulation by commission were described as those "who would brook no restraint on aught that seems to make for their gain," "unanimous in crying out against judicial interference," and "constantly seeking to minimize the power of the courts."

"The argument is that judges are not adapted by their education and training to settle such matters as [tariffs for common carriers]; that they lack acquaintance with affairs and are tied to precedents; that the procedure in the courts is too slow and that no action could be had therein until long after the need of action has passed. It would be folly to assert that this argument is barren of force. . . . But the great body of judges are as well versed in the affairs of life as any, and they who unravel all the mysteries of accounting between partners, settle the business of the largest corporations and extract the truth from the mass of scholastic verbiage that falls from the lips of expert witnesses in patent cases, will have no difficulty in determining what is right and wrong between employer and employees, and whether proposed rates of freight and fare are reasonable as between the public and the owners, while as for speed, is there anything quicker than a writ of injunction?

"But the real objection lies deeper. Somehow or other men always link the idea of justice with that of the judge. It matters not that an arbitrator or commission may perform the same function, there is not the same respect for the office, nor the same feeling that justice only can be invoked to control the decision. The arbitrator and commission will be approached with freedom by many, with suggestions that the public, or the party, or certain interests demand or will be profited by a decision in one way; but who thus comes near to the court or offers these suggestions to the judge? There is the tacit but universal feeling that justice, as he sees it, alone controls the decision. It is a good thing that this is so; that in the common thought the idea of justice goes hand in hand with that of the judge; and that when anything is to be wrought out which it is feared may not harmonize with eternal principles of right and wrong, the cry is for arbitration or commission, or something else whose name is not symbolical or suggestive. . . .

"So it is that the mischief-makers in this movement ever strive to get away from courts and judges, and to place the power of decision in the hands of those who will more readily and freely yield to the pressure of numbers, that so-called demand of the majority."

He was "firmly persuaded that the salvation of the Nation, the permanence of government of and by the people, rest upon the independence and vigor of the judiciary."

Brewer's main ideas were quite similar to the position the American Bar Association took in the 1930's with respect to the activities of the regulatory commissions. The alleged inherent arbitrary character of administrative agencies, their tendency toward "absolutism" and denial of justice, the exclusive capacity of judges to dispense justice, the role of the courts in protecting the rights of private property against attack by the majority, by mere "numbers," all these ideas have been developed by the American Bar Association, especially since 1933, and have been adapted to a situation in which the regulatory commission had become well established as an integral part of the institutional structure of regulated industries.

### CHAIRMAN COOLEY OF THE ICC

In one respect Justice Brewer's views about the arbitrary nature of regulatory commissions must have sounded strange to Judge Cooley. As the famous author of the treatise on *Constitutional Limitations*, published in 1868, and the former chief justice of the Michigan Supreme Court, Cooley could scarcely be described as an enemy of private property. Cooley, like Brewer, regarded the judges as the spokesmen for the principle of the unfettered rights of property and as protectors of the *status quo* against the threat of popular power. Regulatory legislation, he felt, violated the law of supply and demand and the higher constitutional law upon which a free government was based. "It is not understood," he wrote, "to be now pretended that any general right to fix the price of commodities or to limit the charges for services can exist as a part of any system of free government."[17] Cooley, however, did not support the proposition that the government did not have a right to interfere in economic affairs under any conditions. "There are some cases in which the legislature is accustomed to limit the charges for services and for the uses of property," and "the exercise of the power is acquiesced in as being rightful."[18] But Cooley insisted that the government had no right to limit the profits earned by economic enterprise. ". . . the capability of property, by means of the labor or expense or both bestowed upon it, to be made available in producing profits, is a potential quality in property, and as sacredly protected by the constitution as the thing itself in which the quality inheres."[19]

In the half-dozen years or so before his appointment to the ICC, Cooley's views on the appropriate limits of government action became more flexible. In 1883 he supported greater regulation in railroad transportation,[20] and in 1886 he advocated arbitration in labor disputes.[21] Cooley was certainly a "safe conservative";[22] as he himself wrote, "Like everything else, to grow soundly, the law must grow slowly, and changes should not come unless their necessity is perfectly clear."[23] When Cooley reluctantly accepted member-

[17] Thomas M. Cooley, "Limits to State Control of Private Business," *The Princeton Review*, March 1878, p. 243.

[18] *ibid.*, p. 243.     [19] *ibid.*, p. 271.

[20] T. M. Cooley, "State Regulation of Corporate Profits," *North American Review*, September 1883.

[21] T. M. Cooley, "Arbitration in Labor Disputes," *Forum*, June 1886.

[22] See the essay on Cooley by Harry B. Hutchins, in William Lewis Draper, ed., *Great American Lawyers*, vol. 7, John C. Winston Co., Philadelphia, 1909, pp. 431-491. According to Hutchins, "Judge Cooley's opinions clearly indicate a safe conservatism" (p. 461).

[23] *American Law Review*, vol. 32, p. 916. For a sympathetic account of Cooley's political views, see O. Douglas Weeks, "Some Political Ideas of

ship on the ICC,[24] his conception of property was altered to the extent that he no longer maintained that public regulation of railroad rates violated sacred property rights and constitutional limitations. His responsibility for enforcing the Interstate Commerce Act ran counter to his earlier published views on the regulation of prices, tariffs, and profits of business enterprise, and his earlier writings were frequently cited against his actions. However, Cooley never gave up his conception of the judicial process as a guarantor of free government, and he succeeded in establishing a judicial pattern of operation for the ICC which has never been basically altered.

Always regarded highly as a man of the utmost integrity, Cooley retired from the Commission in September 1891, broken in health. A fellow commissioner wrote to Cooley on his retirement: "You have organized the National Commission, laid its foundations broad and strong and made it what its creators never contemplated, a tribunal of justice, in a field and for a class of questions where all was chaos before."[25] During the four years he served as chairman of the ICC, Cooley dominated the Commission. He is often cited as being responsible for turning the ICC into a quasi-judicial body and for providing a precedent which future commissions have followed.[26] The quasi-judicial character of commissions would probably have devel-

---

Thomas McIntyre Cooley," *The Southwestern Political and Social Science Quarterly*, vol. 6, 1925-1926, pp. 30-39.

[24] Dorfman writes that "Cooley, in fact, did not want the Interstate Commerce Commission job. He wrote to his wife when rumors of his appointment appeared: 'I really begin to think that I am in danger of being named on the Railroad Commission. . . . I don't think there is anything in it for me to feel elated.'" Joseph Dorfman, *The Economic Mind in American Civilization, 1864-1918*, vol. III, The Viking Press, New York, 1949, p. xx. The Cooley quotation is from a letter of Cooley to his wife on February 11, 1887, and is found in the Thomas McIntyre Cooley Papers, University of Michigan Library.

[25] Quoted in the sketch of Cooley by A. C. McLaughlin, in the *Dictionary of American Biography*, vol. 4, Charles Scribner's Sons, New York, 1930, p. 393.

[26] See William Seagle, in his article on Cooley in *Encyclopedia of the Social Sciences*, vol. 4, The Macmillan Co., New York, 1931, p. 357.

oped with or without Cooley. The commission seemed to threaten the monopoly of judges to say what the law is. In order to overcome the hostility of the courts, the commission assumed the protective coloration of the judicial environment. Moreover, the Supreme Court was on the way toward making reasonableness of rates a judicial question at the time the ICC was establishing itself. Cooley was following, therefore, an emerging pattern of governmental regulation, and, at the same time, he was contributing to its design.

The early history of the Interstate Commerce Commission reveals that the first national commission developed during a period in which the political majority effectively demanded reform but did not know how to translate its demands into regulatory policy and administrative operations. Congress willingly passed on to the Commission the burden of resolving policy issues that it could not resolve itself. The unsympathetic attitude of the courts toward administrative regulation, the opposition of the railroads, and the prevailing conservatism with respect to expanding governmental powers produced an atmosphere hostile to regulation. The Commission's survival in such an environment was defined in terms of a slow evolution of regulatory policy within the framework of judicialized operation. The Commission's adjustment to political antagonism was symbolized by its emphasis on expert, impartial, passive administration.

## *1906-1917: The Progressive Reform Movement*

The second period in the development of the independent regulatory commission was the period of Progressive reform from 1906 to 1917. The Progressive reformers were mainly middle-class, urban citizens who were shocked by the corruption and fraud of American politics at the turn of the century. Progressive reform was a manifestation of moral uplift and indignation directed at the degradation of American politics. Its principal preoccupations were the purification of political life and the achievement of a higher measure of social justice for most Americans. It embraced government as a primary instrument of social reform, provided honest men could obtain power. It fought for decency and against corruption and privilege.

The struggle of the Progressives against fraud and corruption led them to regard politics as essentially evil and venal. They offered three techniques for purifying the political process. The first was to reform the electoral process by tinkering with the machinery of voting. The secret ballot, the short ballot, the direct primary, the direct election of senators, and the initiative, referendum, and recall were relied upon to eliminate the grafter and the crook from political dominance. The second was to make government more efficient and economical through the use of principles of sound management and business methods. The third technique was to escape from politics by allocating major governmental responsibilities to regulatory commissions which would somehow be kept out of "politics" and would be free to make decisions on the basis of expert knowledge and impartial judgment.

KEEPING OUT OF POLITICS

The Progressives had an abiding faith in regulation, expertness, and the capacity of American government to make rational decisions provided experts in the administrative agencies could remain free from partisan political considerations. They confidently believed that regulation would overcome privilege, restore decency, and save industry from its own avarice and self-destruction. The modern commission movement was given a great impetus by the establishment of the state public utility commissions of New York and Wisconsin in 1907 and the Federal Trade Commission in 1914.

The great error of the Progressives was their belief that it was possible to avoid corruption by taking regulation of economic affairs out of politics. Escape from politics became a panacea to purify and uplift the political process. The Progressives made the mistake of assuming and hoping that economic regulation by government can and should be made nonpolitical. As Herring has stated, ". . . the control of business remains too controversial and too vital a political issue to be entirely relegated to any commission independent of close control by the policy-formulating agencies of the government. Administrators cannot be given the responsibilities of statesmen without incurring likewise the tribulations of politicians."[27]

The genteel reformers of the Progressive period made their most significant contribution to American politics in their analysis of specific problems in the fields of conservation, industrial competition and monopoly, adulteration of foods and drugs, regulation of railroads and public utilities generally, and financial manipulations. While their analysis of contemporary problems was frequently sound and sometimes brilliant, their cures were often naïve and simple-minded. Most of them believed that the key to effective regulation lay in the creation of a commission that would act in behalf of the public interest but nevertheless remain aloof from and untouched by regulated groups. Regulation by commission was to be regulation without tears.

## THE CASE OF THE PROGRESSIVES FOR THE COMMISSION

The typical Progressive position on the regulatory commission was summarized by Samuel Dunn in 1914:

"The development of the policy of regulation by commission has grown out of the belief that lawmaking bodies, courts, and the ordinary executive officials are incompetent to deal with problems raised by unsatisfactory relations between public utilities and the public. The legislatures cannot deal with these problems intelligently and effectively, because to do so requires a body possessing expert knowledge and in practically continuous session. In both of these respects lawmaking bodies are deficient. The courts cannot satisfactorily deal with these problems because they

27 E. P. Herring, *Public Administration and the Public Interest*, McGraw-Hill Book Co., Inc., New York, 1936, p. 138.

lack expert knowledge and have many other kinds of business to transact, and because their slow, cumbrous, and formal process excludes classes of evidence which, while logically irrelevant to a lawsuit, are precisely the considerations that would influence a business man in deciding a business proposition. The ordinary executive or law-enforcing officials are incompetent to deal with the problems of regulation because they lack expert knowledge, because they have other and entirely different duties to perform, and because a regulating body should approach its work in a judicial spirit which is incompatible with the executive spirit by which the ordinary law-enforcing officials should be animated.

". . . The disqualifications of legislatures, courts, and ordinary executive officials for the regulation of business suggest some of the qualifications that ought to be possessed by the members of regulating commissions. Ability, expert knowledge, fairness in utterance and act, moral courage to resist public opinion when it is wrong, as well as to enforce their duty on refractory public utility managements when they are wrong—these are the prime essentials."[28]

However, Dunn found that the members of the commission usually lacked the desired qualifications and had little or no expertness or business experience. He concluded his statement in this manner: "The true theory of regulation seems to be this: The management of public utilities should be left in the hands of the owners or those that they choose to represent them. The regulating commissions should be strong enough in personnel and statutory power to exercise corrective authority over the managements when the acts of the managements are unreasonable and unjust to the public. And such commissions having been created, should be left free to perform their duties without interference from the public or any public body except the courts, and then only when it can be shown that the commissions have exceeded their constitutional authority in a manner plainly

[28] Samuel O. Dunn, "Regulation by Commission," *North American Review*, vol. 199, February 1914, pp. 205-206.

unreasonable and unjust to the concerns over which their jurisdiction extends. The success of regulation will probably be in proportion to the consistency, fairness, and integrity with which we carry out these principles."[29]

Justice Brandeis supported the commission idea strongly. He advised Wilson during his campaign for the Presidency in 1912 that the Sherman Act, whose economic soundness he upheld, should be supplemented by additional legislation which would be enforced "by a Federal Board or Commission."[30] Brandeis was concerned primarily with the capacity of the government to deal effectively with the monopoly problem. He recommended to Wilson the creation of a board or commission to aid in the enforcement of the Sherman Act and did not question the advisability of relying on such a body. He was content to recommend that the board or commission should have ample powers of investigation, should cooperate with the Department of Justice in enforcing the Sherman Act, and should lend its aid to small businessmen who had been injured by the large corporations. In Brandeis' view, a commission would be successful if it had "knowledge, comprehensive, accurate, and up to date, of the details of business operation."[31]

OPPOSITION TO THE COMMISSION IDEA: 1906-1917

Despite the general trust in the device of the independent regulatory commission, the commissions and the commission idea were not free of criticism. Justice Holmes was one of those who had little confidence in the work of a commission. In a letter to Pollock in 1910, Holmes wrote: "Of course I enforce whatever constitutional laws Congress or somebody else sees fit to pass—and do it in good faith to the best of my ability—but I don't disguise my belief that the Sherman Act is a humbug based on economic ignorance

29 *ibid.*, p. 217.

30 From a letter from Brandeis to Governor Wilson on September 30, 1912, containing some suggestions for a letter by Wilson on trusts, p. C, in the Baker Manuscripts, Harvard University Library.

31 *ibid.*, pp. J and K.

and incompetence, and my disbelief that the Interstate Commerce Commission is a fit body to be entrusted with rate-making, even in the qualified way in which it is entrusted. The Commission naturally is always trying to extend its power and I have written some decisions limiting it (by constructions of statutes only)."[32]

One of the sharpest attacks on the commission form came from the proponents of municipal as opposed to state regulation of public utilities. In 1913 the Minnesota Home Rule league studied regulatory legislation and administration in Wisconsin, New York, New Jersey, and Maryland. In view of its earnest bias against state regulation, it was not surprising that the League found the state commissions defective. It accused the utility companies of preferring state regulation of utilities on the ground that they could influence state regulation more effectively than municipal administration. The report of the League charged "that the public utilities sought to write the laws and have done so in some cases, and modified the laws in others; have used their influence upon the appointing power to name men of 'right' minds on the commission; have sought to influence the attitude and to control the action of the commissions after appointment." The League found that "with few exceptions the men occupying positions on state commissions had no technical or special qualifications for the work, and in most cases were selected for services past or prospective to the appointing power, and in other cases were men with public utility or allied affiliations, or men known to have a strong corporation or property bias." As a final thrust, the League charged that "the public utilities have found that state regulation serves their purposes admirably; that it protects them from unreasonable rates, assures them liberal dividends, imposes no unreasonable service obligations, by means of the indeterminate permit assures the permanency of their investment with opportunity to get out in the event of purchase by the city at a

[32] Mark DeWolfe Howe, ed., *Holmes-Pollock Letters*, vol. I, Harvard University Press, Cambridge, 1941, letter of April 23, 1910, p. 163.

price considerably above the legitimate investment in the property, increases the market value of their securities, and, finally, in effect, through state supervision of bond and stock issues, guarantees the integrity of their securities."[33]

In *The Promise of American Life* Herbert Croly, the leading political thinker of the Progressive movement, expressed a qualified dissent from the general approbation of the commission: "One may well hesitate wholly to condemn this government by commission, because it is the first emphatic recognition in American political and economic organization of a manifest public responsibility. In the past the public interests involved in the growth of an extensive and highly organized industrial system have been neither recognized nor promoted. They have not been promoted by the states, partly because the states neither wanted to do so, nor when they had the will, did they have the power. They have not been promoted by the central government because irresponsibility in relation to national economic interest was, the tariff apart, supposed to be an attribute of the central authority. Any legislation which seeks to promote this neglected public interest is consequently to be welcomed; but the welcome accorded to these commissions should not be very enthusiastic. It should not be any more enthusiastic than the welcome accorded by the citizens of a kingdom to the birth of a first child to the reigning monarchs,—a child who turns out to be a girl, incapable under the law of inheriting the crown. A female heir is under such circumstances merely the promise of better things; and so these commissions are merely an evidence of good will and the promise of something better. As initial experiments in the attempt to redeem a neglected responsibility, they may be tolerated; but if they are tolerated too long, they may well work more harm than good."[34]

[33] These quotations are taken from Stiles P. Jones, "State versus Local Regulation," *Annals*, vol. 53, May 1914, pp. 96-97. The reply to these charges is in G. C. Mathews, "The Truth about State Regulation of Utilities in Wisconsin," *Annals*, vol. 54, July 1914, pp. 303-320.
[34] Croly, *op.cit.*, p. 361.

Croly's criticism of the commission movement stressed two points. First, he felt that the commissions would divide responsibility for business decisions between public and private officials and would be driven to harmful interference with business efficiency. He thought that commission supervision of an industry would destroy its flexibility and spirit of enterprise. Second, he thought that the approach of the regulatory commissions was too limited. "They endeavor to solve the corporation problem merely by eradicating abuses, the implication being that as soon as the abuses are supervised out of existence, the old harmony between public and private interest in the American economic system will be restored, and no more 'socialistic' legislation will be required."[35]

Croly did not find the experience of the state regulatory commissions either hopeful or edifying, primarily because of the success of the railroads in dominating the state commissions and in acquiring political influence. He wrote: ". . . once the railroads had acquired their political influence, they naturally used it for their own purposes. They arranged that the state railroad commissioners should be their clerks, and that taxation should not press too heavily upon them. They were big enough to control the public officials whose duty it was to supervise them; and they were content with a situation which left them free from embarrassing interference without being over-expensive."[36]

More than any other contemporary analyst of the political scene, Croly understood the requirements of effective regulation in the public interest. He realized that the commission was not merely a pawn in the struggle between private interests but had a part to play in the definition of public policy and the identification of the public interest. He had no simple pressure group theory about the nature of the political process. He appreciated the need for expertness in administration but insisted that the expert in administration must also be a promoter of and propagandist

[35] *ibid.*, p. 367.     [36] *ibid.*, p. 353.

for the public welfare. He must, said Croly, "share the faith upon which the program depends for its impulse." The expert, he said, "qualifies for his work as an administrator quite as much by his general good faith as by his specific competence." Effective regulation must be based on "an honest popular aspiration for social improvement, a sufficient popular confidence in the ability of enlightened and trained individuals to find the means of accomplishment, and the actual existence for their use of a body of sufficiently authentic social knowledge." Croly urged the commissions to abandon their passive role of deciding the individual cases brought to their attention by the private parties and instead to assert the public interest aggressively. The duty of the commission, according to Croly, "is not to prevent injustice to individuals and, consequently, to society, but to discover and define better methods of social behavior and to secure cooperation in the use of such methods by individuals and classes. It is, as we have seen, a social promoter, and its whole work is one of circumspect but intrepid social enterprise."[37]

Among the Progressive reformers of his day, Croly was one of the very few who did not regard the commission as the ideal type of government agency for the administration of economic controls. He understood that technical competence alone was not sufficient to bring about effective regulation, and he appreciated the need for a more positive approach toward the formulation of regulatory policy. In his judgment, informed, popular support for regulation was a prerequisite of satisfactory performance. He had at least an inkling of the problem of securing the compliance of the regulated.

The case which the Progressive reformers made for regulation by commission throws considerable light on the Progressive reform movement as a whole. Jane Addams, one of the leaders of the humanitarian movement which became part of the Progressive reform movement, had a

[37] Herbert Croly, *Progressive Democracy*, The Macmillan Co., New York, 1914, pp. 361-369.

deeper understanding than her reform colleagues of the nature of the reform movement itself. She was critical of the well-to-do men of the community who "think of politics as something off by itself; they may conscientiously recognize political duty as a part of good citizenship, but political effort is not the expression of their moral or social life. As a result of this detachment, 'reform movements,' started by business men and the better element, are almost wholly occupied in the correction of political machinery and with a concern for the better method of administration, rather than with the ultimate purpose of securing the welfare of the people. . . . This accounts for the growing tendency to put more and more responsibility upon executive officers and appointed commissions at the expense of curtailing the power of the direct representatives of the voters." These reform movements, said Miss Addams, tended to become negative and to lose their educational value for the mass of the people. In their drive for reform, the reformers, she said, "have in mind only political achievements which they detach in a curious way from the rest of life, and they speak and write of the purification of politics as a thing set apart from daily life."[38]

Jane Addams' view of the politician diverged sharply from the prevailing reformist view. She regarded the politicians as genuine leaders of the community because they give "a social expression to democracy." As she stated, "They are often politically corrupt, but in spite of this they are proceeding on a sounder theory." They may often do their work badly, "but they at least avoid the mistake of a certain type of business men who are frightened by democracy, and have lost their faith in the people." In her analysis, corruption was not an adventitious growth in society but a reflection of one of its basic elements. "We are all involved in this political corruption," she said, "and as members of the community stand indicted. This is the

[38] These quotations and those which follow are from Jane Addams, *Democracy and Social Ethics*, The Macmillan Co., New York, 1915, pp. 221-277.

penalty of a democracy,—that we are bound to move forward or retrograde together. None of us can stand aside; our feet are mired in the same soil, and our lungs breathe the same air."

Perhaps Miss Addams' most cogent point is the charge that the reformers by and large misunderstood the nature of the political process. She wrote: "Would it be dangerous to conclude that the corrupt politician himself, because he is democratic in method, is on a more ethical line of social development than the reformer, who believes that the people must be made over by 'good citizens' and governed by 'experts'? The former at least are engaged in that great moral effort of getting the mass to express itself, and of adding this mass energy and wisdom to the community as a whole." Miss Addams recognized that the good citizen found it hard to grasp the character of the democratic process. The good citizen, she said, "is more or less a victim to that curious feeling so often possessed by the good man, that the righteous do not need to be agreeable, that their goodness alone is sufficient, and that they can leave the arts and wiles of securing political favor to the self-seeking." She concluded finally that: "The success of the reforming politician who insists upon mere purity of administration and upon the control and suppression of the unruly elements in the community, may be the easy result of a narrowing and selfish process. For the painful condition of endeavoring to minister to genuine social needs, through the political machinery, and at the same time to remodel that machinery so that it shall be adequate to its new task, is to encounter the inevitable discomfort of a transition into a new type of democratic relation. . . . The mass of men seldom move together without an emotional incentive. The man who chooses to stand aside, avoids much of the perplexity, but at the same time he loses contact with a great source of vitality."

In its belief in the efficacy of changes in the machinery of government, its faith in the expert, its distrust of the politician, and its habit of viewing government as separate from the rest of society, the movement for the expansion of regulation by commission typified the broader Progressive reform movement of which it was a part.

Mr. Dooley substantially agreed with Jane Addams about the uses of reformers. The reformer, said Mr. Dooley, tries to prevent us from assuming "our nachral condition iv illegal merrimint." He is good at "tellin' us where we are wrong. . . . On'y he don't undherstand that people wud rather be wrong an' comfortable thin right in jail."[39]

In 1906 Mr. Dooley commented:

"Ivry year, whin th' public conscience is aroused as it niver was befure, me frinds on th' palajeems iv our liberties an' records iv our crimes calls f'r business men to swab out our goermint with business methods. We must turn it over to pathrites who have made their pile in mercantile pursoots iv money wheriver they cud find it. We must injooce th' active, conscientious young usurers fr'm Wall Sthreet to take an inthrest in public affairs. . . . Th' wather department is badly r-run. Ilict th' presidint iv th' gas comp'ny. Th' onforchnit sthreet railroads have had thimsilves clutched be th' throat be a corrupt city council an' foorced to buy twinty millyon dollars' worth iv sthreets f'r sixty-four wan-hundherd dollar bills. Oh, for a Moses to lead us out of th' wilderness an' clane th' Augeenyan stables an' steer us between Silly an' What's-its-name an' hoist th' snow-white banner iv civic purity an' break th' feathers that bind a free people an' seize th' hellem iv state fr'm th' pi-ratical crew an' restore th' heritage iv our fathers an' cleanse th' stain fr'm th' fair name iv our gr-reat city an' cure th' evils iv th' body pollytick an' cry havic an' let loose th' dogs iv war an' captain th' uprisin' iv honest manhood again th' cohorts iv corruption an' shake off th' collar riveted on our necks be tyrannical bosses an' prim'ry reform.

". . . What th' business iv this counthry needs . . . is f'r active young pollyticians to take an' inthrest in it an' ilivate

[39] Finley Peter Dunne, *Observations by Mr. Dooley*, R. H. Russell, New York, 1902, p. 172.

it to a higher plane. Me battle-cry is: 'Honest pollytical methods in th' administhration iv business. . . .' "

Mr. Dooley concluded: "It seems to me that th' on'y thing to do is to keep pollyticians an' business men apart. They seem to have a bad infloonce on each other. Whiniver I see an aldherman an' a banker walkin' down th' sthreet together I know th' Recordin' Angel will have to ordher another bottle iv ink."[40]

[40] Finley Peter Dunne, *Dissertations by Mr. Dooley*, Harper and Brothers, New York, 1906, pp. 275-281.

# CHAPTER 2

# The Intellectual Development of the Regulatory Movement: Since 1920

### *1920-1929: Postwar Normalcy*

FROM 1917 to 1920 the commissions were eclipsed by World War I. The task of mobilizing the economy of the country for war overshadowed the activities of the FTC, and the ICC was for all practical purposes abandoned while the U.S. Railroad Administration assumed control of all rail transportation. The political climate of the twenties was distinctly unfriendly to efforts to extend regulation of economic affairs and hostile to the maintenance of current programs of regulation. The period was one of material fulfillment and industrial expansion on a grand scale. But Americans caught in the degradation of the Great Depression, which followed on its heels, remember it for drift and complacency in domestic and international affairs. They remember it for its weak and badly equipped presidents, for its easy acceptance of corruption in high places, for crass selfishness and disastrous isolationism in foreign affairs. As the depression years grow dimmer, historians are more likely to recall the twenties as a period of tremendous growth in corporate wealth, of the application of the techniques of mass production to rich natural resources, and of the great expansion of trades and service industries. As Allan Nevins has remarked, "It was not merely Harding and Coolidge who wanted to go back to the ideas of Herbert Spencer and the policies of William McKinley. A majority of the American people wanted the same."[1]

During the twenties, businessmen acquired a prestige and status in the American community at large which they may never attain again. Interference with the sound judg-

---

[1] Allan Nevins, review of Karl Schriftgiesser, *This Was Normalcy*, in *New York Times Book Review Section*, April 25, 1948.

ment of business leaders was a sin which the country could tolerate only at the price of economic collapse and the loss of individualism. The political figures of the twenties in both parties were essentially dull, unimaginative, cautious men incapable of vigorous leadership. Only Alfred E. Smith and Herbert Hoover among the national politicians commanded respect and admiration as able, competent political leaders. But even Hoover was admired not so much for his political accomplishments as for his stature as an engineer, able bureaucrat, and humanitarian. As Hofstadter has written, "Hoover was one of those bright and energetic businessmen who, precisely because of the ease with which success has been attained in their immediate experience, refuse to learn deeply from anything outside of it."[2]

The decade of the twenties did little to restore the vitality of commissions. Although the Interstate Commerce Commission became more firmly established with expanded authority under the Transportation Act of 1920, it did little to utilize its new powers. The Federal Trade Commission was reduced to an investigative body and was unable to make any progress in developing the law governing unfair trade practices. The Federal Water Power Act of 1920 established a weak, ex officio Water Power Commission with some authority to license water power developments by private interests on public lands and to fix interstate power rates and regulate the security issues of interstate power companies. Until 1928 the Water Power Commission was unable to persuade Congress to appropriate adequate funds for its staff, and it had to depend on a staff borrowed from other agencies. It was finally reorganized as an independent commission in 1930.

Perhaps the most interesting development in the decade of the twenties was the creation in 1927 of the Federal Radio Commission, which was succeeded in 1934 by the Federal Communications Commission. After the federal courts declared invalid in 1926 and 1927 the attempts of

2 Richard Hofstadter, *The American Political Tradition*, Alfred A. Knopf, New York, 1948, p. 289.

the Secretary of Commerce to regulate radio broadcasting through the issuance of licenses, utter chaos developed in that field. As a result, the radio industry demanded some form of public regulation to restore order.

## THE VIEWS OF JOSEPH B. EASTMAN IN THE TWENTIES

There was little critical analysis of, or critical thought devoted to, the subject of regulation by commission during the twenties. One of the few persons who considered the role of the commission in economic regulation was Joseph B. Eastman, almost universally regarded as the most distinguished member of any federal regulatory commission.

In January 1919 Eastman was confirmed as a member of the Interstate Commerce Commission. Although he was only thirty-eight years of age, he had already acquired four years' experience as a member of the Public Service Commission of Massachusetts and spent eight years of devoted effort as secretary of the Public Franchise League in Boston. In the latter capacity he was associated closely with Louis Brandeis, Edward Filene, and other leaders in the fight for adequate regulation of public utilities in Massachusetts. Although he became a leading advocate of public ownership of railroads, a policy which received little support during the twenties, he gradually won distinction as a leading member of the ICC by sheer ability and hard work. His early years on the Commission were rather disappointing because he found the Washington environment uncongenial to his habit of thinking about regulation in broad terms. He wrote to a close friend in 1922: ". . . I am constantly impressed by the difficulty down here of any constructive thinking along broad lines."[3] During the Harding regime Eastman remained aloof from political intrigues. His desire was to keep railroad regulation free from the "turmoil of politics."

In an address before the American Political Science As-

[3] From a letter from Eastman to Judge G. W. Anderson, December 1922, quoted in Claude Moore Fuess, *Joseph B. Eastman—Servant of the People,* Columbia University Press, New York, 1952, p. 125.

sociation in Washington late in December 1927, Eastman stated the accepted concept of the commission as the most appropriate device for public regulation of the economy. "The need for a commission arises . . . when the legislative body finds that particular conditions call for continual and very frequent acts of legislation, based on a uniform and consistent policy, which in themselves require intimate and expert knowledge of numerous and complex facts, a knowledge which can only be obtained by processes of patient, impartial, and continual investigation." Congress itself, said Eastman, could not handle the "vast and painful detail" of railroad rate regulation. Furthermore, ". . . where it is necessary for the Congress to impose upon some agency duties of a strictly executive character, it is both logical and appropriate that an independent commission should be selected as the agency when such duties relate to its sphere of activity." Eastman regarded the commissions as "creatures of the Congress sworn to the faithful per- formance of certain specific duties by impartial, judicial methods." He was opposed to transfer of the commissions to the executive departments on the ground that this would expose the commissions to considerations of partisan poli- tics. ". . . the cold neutrality of the commission . . . ought rather to be safeguarded jealously against precisely such extraneous influences. They are as out of place in the case of a commission as they would be in the case of a court."[4]

Eastman was constantly dismayed by the attempts of the presidents to influence the activities of the commissions through the appointment process. He regarded partisan political appointments as dangerous meddling with mat- ters better left to the impartial discretion of commissioners qualified by experience and training to serve as judicial arbiters. The more evidence was accumulated indicating that appointments to commissions were usually dictated by "political" factors, the more Eastman insisted on the

[4] This address was published in the *Constitutional Review*, vol. 12, April 1928, pp. 95-102, as "The Place of the Independent Commission." Quoted with permission of *The George Washington Law Review*.

overriding need to appoint only qualified commissioners. Even in the case of the ICC, the evidence showed that "while some admirable choices have been made, in a majority of cases political considerations have dominated."[5] Eastman apparently did not consider the possibility of any other kind of adjustment to the intrusion of so-called political factors into a process which was predicated on the unique capacity of the commission for expert, impartial, nonpolitical administration. Since political considerations were antithetical to the commission idea, they had to be rooted out. The fact that they had not been eliminated called only for renewed determination by reformers to restore the integrity of the commissions.

Eastman's concept of the commission was consistent with the arguments made in behalf of the commission idea since the debates on the railroad regulation bills of the 1880's. Although Eastman had a deep understanding of railroad problems, an abiding appreciation of the importance of facts, and a forward-looking attitude on the public questions of the day,[6] he remained true to the tradition of Brandeis and other Progressives in searching for an escape from politics. As a commissioner who stood for more effective regulation of the railroad industry, he did not question either the possibility or the desirability of removing regulation from politics. In his regulatory world, expertness, judicial impartiality, and farsighted action could be achieved only in the nonpolitical atmosphere in which the commissions were supposed to operate. They were incompatible with a political-minded administration.

## The 1930's: Depression Decade

During the 1930's there were significant changes in the

---

[5] Harvey C. Mansfield, *The Lake Cargo Coal Rate Controversy*, Columbia University Press, New York, 1932, p. 193.

[6] Eastman championed government ownership of railroads in the twenties, the prudent investment theory of valuation, programs to prevent holding companies and dummy corporations from exploiting investors, open-market bidding for railroad securities, etc. In 1928 he voted for Alfred E. Smith for president.

place of the independent regulatory commission in the national government and in thinking about its role. The commission developed originally in a period when its activities were the most significant ones undertaken by the national government in the area of economic affairs. However, the demand for governmental activity to provide relief from the effects of the Great Depression and the imperatives of economic recovery turned the spotlight away from the independent commissions and toward new emergency agencies and the expanding programs of older departments, such as the Departments of the Interior and Agriculture.

Despite the greater economic significance of the emergency and recovery activities of the new agencies and the executive departments, interest in the independent commissions did not decline, for several reasons. First, the country was aroused by the stock exchange scandals of 1931-1932 and followed closely the Senate investigation of stock exchange practices. The Securities and Exchange Commission captured the imagination of citizens anxious to prevent fraudulent manipulation of the securities markets and to fix the blame for the depression. Similarly, the establishment during this decade of the Federal Communications Commission, the U.S. Maritime Commission, the National Labor Relations Board, and the Civil Aeronautics Board maintained the interest of the public in regulation by commission. Second, many influential senators and representatives supported the commission as a device for counteracting the trend toward concentration of power in the executive branch under a strong president. During the 1930's Congressional documents dealing with regulatory problems contained many references to the close association of Congress and the commissions and the need to prevent the president from obtaining excessive control over economic regulation. To Congress the commission remained a bulwark against presidential domination.

Third, the American Bar Association spearheaded a campaign to surround the regulatory process with procedures and rules to protect private parties from the possibility of unfair or arbitrary action by the commissions. The lawyers succeeded in focusing the attention of Congress, the courts, and law schools on the growth of administrative discretion and the problems of judicial review and procedural due process growing out of the tremendous expansion of the economic activities of the national government. A succession of reports on administrative law issued by the American Bar Association, debates over the proposal to establish an administrative court to specialize in the review of the decisions of the regulatory agencies, and subsequent attempts to devise a judicialized code of regulatory procedure gave a strong legal cast to public discussion of the role of the independent commission.

During this period two important points were added to the classic controversy on the merits and prospects of the independent commission. First, even though the commission was widely acknowledged to be uniquely suited to the task of adjudicating regulatory controversies, some attacked it as being unfit for this task unless its activity were safeguarded at every point by laws prescribing rules of fair procedure and judicial review. "Administrative absolutism" was the term employed by conservative lawyers to characterize the alleged deficiencies of the independent commissions and other agencies exercising regulatory powers. Interestingly enough, those who criticized the commissions as arbitrary and unfair simultaneously maintained the orthodox position that the impartiality, expert staff, and nonpolitical character of the commissions equipped them well for the task of economic regulation and adjudication. As a result, the commissions were isolated from the support of the general public and then placed on the defensive by attacks on their capacity for fairness.

The second major development in public thinking about the commission during the 1930's was the interest in improving coordination in the administration of governmental activities generally and in the coordination of the regulatory activities of the commissions and national economic policies. The creation of new commissions, the enlargement of the scope of statutory powers of the older commissions, and the increase in the degree of discretion exercised established a prima-facie case for the coordination of regulatory policies governing various forms of transportation and for the coordination of public functions of promotion and regulation of economic affairs. While the regular departments administered promotional rather than regulatory programs it became extremely difficult to maintain a strict classification of regulatory and promotional programs. What was regulatory to one industry might be promotional in its effect on another industry, especially if the industries were rival forms of transportation. The federal aid program for highway construction promoted the motor trucking industry but also made the competitive position of the railroads, at least for the moment, more precarious.

The rising profession of public administration and the great interest generated by the New Deal in the affairs of government focused attention upon the possibilities of achieving a higher level of efficiency in the operation of the national government. Coordination through the administrative supervision of the president presented one of the most attractive and persuasive proposals for strengthening the administrative capacity of the government and for creating a firm line of political responsibility from the president to Congress. Concentration of administrative authority in politically responsible officials was advocated as a major goal of administrative reorganization. "Executive integration" became a byword of administrative practice.

Contradictions seemed to plague the public discussion of regulation. Commissions were alleged to have a capacity for both impartiality and unfairness. They were said to be uniquely appropriate to the administration of regulatory policies because they compensated for deficiencies in the legislative and judicial branches and were safeguarded from the political environment of the executive branch. However, their virtues could be translated into administrative reality only by making them as much like the courts as possible. Their advocates argued that commissions have special advantages in the recruitment of expert personnel, in continuity of policy through the long, staggered terms of the commissioners, and in development of specialization in the handling of complex, technical problems; but evidence failed to support the validity of these claims. The success of state commissions was cited in support of the creation of more national commissions; but the record of state regulatory commissions was generally one of inadequate staffs, low appropriations, meager salaries, and short tenure and highly partisan appointments of commissioners. Commissions were overburdened by details and subservient to their regulated clientele.[7]

The assignment of regulatory duties to commissions was held to be one way of checking the discretionary powers of the president. However, the scope of discretion exercised by the commissions often aroused Congressional suspicion. Vague standards in most regulatory statutes inevitably gave commissions a broad grant of discretionary power. While the business community generally opposed the expansion of governmental authority, it frequently resisted Congressional efforts to restrict the powers of commissions. During the debate on the passage of the Investment Trust bill, Senator Taft expressed concern because pressure for the grant of broad discretionary authority to the SEC came not from the supporters of the SEC or the President but from businessmen who feared that their activities would be hamstrung if the statutory standards became more specific or if the commission circumscribed them with rigid rules. The Senator said: "I may say that one of the great difficulties of the Congress in attempting to avoid the detailed regulation of business, with indefinite power in a Federal bureau, is the fact that in many cases the business-

---

[7] See, for example, Felix Frankfurter, *The Public and Its Government*, Yale University Press, New Haven, 1930, pp. 81-122; William Mosher and Finla G. Crawford, *Public Utility Regulation*, Harper and Brothers, New York, 1933.

men themselves seem to want that kind of regulation. It is so in this case, and so it has been in other cases."[8]

During the depression decade, regulatory commissions, especially new ones, were relied upon for minor patrol duties to prevent American business from destroying itself. But the economic problems facing the country went far beyond the limited scope of economic regulation. The NRA replaced the antimonopoly programs of the FTC and the Department of Justice until 1937, while public works and other programs designed to stimulate recovery took precedence not only in significance but in popular imagination as well.

The history of the commissions throws some light on the American political process. The evolution of the Morgan cases from 1936 to 1941,[9] the reports of the administrative law committee of the American Bar Association, the debate over separation of functions and judicialized procedure, and the strong interest of law schools in administrative adjudication all revealed a strong preference for allowing lawyers to preempt the field of politics as their area of specialization. The report of the President's Committee on

[8] 86 *Congressional Record*, August 8, 1940, pp. 15413-15414. Quoted in Jerome Frank, *If Men Were Angels*, Harper and Brothers, New York, 1942, p. 149; and in Kenneth C. Davis, *Administrative Law*, West Publishing Co., St. Paul, 1951, p. 23.

[9] The Morgan cases include the following: (1) Morgan v. United States, 298 U.S. 468 (1936); (2) Morgan v. United States, 304 U.S. 1 (1937); (2a) petition for rehearing denied, 304 U.S. 23; (3) United States v. Morgan, 307 U.S. 183 (1939); (4) United States v. Morgan, 313 U.S. 409 (1941). They involved the validity of the proceeding before the Department of Agriculture establishing rates for a group of Kansas City market agencies under the Packers and Stockyards Act of 1921. The Supreme Court took the opportunity in these cases to lecture the administrative agency and the Secretary of Agriculture on the essential elements of fair procedure in administrative adjudication. The cases attracted widespread attention and became the occasion for extravagant statements made both by those who favored and by those who opposed the decisions of the Court. Today the cases are significant not because they have established important precedents, but because they are a critical episode in the struggle to balance the administrative requirements for speed and flexibility in adjudicating controversies, on the one hand, and protection of the rights of the private parties against arbitrary and unfair procedure by the regulatory agency, on the other.

Administrative Management provided evidence of the growing concern about the administrative organization of the national government and the role of the president as coordinator and general manager of administrative activity. Lack of interest in systematic development of political ideas is illustrated by the general refusal to take criticisms of commissions seriously enough to force a general reappraisal of traditional Progressive faith in regulation by commission. The battle over proper organization and procedures of commissions was important but somewhat peripheral to the overriding problems of economic recovery—the relief of unemployment and the elimination of poverty in the United States.

CRITICISMS OF THE COMMISSIONS DURING THE 1930'S

The deficiencies of state as well as national regulatory commissions were neither ignored nor unknown in the 1930's. Felix Frankfurter wrote in 1930 that commissions had not achieved the aims for which they were designed and they defeated the purposes for which they were created.[10] In their study of public utility regulation in 1933, Mosher and Crawford found that commissions were swamped with routine work, bound by stereotyped methods, understaffed, and unable to keep pace with problems of regulation.[11] In their judgment, the most serious shortcoming of the commission was the tendency to follow the judicial pattern: "The original conception of the commission as an administrative agency representing the public must be reborn; it must permeate commission practice and procedure in all of its ramifications."[12]

A National Transportation Committee was formed in 1932 on the invitation of a large group of insurance companies, Columbia University, Harvard University, the University of Chicago, and Yale University to study regulatory

[10] Frankfurter, op.cit., p. 93. But he thought that the key problem was the judicial chaos concerning the meaning of fair value (see p. 113).

[11] Mosher and Crawford, op.cit., p. 560.

[12] ibid., p. 40.

problems in transportation. The Committee, consisting of Calvin Coolidge, chairman, Bernard Baruch, Alfred E. Smith, Alexander Legge, and Clark Howell, was similarly aware of the operating deficiencies of the Interstate Commerce Commission. The majority report of the Committee, signed by Baruch, Howell, and Legge, stated that the judicial type of organization of the Interstate Commerce Commission was inappropriate to its work and wholly inadequate to a broader jurisdiction. The Committee found a "lack of incentive or authority in the Commission to plan and to act affirmatively." It characterized the 1932 annual report of the ICC as "eloquent of a somewhat passive attitude toward acknowledged evils."[13]

Former Governor Smith was in substantial agreement with the Committee's report but wished to supplement it as follows: "I find, however, little in recent history to justify the continuance of the ICC as now organized. This implies no criticism of its members. They have attempted to function under an obsolete and unworkable law, and in the face of conditions which call for intelligent planning and leadership as distinguished from endless debate on details. . . . I believe that too much emphasis has been placed on the judicial functions of the ICC, especially on valuation and rate making, and too little on planning and administration. . . . I favor the abolition of the ICC and the creation in its place of a new department of transportation headed by one man, or a one-man bureau head in the Department of Commerce determining policies with the approval of the Secretary of Commerce. What we need is a new transportation system, not endless hearings on a system that does not work."[14]

The Brookings Institution study of national transportation problems in 1933 found that the most serious problem of regulatory policy was the dispersal of regulatory and pro-

13 Report of the National Transportation Committee, reprinted in Harold G. Moulton and Associates, *The American Transportation Problem*, copyright by The Brookings Institution, Washington, 1933, pp. xlix-li.
14 *ibid.*, pp. lxi-lxii.

motional controls over the various forms of transportation among several agencies. It recommended that all transportation functions be centralized under the ICC. It regarded the ICC as competent and thought that through proper "delegation of routine administrative tasks," the commissioners would be able "to plan constructively in national terms."[15]

## THE DEVELOPMENT OF EASTMAN'S VIEWS

The ability of the ICC to plan and develop a broad concept of its regulatory duties was a major concern of Joseph B. Eastman during his term as Federal Coordinator of Transportation from 1933 to 1936. In his speeches and reports to Congress, he developed his mature philosophy of regulation. For Eastman the aims of railroad regulation were broad and comprehensive. "Public regulation used to be thought of merely as a means of protecting the public against extortionate charges. It has that purpose, but it also has a much wider sphere of usefulness. It is needed for the welfare of the industry itself, to promote order and stability, prevent exploitation, and curb destructive competition and waste. The public served needs it, not only as protection against extortionate charges, but to prevent unjust discriminations, promote safety, reliability, and responsibility of service at known and stable rates, reduce expense both direct and overhead, and avoid a financial demoralization which in the end is as destructive to the public interest as it is to the private investors. . . . Our regulation in the past has operated too much on the cure basis, dealing with complaints after they arise but not forestalling them. National planning has been conspicuous by its absence."[16] Eastman deplored the practice of creating separate agencies to deal with different forms of transportation not only because it made planning almost impossible, but because "each regulatory authority will become the

15 *ibid.*, p. 895.
16 Joseph B. Eastman, address before the American Life Convention, Chicago, October 10, 1934, mimeo., pp. 8-9.

partisan of its own form of transportation, and there will be much less chance of proper coordination."[17] Several "separate commissions would each have a partial and fragmentary insight into the situation. . . . Policies would pull in conflicting directions. Those invoking regulation would have a series of tribunals to deal with, with no assurance that what was done by one might not, in effect, be undone by another."[18]

Eastman's comments on the administrative approach of the ICC were meaningful:

"Regulation is essentially a means of curing evils after they arise. It would be better, of course, if they could be prevented in advance. There is need for foresight—for consideration and comprehension of tendencies and trends and where they are leading in order that those that are desirable may be encouraged and those that are undesirable discouraged.

"Anyone who has served on the Commission knows that it is not well adapted to such work. Its functions are performed under quasi-judicial procedure. Its attention is occupied with specific causes which must be decided. It has little time for thought and research on broad lines. It is difficult for commissioners to confer with parties on controversial issues, without constant need of protecting their own position in the event that they are called upon to play the part of judges in actual litigation. Planning and prevention are not matters which can well be handled at off times, or as side issues. They require single-minded, concentrated attention."[19]

Eastman saw no incompatibility between a public-minded, broad-gauged commission and the insistence on maintaining its nonpolitical character. He said: "Experience has shown that public regulation of transportation,

17 Joseph B. Eastman, address before the Bus and Truck Conference, Harrisburg, Pennsylvania, October 20, 1933, mimeo., pp. 12-13.

18 Federal Coordinator of Transportation, *Third Report*, House Document No. 89, January 23, 1935, 74th Congress, 1st session, p. 14.

19 Federal Coordinator of Transportation, *Fourth Report*, House Document No. 394, January 21, 1936, 74th Congress, 2nd session, p. 42.

in view of the many conflicting interests, must be administered by a permanent, independent, and nonpolitical body
having a continuous and dependable policy, and through
definite statutory provisions which register the will of
Congress. This body must not be subject to sudden political
reorganizations; it must act in controverted matters on a
record openly and publicly made—and state the reasons for
its action; and, apart from statutory direction, it must be
as removed from influence by the President, Congress, or
any political agency as the Supreme Court itself. In feverish
times like these, it is easy to lose sight of such principles,
but they are fundamental."[20]

"Keeping out of politics" remained a major preoccupation for Eastman and could be counted on to stimulate
comments on the necessity of maintaining the nonpolitical
character of commission regulation. For example, in his
*Third Report* as Federal Coordinator of Transportation,
he opposed a federal Department of Transportation:

"Transportation is essentially a technical subject and
should be dealt with accordingly. It is vital that it be kept
out of politics, so far as possible. A Cabinet member, concerned with general affairs of State as well as with transportation, would have difficulty in mastering the subject.
Necessarily, also, he is in politics and has no greater permanence than the administration of which he is a part. Thus
there would be frequent shifts in the personnel of a Secretary of Transportation, militating against any continuity
of policy and development of wisdom from experience.

"Here [in the United States], the President and Congress
are often in discord. In these circumstances, a nonpolitical
officer would have an advantage over a Cabinet member
in dealing with the two branches of the Government.

". . . If independent, nonpolitical control over planning,
prevention, and coordination is desired, as it should be,
the Commission is the logical body for this work."[21]

[20] Federal Coordinator of Transportation, *Second Report*, Senate Document No. 152, March 10, 1934, 73rd Congress, 2nd session, p. 37.
[21] Federal Coordinator of Transportation, *Third Report*, *op.cit.*, pp. 28-
29.

Eastman's general views about independent commissions were expressed at a meeting of the National Emergency Council, which was established during the early New Deal days to assist the president in coordinating the policies and activities of executive agencies. At the Council's meeting of December 17, 1935, the problem of conflicting testimony of administration officials before Congressional committees was discussed. President Roosevelt and Postmaster-General Farley emphasized the need for a clear administration policy which all department heads would support. Mr. Eastman, however, opposed prior clearance of testimony of ICC commissioners before Congress:

MR. EASTMAN. I am sure it is not the intention to apply that policy to the independent agencies, such as the Interstate Commerce Commission. That is the servant of Congress and is directed by law to make reports to Congress. The report of the Interstate Commerce Commission does not go to the President. It goes to Congress, and it is in the habit of committees of Congress to ask our opinion on almost every bill that comes up.

PRESIDENT ROOSEVELT. But, again, there you forget that the Constitution provides that the President is head of the Executive branch of the Government. Congress cannot set up the Interstate Commerce Commission as a separate agency and not in any way related to the President. Therefore, the Interstate Commerce Commission I think would be on the wise side if, when asked for an opinion on a matter of policy, they would consult the President.

MR. EASTMAN. Of course there is a question whether the Interstate Commerce Commission is a member of the Executive branch. Its work is largely legislative, established by law. I have served not only in a Democratic Administration, but in a Republican as well. I know it has certain judicial functions.

PRESIDENT ROOSEVELT. Of course it has judicial functions. It has a great many executive functions, and therefore it cannot be wholly disassociated from the Executive.

MR. EASTMAN. It is a sort of mixture of several things.

PRESIDENT ROOSEVELT. It cannot set itself up as a whole department of the Government.

MR. EASTMAN. No, but it does do certain things when it is asked by Congress.

PRESIDENT ROOSEVELT. At the same time, who could say that it meets with the approval of the Executive branch of the Government?

MR. EASTMAN. I think it would cause a great deal of trouble if all the bills referred to the Commission were referred here.[21a]

While Eastman recognized a need to centralize transportation regulation in one agency, he saw no need to coordinate regulatory policy with other economic policies of the government. His conception of the aims of regulation was broad, but his view of techniques and methods was limited. He demanded that the ICC adopt a more aggressive, less passive attitude toward regulation and pay more attention to the prevention of abuses. Eastman understood, however, that the ICC was primarily an administrative tribunal and therefore was unsuited to planning and administrative operations. In his view the commissioners of the ICC could be proper custodians of the public interest provided they remained nonpolitical and impartial and approximated the revered status of the Supreme Court.

THE PROGRESS OF RESEARCH

The 1930's produced the first sizable collection of research studies on the activities of the independent commissions. Sharfman's monumental study of the ICC, Landis's

[21a] This excerpt is from the minutes of the National Emergency Council meeting of December 17, 1935. I am indebted to Professor Lester R. Seligman for bringing these minutes to my attention and for supplying a copy of them.

*64*

*The Administrative Process,* Herring's *Public Administration and the Public Interest,* and other writings provided the beginning of a literature of administrative regulation which went beyond the consideration of narrow legal problems. By 1941 a number of textbooks on government regulation were available, of which the most notable were probably *Government and the American Economy,* by Merle Fainsod and Lincoln Gordon, and *Government and Economic Life,* by a group of Brookings Institution economists headed by L. S. Lyon, M. W. Watkins, and V. Abramson. The first full-scale study of the adjudicatory practices of regulatory agencies was completed in 1941 by the Attorney General's Committee on Administrative Procedure. In 1940 William O. Douglas, the vigorous former chairman of the SEC, published his addresses and public statements about governmental regulation, particularly of financial practices, under the title *Democracy and Finance.* And the first effort to develop a concept of the regulatory process that went beyond a simple application of Bentley's theory of pressure groups was presented by Fainsod in 1940. In a suggestive essay, Fainsod proposed that regulation could be understood as a process if the analysis proceeded on three levels: the conditioning factors which make up the context of regulation, the parties in interest who are concerned with regulation, and the political instruments which provide the regulatory controls. Fainsod was skeptical about proposed reorganizations of the regulatory commissions; he stated that the effectiveness of the commissions goes far deeper than the problem of their relationship to the president and depends on a variety of factors: "It involves personnel reforms, improved relations with Congress and the courts, as well as the president; it requires changes in internal organization and procedure as difficulties are disclosed. In a more profound sense, however, it also involves the existence of a social and economic environment in which regulators can function without meeting frustration. Improvements in the instruments alone and readjustments of their relationships may be powerless to achieve the purposes which they are intended to serve in the absence of a milieu congenial to the realization of these purposes."[22]

Although it may tend to identify the public interest with the interest of its regulated clientele, the commission can be a creative factor in the determination of public policy. It has some opportunity to alter the equilibrium of interests in the process of regulation. It has the capacity to encourage certain interests and to discourage others. Noting that various national commissions have had different experiences in influencing the content of public policy, Fainsod suggested that the ability of a commission to mold the behavior of regulated groups may depend largely upon the strength and clarity of the communal support for effective regulation.[23] Fainsod emphasized the historical and institutional forces that influenced and molded the evolution of regulatory policy and the operations of commissions. He focused attention upon the political and social environment of regulation and the degree of clarity and agreement in the public purposes of regulation. His analysis made the commission meaningful in terms of its political and social milieu and not in terms of its ability to remain aloof from politics.

The period 1930-1941 closed with the publication of Cushman's *The Independent Regulatory Commissions.* Drawing on his researches made for the President's Committee on Administrative Management, Cushman wrote a definitive legislative history of the independent commissions and analyzed the legal position of the independent commission in American politics.[24]

The expanding literature of administrative regulation and the analysis of the activities of the independent commissions had little immediate effect on prevailing views about the commissions. In an address in 1941 on the role

[22] Merle Fainsod, "Some Reflections on the Nature of the Regulatory Process," in C. J. Friedrich and E. S. Mason, eds., *Public Policy, 1940,* Harvard University Press, Cambridge, 1940, pp. 299-320.

[23] *ibid.*, p. 321.

[24] Robert E. Cushman, *The Independent Regulatory Commissions,* Oxford University Press, New York, 1941. Discussed in Chapter 1, above.

of Congress, Speaker Rayburn of the House of Representatives made a typical statement of the fundamentalist view of the commission: "Far from undermining the constitutional authority of the Congress, delegation of authority to administrative agencies is one of the surest safeguards to effective legislative action. It is a procedure which conserves the vital powers of the Congress for vital matters. It removes rather than creates the danger of dictatorship by providing means of making democracy work under the complex conditions of modern life. I am proud to have taken active part in the creation of those commissions and boards. I might name the Federal Trade Commission, the Federal Power Commission, the Tariff Board, the Securities and Exchange Commission, the Federal Communications Commission, and the Federal Reserve Board. The Interstate Commerce Commission is an agency of Congress. It does not perform any act that the Congress has not the power and authority to perform itself. Members of Congress are too busy with other duties, among them fixing great legislative policies, to take the time to go into the finer technicalities of a rate structure or granting the right to a railroad to issue new securities, whether in the form of stocks or bonds. Congress therefore delegated this responsibility to a commission of eleven men with trained experts to work out the details for them. The same might be said of every board and every other commission formed in the government." Rayburn understood the basic dynamic behind Congressional delegation of discretionary authority to administrative agencies. As a Congressman of long tenure, he accepted without question the view of the commission as a creature of Congress, independent of the president, impartial and objective in the performance of its duties, and expert in the handling of complex, difficult matters beyond the capacity of Congress to handle effectively.

## Developments since 1941

Since 1941 five major developments have occurred in the commission system of regulation. First, the overriding demands of mobilization for war and later for defense have effectively dramatized those economic policies and programs that fall outside the scope of the national commissions. The expansion of productive capacity, the acquisition of raw and fabricated materials, the stockpiling of strategic and critical materials, the scheduling of production and the allocation of materials, the stabilization of prices and wages, and the advisory allocation of manpower into priority industries—these dwarfed the programs of the commissions. During World War II some commissions helped to maintain themselves by performing specific tasks for the emergency agencies or by organizing programs that contributed to the successful prosecution of the war. For example, the FTC and the SEC aided the Office of Price Administration in the compilation and analysis of financial and accounting data, while the FCC organized a foreign-broadcast intelligence service. Nevertheless, commissions tended to decline in employment, and the Bureau of the Budget and Congress treated the commissions' requests for appropriations with skepticism.

Second, despite the continuing decrease in the significance of regulation by commissions, their activities frequently affected the programs of the emergency mobilization agencies. For example, the rate-making activities of the ICC led to conflicts with stabilization policies of the Office of Price Administration. The impossibility of insulating the activities of commissions from the impact of the policies of the wartime agencies raised again the problem of coordinating the regulatory programs of commissions with the functions of executive agencies.

Third, in accordance with the Employment Act of 1946, the government undertook, through the machinery of the Council of Economic Advisers and the Congressional Joint Committee on the Economic Report, to promote maximum production, employment, and purchasing power consistent with the maintenance of a free-enterprise economy. Even though achievement under the Act, during the first few years of the existence of the Council and the Joint Committee, has been limited, this legislation marks a significant change in the conception of the responsibility of the national government for promoting and maintaining a prosperous and stable economy. The stabilization commitment of the national government has reduced even further the impact of the commissions' activities and has highlighted the need to coordinate the economic policies of the commissions and the executive departments.

Fourth, in 1946 the campaign to regularize the procedures of the regulatory agencies culminated in the passage of the Administrative Procedure Act. By establishing certain procedures governing the operations of rule making and adjudication by national commissions and other agencies, the Act tended to codify the practices of the commissions. The major effect of the Act was to "strengthen, dignify, and increase the independence of, the position of the officers of the commissions or departments who conduct hearings."[25]

Fifth, and by no means least important, the literature of economic regulation has continued to grow. In his monograph on *The Independence of State Regulatory Commissions*, James Fesler carefully analyzed the record of experience of state public utility commissions and the state commissioners. In *Regulatory Administration*, edited by George Graham and Henry Reining, Jr., a group of scholars and practitioners reviewed the process of regulation in a variety of fields.[26] The development of administrative law has been documented and analyzed in a number of casebooks.[27] A volume of essays in *Administrative Law* by

[25] Emmette S. Redford, *Administration of National Economic Control*, The Macmillan Co., New York, 1952, p. 300.

[26] James W. Fesler, *The Independence of State Regulatory Agencies*, Public Administration Service No. 85, Public Administration Service, Chicago, 1942; George A. Graham and Henry Reining, Jr., *Regulatory Administration*, John Wiley and Sons, Inc., New York, 1943.

[27] See, for example, Walter Gellhorn, *Administrative Law: Cases and Comments*, 2nd edn., Foundation Press, Chicago, 1947; Carl McFarland and Arthur T. Vanderbilt, *Cases and Materials on Administrative Law*, Matthew Bender and Co., Albany, 1947; E. Blythe Stason, *The Law of Administrative Tribunals*, 2nd edn., Callaghan and Co., Chicago, 1947; James

Kenneth C. Davis, published in 1951, provides an excellent analysis of the key legal problems of administrative regulation and incisive comments on the process of regulation in general. The Hoover Commission Task Force on Regulatory Commissions produced a series of monographs on the operations of the national independent commissions which provide basic data on their current activities and administrative practices. In addition, an increasing number of doctoral dissertations and other monographs have described and analyzed the activities of various government agencies in the regulatory field.[28]

As of 1950, the classic case for the independent commission had remained relatively unchanged since its development in the period immediately before and after the enactment of the Interstate Commerce Act of 1887. The Hoover Commission Task Force restated the standard case for the commission. It included the following points in its list of advantages of the commission: (1) its capacity for impartiality and the necessity that regulatory administration remain free from partisan political considerations; (2) the possibility of obtaining better judgment and wisdom from a group than from a single-headed agency; (3) the possibility of achieving a higher level of expertness from commissioners with long, overlapping terms; and (4) the desirability of continuity of policy, which an independent board allegedly could demonstrate better than a single-headed agency. The Task Force, as well as the Hoover Commission itself, recognized the weaknesses of commissions: the delay and slowness inherent in group action, the excessive turnover in commission membership, and the failure of commissions to plan their regulatory work. After weighing the advantages against the weak-

---

Hart, *An Introduction to Administrative Law*, 2nd edn., Appleton-Century-Crofts, Inc., New York, 1950.

28 For an analysis of the current research in the United States on the relations of government and business, see Merle Fainsod, "The Study of Government and Economic Life in the United States," *Contemporary Political Science*, Publication No. 426 of the United Nations Educational, Scientific, and Cultural Organization, Paris, 1950, pp. 465-480.

nesses, the Hoover Commission accepted the conclusion of its Task Force that the independent commission "has an essential place for certain types of government regulation."[29]

## Some Conclusions

The historical context for the study of regulatory administration provides a number of clues for understanding the American experience with the independent commission. These clues can be summarized as follows:

1. Since 1880 Americans have shared a faith in the independent regulatory commission as an efficient and effective instrument of business regulation and as a suitable agent for adjusting economic relationships. Although in each stage of their development commissions have been attacked as inappropriate instruments of governmental regulation, there has been a remarkable predominance of the opinion that the commission form is the best organizational device for such regulation.

2. Commissions have been supported by those who sought to insulate the process of governmental regulation from partisan political forces. In their belief in the possibility and desirability of keeping regulation "out of politics," the advocates of commissions revealed a naïve view of the political process. Since corruption was identified with political life, competent, honest administration could be achieved only in an atmosphere of judicial detachment. They wanted to achieve statesmanship without politics and sought to avoid corruption by diffusing political responsibility.

3. The commission movement has been characterized by a faith in expertness and rational solution of controversial regulatory problems. Regulation has been viewed as a matter of collecting facts and of deciding issues in an unbiased way by examining the facts and applying a rule of law.

4. In contrast to the rapidity of change in technology, in

[29] Task Force on Regulatory Commissons of the Commission on Organization of the Executive Branch of the Government, *Task Force Report on Regulatory Commissions*, 1949, p. 28.

business practices, and in economic organization, regulatory policies have evolved slowly and hesitantly.

5. The faith in regulation of business is based, in part, on the belief that regulation is a process which minimizes governmental interference in economic affairs. There seems to be an implicit belief that the objectives of regulation are narrow in scope and rather self-contained and that the process of regulation is separable from the general context of public economic policies.

6. Original preoccupation with the inadequacies of the legislative and judicial processes gave way gradually to skepticism about the judicial capacity of the commissions and even to charges that they were by nature inherently absolutist and arbitrary. Commissions, it was claimed, could achieve fairness only by following the pattern of the courts in handling cases. Kept on the defensive by the attacks of the bar and the courts, commissions have judicialized their procedures.

7. Commissions have been relegated to minor roles during periods of economic and military emergency and have been regarded as unsuitable instruments for the administration of economic regulations governing retail and industrial prices, industrial and agricultural production, rationing, and other economic transactions.

8. The commission system has altered the concept of private property in regulated areas. In accordance with vague statutory standards, the rules and orders of commissions have established restrictions and conditions concerning the use of property. Thus the commission has become an important factor in the changing concept of property.

9. While criticism of commissions has not been uncommon, it has scarcely influenced opinions and attitudes concerning them. The case against the commission has been ignored for a number of reasons. Public concern with regulation has usually declined shortly after the establishment of a commission, and widespread interest in matters of organization and administration in government has been short-lived. The success of the bar in emphasizing the proc-

ess of adjudication has turned the regulatory process into a technical, legal matter that presumably lies outside the area of experience of the layman. Finally, the attempt to "take regulation out of politics" by assigning regulatory responsibilities to a commission does not insulate the regulatory process from political forces. Instead, it removes the commission from the public spotlight and allows public support for regulation to wither and die.

10. Finally, "taking things out of politics" begins to take on additional meaning. Although regulated industries have usually maintained a steady opposition to proposals to establish additional or more stringent controls over their industries, they have become stout defenders of the commission as the most appropriate instrument of public regulation. The history of commissions indicates that they may have survived to the extent that they have served the interests of regulated groups. As Paul Appleby has suggested, "taking things out of politics" means "taking things out of popular control. This is a frequent device of special-interest groups to effect the transfer of governmental power away from the large public to the special-interest small public."[30]

[30] Paul Appleby, *Policy and Administration*, University of Alabama Press, University, Alabama, 1949, p. 162.

CHAPTER 3

# 'he Life Cycle of Regulatory
# Commissions

Aᴅᴅ.. ᴊɴᴀʟ light can be shed on the process of regulation by the historical pattern followed by commissions from birth to decay. While the experience of each commission has unique elements, the history of commissions reveals a general pattern of evolution more or less characteristic of all. Despite variations in time sequence and the particular circumstances surrounding the creation of each one, the national independent commissions have experienced roughly similar periods of growth, maturity, and decline. These common experiences can be generalized into a rhythm of regulation whose repetition suggests that there is a natural life cycle for an independent commission.

The life cycle of an independent commission can be divided into four periods: gestation, youth, maturity, and old age. The length of each phase varies from one commission to another, and sometimes a whole period seems to be skipped. Some commissions maintain their youthfulness for a fairly long time, while others seem to age rapidly and apparently never pass through a period of optimistic adolescence. Some are adventurous, while others are bound more closely to the pattern established by the oldest commission, the ICC. Such differences add an element of interest and reality to the evolution of commission regulation, but they do not invalidate generalizations about the administrative history of regulation.

### Gestation: Phase 1

Frequently twenty years or more may be required to produce a regulatory statute. First, there is a period of slowly mounting distress over a problem. When the strain or oppression is felt by organized groups or is dramatized

74

by public scandal or economic depression, it may gather momentum quickly. Recognition of acute distress promotes discussion of complaints and abuses and may lead to the organization of groups to fight for governmental regulation to eliminate the source of complaint. Organized groups will seek to widen their membership and strengthen their resources for the legislative battle ahead. Demands will be made on the legislature for corrective action to protect the interests of the groups affected. Throughout this period the organized groups favoring regulation intensify the search for a proposed public policy around which they can rally.

If distress over a problem is sufficiently acute, response to it becomes more articulate. Reform elements agitate vigorously for corrective legislation, while opposition groups battle to maintain the *status quo*. Agitation for reform becomes labeled as socialism, as a denial of freedom and liberty, and as an assault on the American way. Advocates of regulatory reform usually follow a rather "common sense" approach. They demand some specific action to cure a specific evil and avoid philosophical notions about the role of the government, relations between liberty and property, and the advantages of self-reliance and individual independence.

After a period of earnest agitation for enabling legislation, the statute is finally enacted. It represents the culmination of study of what has come to be recognized as an acute public problem. Usually the legislature can be galvanized into action only after the problem has become extremely serious. At first the objectives of the legislation are limited and generalized in somewhat vague language. The approach of the statute tends to be restrictive and to concentrate attention on eradicating abuses. The prevailing view is that the elimination of abuses will bring public and private interests into harmony again.[1]

The statutory mandate lacks clarity. Although it climaxes a prolonged struggle for reform, the policy which it estab-

[1] See comment of Herbert Croly, *The Promise of American Life*, The Macmillan Co., New York, 1909, p. 367, quoted in Chapter 1, page 42, above.

lishes rarely provides clear directions to the new agency. Despite the effort to produce a consensus in favor of *regulation*, the legislation reflects unsettled national economic policy. The agency of regulation is created at the peak of organized fervor for reform. But agitation for regulation rarely produces a first statute that goes beyond a compromise between the majority favoring and the powerful minorities opposing regulation. As Latham has described the commissions, they "carry out the terms of the treaties that the legislators have negotiated and ratified. They are like armies of occupation left in the field to police the rule won by the victorious coalition."[2]

Throughout the period of gestation, there is intensive study by interested groups of a difficult problem of economic relations which has been recognized finally as sufficiently serious to require governmental action. The forces resisting regulation are powerful and ingenious, and are overcome only by the effective efforts of advocates of reform, sustained by a favorable public response to their demands and led by a strong president. These proponents lay their emphasis on securing the enactment of a law and obtaining public recognition of the claims of certain groups for protection against abusive business practices. The desire for regulation in this early period takes precedence over attempts to refine regulatory goals and basic policies. It is the battle for legislation that captures public attention, not the hammering out of a carefully articulated set of regulatory goals. What is wanted is immediate relief from an intolerable situation, not the development of a philosophy for ordering economic relations. It is the short-run, rather than the long-term, implications of regulatory policy which preoccupy the advocates of regulation.

Because of the long struggle which must preface regulatory reform, the first statute is apt to be seriously out of date at the time it is enacted. It may not deal with the most significant current industrial problems. Because of the

[2] Earl G. Latham, "The Group Basis of Politics: Notes for a Theory," *The American Political Science Review*, vol. 46, June 1952, p. 391.

rapidity of technological and industrial change and continuing modifications in the economic structure of industry, the regulatory treaty finally hammered out by House and Senate conferees will be focused on remedying problems that have been acute for many years. The battle to adapt regulatory policy and practices to problems currently emerging in the industrial scene will be fought bitterly during subsequent decades. As Redford noted, "too little and too late" are inherent weaknesses in governmental efforts to regulate a complex and rapidly moving economy.[3]

THE ICC IN GESTATION

The events leading to the establishment of the Interstate Commerce Commission illustrate the general trend in the phase of gestation. At least twenty years of political agitation preceded the creation of the ICC in 1887. Shippers and farmers for years had used all available political devices to secure protection against discriminatory railroad practices. As agricultural distress mounted in the 1870's, Congress considered a variety of legislative proposals designed to provide more certain and cheaper transportation. As it became clear that Granger legislation passed in several midwestern states could not alleviate the economic distress of farmers, advocates of state railroad legislation devoted more effort to the campaign for favorable national legislation. The House of Representatives passed corrective legislation in 1874 and 1878, but the Senate refused to take any action.

By 1880 farmers were joined by manufacturing and mercantile groups, and the "railroad question" became a major Congressional concern. As the House continued to vote for railroad legislation, the Senate was forced into action. In 1885 it appointed the Cullom Committee to investigate and report on the necessity for regulating railroad and water rates. The political strength of agrarians and small shippers was bolstered first by a report of the Cullom Com-

[3] Emmette S. Redford, *Administration of National Economic Control,* The Macmillan Co., New York, 1952, p. 384.

mittee favoring national regulation of interstate commerce and then by the decision of the Supreme Court in the Wabash case in 1886 holding that a state could not control that part of an interstate railroad journey within the boundaries of the state. Such regulation, the Court held, could be exercised only by the national government. Finally, the drive for reform was climaxed in 1887 when the Interstate Commerce Act was passed. The prolonged and bitterly fought campaign for railroad legislation ended abruptly with the passage of the regulatory statute. The unity of agrarians, merchants, and industrialists evaporated quickly in the confident expectation that the creation of the Commission would solve all railroad problems.

THE BEGINNINGS OF THE SEC

The establishment of the Securities and Exchange Commission rather closely parallels the drive for railroad legislation. In 1913 Louis Brandeis published his *Other People's Money*, denouncing the machinations of investment bankers and financiers and proposing a policy of full and complete disclosure of all relevant facts in the marketing of securities. Beginning in 1911 with Kansas, many states passed blue-sky laws in an effort to eliminate fraud and dishonesty in the securities market. Finally, the tremendous loss of prestige by the business community after 1929 and the disclosures of fraudulent practices in Wall Street by the famous Senate investigation of stock exchange practices in 1932-1934 helped to mobilize a popular majority in favor of federal legislation to protect investors. With the leadership of President Roosevelt, the drive to reform the securities business produced the enactment of the Securities Act of 1933 and the Securities Exchange Act of 1934.

The devastating effect of the Great Depression, the disclosures of the Senate report on stock exchange practices, and the popular, nation-wide appeal of Roosevelt did not permit public concern to expire immediately after the enactment of the enabling legislation. The original Com-

missioners were earnest, enthusiastic promoters of the public interest in the marketing of securities and helped to
dramatize the regulatory problems of the SEC. Significant
additions were made to the legislative authority and regulatory jurisdiction of the SEC, especially by the enactment
of the Public Utility Holding Company Act of 1935. For
at least three to four years following the establishment of
the SEC, the political environment encouraged forceful
administration.

### Youth: Phase 2

When a regulatory commission is established, its real and
potential capacities contrast sharply with those of the regulated groups. It lacks administrative experience, its policy
and objectives are vague or unformed, its legal powers are
unclear and untested, and its relations with Congress are
uncertain. On the other hand, the regulated groups are
well organized, with vital interests to protect against the
onslaught of the regulators. The regulatory agency usually
begins to formulate its program and to block out its major
policies at a time when the regulated enterprises are highly
developed and their technologies far advanced.

At this stage the atmosphere surrounding the regulatory
process is far from placid or neutral. The animosities generated during the period of agitation and legislative enactment do not subside quickly, and the new administrators
are reminded of the strength of the regulated groups at
every possible opportunity. As Herring has described it:

"The milieu is distinctly one of special interests, and the
regulatory body lives in an environment of conflicts. It
must function here, not in accordance with thin, vague
concepts, but in terms of concrete situations where the real
content of the public interest must be extricated from a
maze of technical detail."

". . . The commission performs its duties in surroundings
far from neutral, and it must cope with pressures too power-

ful to be exorcised by simple exhortation or condemnation."[4]

On the other hand, the agency ordinarily begins its administrative career in an aggressive, crusading spirit. It may resolve to meet the opposition of the regulated with firmness in order to promote the public interest. It tends to take a broad view of its responsibilities; and some members of the commission, at least, will develop a fair measure of daring and inventiveness in dealing with their regulatory problems. The spirit of youthful vigor in the commissions has been described by Kenneth Davis: "Characteristically, the great federal regulatory agencies in the early years of their existence have been fired with an inspiration to achieve the goals laid down for them by Congress. During those years the political pressures which have given birth to the agency are still felt, and the agency is acutely aware of its responsibility. Alertness is natural and necessary, for the agency is pioneering; new paths must constantly be broken. The newness of the tasks and the absence of familiar patterns force the agency and its staff to draw constantly upon their own resourcefulness. Young agencies are dominated by the qualities of youth—energy, ambition, imagination."[5]

In view of the high hopes for administrative regulation and the great faith placed in the commission as an agent of reform, commissioners are urged to define their role in expansive rather than restrictive terms. In the period of Progressive reform politics early in the twentieth century, one commentator observed: "Public service commissions are administrative bodies. They are charged with duties of constant supervision. They are empowered to initiate all proceedings necessary to accomplish the purposes of the laws. Merely passive enforcement of commission laws will not long command public respect and confidence and serve

[4] E. P. Herring, *Public Administration and the Public Interest*, McGraw-Hill Book Co., New York, 1936, pp. 183, 194.

[5] Kenneth C. Davis, *Administrative Law*, West Publishing Co., St. Paul, 1951, p. 164.

as a remedy for abuses, alike on the part of the public and the corporations, which it is the purpose of the commissions to prevent. Aggressiveness should be found in public service commissions."[6]

If the agency is to act in the public interest, it must do so while it still commands public support and can count on sympathetic political leadership both in the Presidency and in Congress. If powerful political support and leadership are available to the commission, it may have "the opportunity—perhaps the only one it will ever have—to make a material contribution to the shape of things."[7] But the opportunity does not last very long. It is remarkable how quickly political interest disappears. If an agency is to take advantage of the favorable political situation, "it must establish its beachheads quickly, and extend and fortify its lines without delay. Standards for conduct of private enterprise, guiding standards for the administrative agency, and the position of the agency may be established before the political force behind the agency's directive is spent and the dissident groups have found ways of moderating or checkmating the new program."[8]

The regulatory commission soon discovers that it can accomplish little until the Supreme Court has passed on the validity and constitutionality of its powers and authority. Immediately the scene of battle changes to the courtroom. Litigation forms the framework for the regulatory process until the courts have issued an authoritative decision or series of decisions outlining the legal scope of regulatory powers. The trial by legal combat gives most of the advantage to the private parties. An untried and untested regulatory statute comes under attack by extremely skillful lawyers traditionally opposed to governmental efforts to control economic affairs. The arena in which the legitimacy of regulation is attacked and defended is highly specialized, technical, and frequently obscure.

---

[6] William D. Kerr, "Qualifications Needed for Public Utility Commissioners," *Annals*, vol. 53, May 1914, p. 28.
[7] Redford, *op.cit.*, p. 386.  [8] *ibid.*, p. 386.

Few nonlawyers are able to follow the legal proceedings, which appear incredulous or mysterious to the uninitiated.

While the enactment of a statute is clear proof that the about-to-be-regulated groups have lost the first round in the struggle against regulation, it is equally clear that they do not give up when the law is passed. Instead, as Graham has suggested, the regulated group ". . . attempts immediately and persistently to get 'sound' men appointed to the independent commission. The distinguished members of the bar who represent it can be most gracious, not to say ingratiating, to members of the commission who seem to deserve the industry's confidence. Some commissioners so win the confidence of industry that industry weans them away from the public service into its own employ. Commissioners who prove 'difficult' are subject to constant attack in the public press, in trade publications, before committees of Congress and on the floor of Congress itself; and their reappointment is bitterly opposed."[9]

It is not difficult to account for the loss of public support and the decline of political leadership on behalf of effective regulation. First, the public support that has been built up laboriously during the period of gestation reaches a climactic peak at the moment that the enabling legislation is passed. Public support can be maintained at this peak for only a short time. Attention has been directed for so long to the issue of whether or not to regulate that the public heaves a sigh of relief when an affirmative decision is made. The organized groups that propagandized in behalf of regulation are tired after their long struggle and believe that they have earned a rest from political turmoil.

Second, after concentration on the enactment of legislation, there is a tendency to regard administration as automatically following legislation. If statutory authority is available, the expectation is that it will be exercised. At least, it is felt, someone else will see that the administrative wheels are set in motion and directed along the prescribed

[9] George A. Graham, *Morality in American Politics*, Random House, New York, 1952, p. 196.

legislative lines. Lack of concern with administration, growing out of its undramatic nature, helps to account for the rapid decline of public interest.

Third, the necessity to defend its powers and methods in the courts forces a commission to operate during its period of youth in a technical environment that defies general comprehension by the public. Fourth, the resourcefulness of regulated groups helps to account for changes in public attitudes and the outlook of the commissioners. Various social opportunities may be open to commissioners who are or may become sympathetic to the position of the regulated groups. The chance to secure an executive post with a firm subject to regulation may urge a certain kind of restraint upon the commissioners. This is not to suggest that there is a conspiracy between the regulated and the regulator but rather a more subtle relationship in which the mores, attitudes, and thinking of those regulated come to prevail in the approach and thinking of many commissioners.

Fifth, Congress can ill afford to perpetuate the acrid animosities and scars of political battle. Senators and representatives hesitate to remain identified as champions of public control of business except in periods when support for such control is overwhelming in their constituencies. Divisions within each major party are aggravated by regulatory controversies, and each party is anxious to heal the wounds to party unity. And finally, the cohesiveness of industrial groups cannot be matched by the inchoate, relatively unorganized (and frequently disorganized) public. Consequently, the new commission may be left in splendid isolation until some new crisis attracts public attention and regulation again becomes a vital public issue.

The spirit and enthusiasm of a commission depends to a large extent on the general political setting. When the ICC was established, the prospect of national railroad regulation seemed to some to be a frontal assault on the structure of American industry. Thus the ICC was established not to take over the management of private enterprise in railroading, but rather to undertake the more limited task of refereeing disputes between carriers and shippers. Charlesworth noted that the ICC was a natural expression of the political philosophy of the limited state, which reserved a legal sphere of anarchy for the individual and the enterprising business corporation.[10] Commissions that were established during the period of Progressive reform and the New Deal began life more aggressively than the ICC. They were nurtured during periods when government was regarded as the legitimate tool of the democratic majority and an agent of social justice and economic rehabilitation. Their youthful days reflect the political views prevailing in the period of their origin.

Most commissions have tried initially to achieve independence from regulated groups. They have embarked on the regulatory task with some exuberance and with a desire to clarify goals and mark out basic policies. But the characteristics of youth have only a transitory existence and soon fade away.

THE FEDERAL POWER COMMISSION:
THE YOUTHFUL STAGE

The origin of the Federal Power Commission can be traced to the gradual development of the national movement to conserve natural resources in the first decade of the twentieth century. Conservationists, supported by Theodore Roosevelt, led the fight for national regulation of water power sites, while power interests fought against control. After two decades of struggle Congress passed the Federal Water Power Act of 1920, which created a Federal Power Commission, composed of the Secretaries of War, the Interior, and Agriculture, to license all water power developments on national public land or on navigable waters subject to national jurisdiction. In the political climate of the 1920's the FPC was not prepared to use its regulatory authority. Its personnel was inadequate, its lead-

---

10 James C. Charlesworth, "The Regulatory Agency: Detached Tribunal or Positive Administrator?" *Annals*, vol. 221, May 1942, p. 17.

ers were burdened with other, more important responsibilities, and there was little demand from Congress, the administration, or the country for national regulation of electric power development. In 1930 the Commission was reorganized as an independent body with five full-time commissioners; but, under extremely conservative direction, it remained largely inactive.

While the FPC existed before 1933, it was in effect recreated by the New Deal. The profound change in the 1930's in public attitudes toward the role of government in economic affairs was quickly reflected in the Commission. Once key personnel changes were made in the Commission and its staff, it began to exert its authority and to expand its operating jurisdiction. In 1935, with the support and leadership of the President, Congress passed the Federal Power Act, providing for regulation of interstate transmission of electrical energy; and in 1938 it passed the Natural Gas Act, conferring upon the FPC the power to regulate the transportation and sale of natural gas in interstate commerce. These successive additions to its jurisdiction and the continued support and leadership of the President were the principal factors in maintaining a spirit of freshness and vigor in the revitalized FPC for a few years. The crusading spirit characteristic of a commission in its first years of regulation was evident in the FPC not in the 1920's, but rather in the early years under the New Deal.

## THE FCC IN ITS YOUTHFUL PHASE

The pattern of development in the regulation of broadcasting in its youthful phase varied somewhat from the conventional pattern. As in the case of the electric power industry, radio broadcasting had become fairly well established before the shape of national regulation was set. Because of technical requirements for some form of governmental allocation of scarce broadcast frequencies, the radio industry became the most powerful advocate of regulation. In order to eliminate the chaos in the use of broadcast channels that threatened to destroy broadcasting in 1926, the industry demanded controls. In accordance with the political conservatism of the 1920's, however, it wanted minimal interference once the frequencies were allocated. In the absence of well-organized public demand for effective regulation of broadcasting, the Federal Radio Commission, which was established in 1927, accepted the existing framework in the industry and used its discretionary authority sparingly. Originally the Commission was created for one year. Its authority was renewed annually until it was made permanent in 1930. Uncertainty of tenure made the Commissioners timid rather than aggressive, and the FRC was given almost no opportunity to display the characteristics of youth.

As a part of the New Deal program, the FRC was abolished in 1934, and its powers were transferred to a new Federal Communications Commission. Two members of the old FRC were reappointed to the FCC, which continued to operate along familiar lines. Repeated charges of corruption or incompetence led to an apparently never-ending series of Congressional investigations that kept the FCC on the defensive. The appointment of a new chairman in 1937 improved the standing of the Commission. It mustered sufficient courage in 1938 to order an investigation of chain broadcasting and monopoly in the broadcasting industry; but its subsequent regulations on chain broadcasting have had little effect on the structure of the industry. The FCC, unlike the FPC, did not reinvigorate itself markedly during its rebirth under the New Deal. The technical complexity of the radio field, the lack of popular demand for regulation, the intense interest of congressmen and senators in radio broadcasting, and the capacity of the industry to dominate the Commission nearly eliminated the phase of youth in the life cycle of the FCC.

*Maturity: The Process of Devitalization: Phase 3*

Gradually the spirit of controversy fades out of the regulatory setting, and the commission adjusts to conflict among the parties in interest. It relies more and more on settled procedures and adapts itself to the need to fight its own political battles unassisted by informed public opinion and effective national political leadership. Redford has described this period as follows: "Later, there comes a period of maturity, when the agency has lost the original political support, when it has found its position among the contending forces in society, and when it has crystallized its own evolved program. It then becomes part of the status quo and thinks in terms of the protection of its own system and its own existence and power against substantial change. Its primary function in government is to operate the mechanisms which have been developed in its creative stage and adjust these as circumstances change. . . . [It] is too much to expect that, after maturity is reached, government will find all the origination and perspective which it needs in its administrative institutions alone."[11]

In the period of maturity, regulation usually becomes more positive in its approach. Its functions are less those of a policeman and more like that of a manager of an industry. The approach and point of view of the regulatory process begin to partake of those of business management. The commission becomes accepted as an essential part of the industrial system. As the program of regulation becomes broader in scope and impinges more directly on the functions of management, the stakes become greater. Hence the struggle to control the formulation of regulatory policies and to influence the conditions surrounding the regulatory process becomes more carefully calculated. The commission becomes more concerned with the general health of the industry and tries to prevent changes which adversely affect it. Cut off from the mainstream of political life, the commission's standards of regulation are determined in the light of the desires of the industry affected. It is unlikely that the commission, in this period, will be able to extend regulation beyond the limits acceptable to the regulated groups.

[11] Redford, *op.cit.*, p. 386.

87

In method as well as policy, the commission loses vitality. Davis describes the pattern in these words: "The early experimentation yields forms, patterns, routines. Problems tend to be solved not by original thought but by digging up precedents. A member of the staff who is abruptly confronted with the question why he follows a particular method, inevitably responds: 'Why, we've always done it that way.' "[12] Precedent, rather than prospect, guides the commission. Its goals become routine and accepted.

Perhaps the most marked development in a mature commission is the growth of a passivity that borders on apathy. There is a desire to avoid conflicts and to enjoy good relations with the regulated groups. Without the spur of Congressional demand for regulatory progress and without prodding and leadership from the White House, a commission is apt to take a rather narrow view of its responsibilities. Troxel's picture of the mature state public utility commission is equally applicable to the national commissions: "A commission can become so firmly attached to certain purposes and procedures of control that the study of new objectives and experimentation with new regulatory methods is [sic] neglected. Like any other organization in our society, a commission acquires some inflexibility as it ages. And a regulator often wants to avoid constant conflicts with utility companies. Reliance on conventional standards and a quiet administrative life are preferable to the turmoil of frequent regulatory changes."[13]

The tendency of commissions to be passive toward the public interest is a problem of ethics and morality as well as administrative method. Graham compares the "passive immorality" of mature commissions to the willingness of many municipal police systems to come to terms with the forces of organized crime. Acceptance by government officials of an alliance with regulated groups is an abdication of responsibility and must be considered a blow to demo-

12 Davis, op.cit., p. 164.
13 Emery Troxel, *The Economics of Public Utilities*, Rinehart and Co., New York, 1947, pp. 69-70.

cratic government and responsible political institutions.[14]

A mature agency cannot count on Congressional support for firm regulation. Congress, in this stage, is reluctant to increase the commission's authority and finds its difficult to overcome its traditional particularism and localism and devote constructive attention to national economic policies. Scarcely a note of concern can be heard from the public. Popular apathy indicates that more energetic action is not desired. Those few concerned with effective regulation are satisfied with the progress made to date and see only disaster ahead if the regulatory program is expanded. Complacency and lethargy become firmly rooted.

The approach of a mature commission is heavily judicialized. It routinely devotes most of its time to the adjudication of individual cases. Any latent ability to reconsider regulatory objectives and formulate programs of action is buried under a burden of cases awaiting decision. In an effort to meet charges of arbitrary action and unfairness toward individuals in the adjudication of disputes, the commission makes available to the private parties almost unlimited opportunities to challenge its position and to persuade it that its contemplated action is incorrect or unfair.

Important developments concerning staff, work load, and appropriations should be noted. A spirit of professionalism gradually becomes entrenched in the staffs of most mature commissions. Lawyers, engineers, and economists vie with each other for dominance in the policy-making channels of the agency. Each professional group likes to have veto power over the policy proposals of the other. Professional interests tend to narrow the point of view adopted with respect to regulatory matters, and the dependence on precedent becomes almost iron-bound. The major result is a myopic view of the public interest which rationalizes the regulatory *status quo*. In terms of work load, the commission tends to get further and further be-

[14] See Graham, *op.cit.*, pp. 193-198.

hind in managing its activities. Backlogs keep attention focused on yesterday's problems. Little or no attention is given to the need for progressive revision of regulatory methods and statutory standards. Both Congress and the Bureau of the Budget tend to be unsympathetic to the commission's plea for larger appropriations for the purpose of hiring more staff to dispose of backlogs. Lack of confidence in the commissions as well-managed agencies results in reduced appropriations and budgetary decline.

The close of the period of maturity is marked by the commission's surrender to the regulated. Politically isolated, lacking a firm basis of public support, lethargic in attitude and approach, bowed down by precedent and backlogs, unsupported in its demands for more staff and money, the commission finally becomes a captive of the regulated groups.

The gradual loss of youthful energy and the transition to the infirmities of old age are not uniquely applicable to regulatory commissions. Because of the economic and political stakes of regulation, however, commissions seem to be more subject than other types of government agencies to passivity and inability to interpret the public interest. Commissions need to be forewarned, more than other agencies, about their prospects. If there are ways of guarding against easy acceptance of the traditional and hesitancy to question its adequacy or propriety, commissions have not yet discovered or applied them.

THE ICC IN MATURITY

The ICC provides the most obvious illustration of maturity in the life cycle of a commission. Its major regulatory functions have been crystallized since 1920. The original support from farmers and small shippers no longer exists. The ICC has become an integral part of the structure of the railroad industry, and its record reflects its commitment to the welfare of that industry. Vitality and independence have petered out in the ICC. Increasingly the Commission has identified itself with the interests of the railroad industry, and it is impossible to deal with the modern evolution of the industry without extensive reference to the ICC. The public is unconcerned with the activities of the ICC, except during intermittent periods when interstate truckers or other competitors of the railroads make effective use of press and radio to state their case for changes in regulatory policies. The apathy that characterizes public opinion seems to extend to the Commission. Acting in accordance with time-honored precedents and judicialized procedures, it is nearly buried under a backlog of cases awaiting its decision. The ICC has been unable to plan its work program. By failing to exercise administrative initiative, it has permitted private parties to control its flow of work. Its appropriations have declined steadily in recent years even though its prestige in Congress and the courts remains high. Because the ICC is unable to deal effectively with the regulatory demands of transportation media other than railroads, there are signs of growing agitation by nonrailroad interests for regulatory changes. The ICC's close attachment to railroad interests for nearly seventy years and its pious lip service to independence, nonpartisanship, and isolation from the Presidency suggest that the Commission may increasingly lack the power to maintain itself.

### *Old Age: Debility and Decline: Phase 4*

All social institutions are subject to inertia and loss of vitality. Procedural patterns tend to become sanctified as unalterable guides for bureaucratic conduct and accepted and defended as the traditional and correct way of behavior. The power to resist debilitating pressures and to maintain administrative vigor varies markedly from one association to another. In governmental activity some agencies develop a sense of mission and attract competent personnel and adequate political leadership that enable them to retain their creative powers for a long period. Other agencies fall victim more quickly to traditional modes of thinking and behavior and become passive instruments of public policy rather early in their administrative career.

The development of the characteristics of old age is not confined exclusively to the independent regulatory commission. But commissions seem more susceptible to debility and eventual collapse than other types of agencies. As multiheaded agencies normally cut off from continuing political support from the chief executive, they tend to lack dynamic administrative leadership. As government agencies operating in a web of controversial and hostile economic relationships, they tend to relate their goals and objectives to the demands of dominant interest groups in the economy. Ignored or abandoned by an unorganized public, commissions tend to play for safety in policy decisions. Passivity deepens into debility.

George Graham has noted that "The tendency to be passive when the public interest requires positive action is so prevalent among regulatory agencies that it now has a name, 'administrativitis,' according to Senator [Paul] Douglas, and 'quasi-judicialitis,' in the lexicon of Louis Brownlow. . . . Regulatory commissions, newly established after a period of intensive study of a recognized problem, retain their original fervor for a time. But sooner or later quasi-judicialitis, to use the Brownlovian term, overtakes them and they settle into the groove of passive conservatism."[15]

During old age the working agreement that a commission reaches with the regulated interests becomes so fixed that the agency has no creative force left to mobilize against the regulated groups. Its primary mission is the maintenance of the *status quo* in the regulated industry and its own position as recognized protector of the industry. The institutionalization of favoritism toward dominant groups in the regulated industries is fostered by the narrow jurisdiction of the commission. Dealing with only one industry or a group of related industries, its vision of the public interest lacks the breadth and scope that a wider jurisdic-

[15] *ibid.*, pp. 194-195. See also U.S. Congress, Senate, Committee on Labor and Public Welfare, *Hearings on the Establishment of a Commission on Ethics in Government*, June-July 1951, 82nd Congress, 1st session, pp. 116, 132-133, 212-214, 222, 558-559.

tion would tend to force upon it. Graham notes that "once quasi-judicialitis grips an independent commission, it is difficult to arrest the course of the disease, which is progressive and leads to chronic invalidism."[16]

The final debilitation of the commission does not go unnoticed in the executive and legislative branches. Congressional appropriations committees and budget examiners of the Bureau of the Budget grow increasingly reluctant to approve funds needed to permit the agency to dispose of its growing backlogs. There is the fear that further additions to budget and staff will not make the agency more efficient and only commit it irrevocably to outworn procedures and policies. If a commission is overtaken by a serious governmental crisis or emergency brought on by war, defense mobilization, or economic depression, it will recede into the background and lose additional budgetary support.

Budgetary decline will in turn have debilitating effects on the personnel of the commission who elect to stay. Employees tend to become less able and imaginative in meeting their responsibilities. The commission will become more dependent than before upon the regulated industries to supply staff. Thus the staff continually reinforces its commitment to the maintenance of the *status quo* in the industry.

Recently a Congressional committee studying ethics in government noted the ethical problems raised by the decline of the independent regulatory commission. In its report on "Ethical Standards in Government," a subcommittee of the Senate Committee on Labor and Public Welfare reported unanimously to the Senate as follows: "A subtle malady which is apparently institutional rather than personal in its incidence is the tendency of the independent regulatory commissions not to die, but to fade away; with advancing age they tend to become the servants rather than the governors of the industries which they regulate, and

16 Graham, *op.cit.*, p. 196.

attain a sort of dignified stability far from the objectives which they originally sought." The subcommittee stated that "the apparent inability of the Government to establish independent regulatory agencies which maintain their original direction and momentum has its ethical aspect" and that "probably a radical remedy (in the medical sense) is required."[17]

Symptoms of debility and old age also include poor management and doubt about regulatory objectives. The managerial qualities of an independent commission decline as the commission passes the first blush of youth. Splintered responsibility at the top level, the growth of passivity, acceptance of the judicial model as sacred, and inability to take the initiative required for planning its operations reduce the commission to managerial ineptitude. The need for commissioners to work as a team makes for certain understandings among them which act as powerful deterrents to efforts to improve their managerial quality. Occasionally a particularly disaffected member may refuse to accept the going relations among commissioners. But his opposition may only unite other commissioners more strongly in their defense of the accepted pattern of operation.

A significant indication of senescence is the failure of regulatory objectives to keep pace with changes in technology, economic organization, and popular views about the proper scope of governmental activity. In the phase of old age the regulatory objectives of a commission are no longer meaningful and appropriate. Not only are there growing doubts about the original objectives laid down vaguely in the enabling statute, but there is even greater doubt about what the objectives ought to be. In their declining days commissions can be described as retrogressive, lethargic, sluggish, and insensitive to their wider political and social setting.[18] They are incapable of securing pro-

[17] U.S. Congress, Senate, Subcommittee of the Committee on Labor and Public Welfare, *Report, Ethical Standards in Government*, 1951, 82nd Congress, 1st session, pp. 60-61.

[18] See Troxel, *op.cit.*, pp. 786-800; David B. Truman, *The Governmental Process*, Alfred A. Knopf, New York, 1951, pp. 416-421; Davis, *op.cit.*, pp

gressive revision of regulatory policies and fall further and further behind in their work.

Administrative apathy received little attention from students of government until a few years ago. A significant commentary on our times is that agencies which are accused by certain groups of excessive zeal and lack of concern with individual property rights should instead become characterized by their apathetic approach to the public interest in regulation of economic life. As Kenneth Davis has stated, "Administrative apathy is all the more insidious because of its silence. A defeat of legislative will through inaction harms only an inarticulate general public and is likely to pass unnoticed. Abuses of an affirmative character are less dangerous because they usually damage interests which are vocal or vociferous. Fear of bureaucracy has over-emphasized excessive zeal and has underemphasized administrative apathy."[19]

The period of old age is unlikely to terminate until some scandal or emergency calls attention dramatically to the failure of regulation and the need to redefine regulatory objectives and public policies. In this fashion, the historical pattern of regulation might come full circle, although no important regulatory function of a commission has actually been eliminated. If a new agency is established to achieve the promise of modifying economic relations in the public interest, it will probably embark on its career full of hope, inspiration, and zeal, alert to its responsibilities, and driven by ambition, ingenuity, and public spirit.

### The Pattern of Attacks on the Regulatory Commission

The life cycle of an independent commission can also be considered from the point of view of the attacks on regu-

---

164-167; Graham, *op.cit.*, pp. 193-198; Redford, *op.cit.*, pp. 381-386; and James W. Fesler, "Independent Regulatory Establishments," in F. M. Marx, ed., *The Elements of Public Administration*, Prentice-Hall, Inc., New York, 1946, pp. 227-230.

[19] Davis, *op.cit.*, p. 167.

lation made by the regulated groups. Such groups have attacked general and specific aspects of regulation in several ways. They have tried to prevent the enactment of legislation, discredit the discretionary activities of the commissions, widen the scope of judicial review of administrative decisions, secure adoption of procedural rules governing the conduct of adjudication, and win popular approval through public relations activities.

The attack on regulation begins with the struggle to prevent Congress from passing legislation establishing a regulatory commission with discretionary powers. Groups that would be affected adversely by proposed legislation use every possible method and technique to influence legislators to vote against regulatory proposals. Failing in this, they will concentrate on making the regulatory provisions as innocuous as possible. The process also works in the obverse. The groups to be regulated will press Congressional committees for amendments to the enabling legislation which provide additional safeguards for the regulated or undermine the work of the commission in securing effective compliance with its rules or in formulating policies. These groups may fight for legislation requiring a particular form of organization that reduces the managerial freedom of the commission and fixes a relatively inflexible operating pattern.

WIDENING THE SCOPE OF JUDICIAL REVIEW

Once legislation is adopted and a commission is established and in operation, the regulated groups combat regulation by accusing the commission of "administrative absolutism." They charge that the commission has no ability to exercise discretionary authority and adjudicate disputes. At this stage the regulated groups hope to reduce the commission to relative ineffectiveness by widening the scope of review of administrative decisions by the courts. The judiciary is regarded as a bulwark against faulty administrative discretion and arbitrary or unfair administrative decisions. For a while in the 1930's, a special court to review the decisions of regulatory agencies was proposed by those who distrusted the regulatory agencies, their capacity for fairness, or their devotion to the public interest. One of the factors accounting for the decision of the American Bar Association and its Special Committee on Administrative Law to cease advocating the establishment of a special administrative court may have been the expectation that a special court might, in fact, become sympathetic to the views of regulatory agencies.

The effort to widen the scope of judicial review ran counter to the principal trend in constitutional interpretation in the late 1930's. The almost revolutionary change in the attitude of the Supreme Court toward New Deal legislation in 1937 reduced the influence of the Court in the field of economic and social legislation. It developed more respect for the views of administrative experts and was less inclined to substitute its judgment for that of the regulatory agency in complicated matters of factual or legal interpretation. Judicial review no longer seemed to promise adequate relief from "liberal" decisions of regulatory agencies.

REQUIRING FAIR PROCEDURE

In the middle thirties the American Bar Association and other groups turned from judicial review as the major device to limit the discretionary activities of regulatory agencies. Instead, they advocated a definition of the requirements of fair procedure to protect adequately the interests of private parties in litigation before commissions. While the reform of adjudication procedures was motivated essentially by a desire to assure private parties and individuals fairness in their dealings with the commissions, some of it reflected a desire to utilize legal rules to inhibit the initiative and competence of the agencies. A relatively inflexible set of uniform procedures for regulatory agencies was proposed. Procedural uniformity was designed to give private parties additional opportunities for challenging the proposed findings, interpretations, and decisions of the agencies and to separate the prosecuting and adjudicating functions. Groups opposed to regulation finally succeeded in securing the passage of the Administrative Procedure Act of 1946, which provided for limited separation of functions and established certain required procedures to insure fairness. However, both those who pointed with pride to the new procedural requirements and those who viewed them with alarm were mistaken in their prophecies. Developments since 1946 suggest that the new legislation neither places the regulatory agencies in a judicial straitjacket nor succeeds in nullifying regulatory efforts.

INFLUENCING PUBLIC OPINION

Efforts to influence public opinion to react unfavorably to governmental regulation of business have been the main stock in trade of those groups combating such regulation. Trade associations, organized to protect industrial interests, keep up a running barrage of attack on commissions to keep them on the defensive as much as possible. In the past the electric utility industry conducted what is now a well-documented effort to influence the writing of college textbooks favorable to privately owned utilities and opposed to governmental regulation and public ownership of electric utilities. Today large companies take full-page advertisements in the metropolitan dailies to proclaim the evils of "bureaucracy," governmental control, and "creeping socialism," the first step to communism. Attacks are made on incumbent commissioners identified with vigorous regulation, and the reappointment of "unfriendly" commissioners is bitterly fought. Organizations of lawyers who practice before particular commissions actively promote procedural and other reforms in the hope that commissions will become more responsive to positions taken by the regulated interests.

Propaganda, as a technique in the fight against regulation, is a continuing phenomenon in the history of American efforts to regulate economic affairs. In this sense it does not properly fit into the life cycle of a regulatory commission. The tactics of persuasion employed by the business community vary to fit the stage of development of regulation. During periods when a commission has not yet been created or is still in the formative stage, it will be portrayed as the instrument which will destroy economic enterprise and liberty. When it becomes apparent subsequently that the economy has not been destroyed and that regulation has strengthened the institutions of capitalism by rooting out some of the worst economic abuses, the attack becomes subtler. At this stage regulated groups attempt to identify their interests with the general welfare. The tactics of propaganda become adapted to preventing regulation from being effective rather than preventing regulation as such.

### Consequences of the Attacks on the Regulatory Process

Even though some of the methods used to combat regulation have not led directly to the weakening of the regulatory process, their over-all impact has been powerful. The commission is placed and kept on the defensive as it passes from youth to maturity. It discovers that its administrative career can be more convenient, less hazardous, and less exhilarating when its activities do not interfere with managerial freedom except as affirmative governmental action is requested by regulated groups. Furthermore, the commission becomes more preoccupied with problems of formal procedure and the handling of adjudication, even though these matters concern only a small share of its total activity. In order to acquire the respectability and social acceptability achieved by the courts, it tends to over-judicialize procedures. Despite sincere efforts to separate the functions of prosecution and adjudication, the commission finds that it cannot avoid the "stigma" of interfering unduly with private economic initiative. For example, the Office of Price Administration during World War II organized the conduct of administrative suspension hearings in the rationing program in order to dissociate the functions of investigation and prosecution from those of the hearing officer, but clear-cut separation of functions did not gain increased acceptance for its program. Separation of functions may achieve a higher degree of fairness for the private parties, but it does not necessarily win approval of a regulatory program which is bitterly resented on economic grounds.

Under sustained attack, commissions turn their attention from such urgent tasks of regulation as the formulation of regulatory policies, winning acceptance of regulations, and securing the compliance of the regulated groups. Attacks on the commission change it from an aggressive, alert body eager to promote the public interest into an agency which is extraordinarily sensitive to the demands of regulated groups and insensitive to growth and change in economic life.

### Outstanding Characteristics of Regulation by Commission

Certain characteristics of governmental regulation emerge from the analysis of the life cycle of commissions and the nature of the attacks made upon the regulatory process:

1. Conventional methods, mechanisms, and policies have been devised and applied in an incomplete, fragmentary manner. They have failed to keep abreast of industrial and technological developments. Consequently, the regulatory mechanism has an air of obsolescence. It has little or no capacity to stimulate industry to adopt improved methods and practices and has failed to overcome judicial hostility.

2. The static quality of regulation and the inertia and apathy that gradually overtake the regulatory process contrast sharply with the dynamic development of industry and technology and the productive ingenuity of American industrial enterprise.

3. The hostile environment in which regulation operates is pervasive. It provides the frame of reference for the regulatory process and makes the process conditional upon the acceptance of regulation by the affected groups. It forces

a commission to come to terms with the regulated groups as a condition of its survival.

4. The struggle to gain judicial acceptance carries a heavy price. Procedural uniformity may perform the essential task of safeguarding individual rights. But it also reduces the effectiveness of a commission, not because procedural requirements are inimical to effective regulation but because the agency becomes preoccupied with judicialized procedure to the neglect of other matters.

5. "Independence" is a device to escape popular politics. It facilitates maximum responsiveness by a commission to the demands and interests of regulated groups. It provides maximum freedom from exposure to popular political forces. It tends to alienate commissions from sources of political strength, especially the president, upon whom regulatory progress may largely depend. Independence acquires a sacred inviolability because it reduces the effectiveness of regulation and seems to satisfy the Congressional desire to lessen the power and authority of the president.

6. The single most important characteristic of regulation by commission is the failure to grasp the need for political support and leadership for the success of regulation in the public interest. Without pressure from the president, Congress is unlikely to undertake progressive reform of regulatory policies. This task falls to the president, who has a broader comprehension of the task of winning public support than either Congress or the commissions.

7. Complacency and inertia appear as inevitable developments in the life cycle of a commission. Although tradition, precedent, and custom can harden into blind routine in all types of social organization, the commission seems to be peculiarly susceptible to the disease of "administrative arteriosclerosis."[20]

8. The limited jurisdiction of most commissions narrows the administrative vision of the public interest. For administrative purposes, it artificially isolates a set of eco-

20 The phrase is found in *ibid.*, p. 183.

nomic relationships from the wider political and economic setting that gives it meaning.

As these characteristics suggest, regulation by commission is a process involving many serious problems of personnel and of regulatory theory and practice. It is these problems which are discussed in the following chapters.

# CHAPTER 4

# Commissioners and the Problem
# of Expertness

THE importance of obtaining qualified commissioners on independent regulatory commissions can scarcely be overstated. Most analyses of administrative and policy problems of commissions conclude with the observation that regulatory success hinges more on the quality of the commissioners than upon any other single factor. The conclusion of the report of the Board of Investigation and Research is typical: "If administrative regulation is to be successful, the greatest care and the most high-minded purpose must guide the selection of those who will be vested with administrative power. This is an absolute essential; all other requirements of the administrative system are minor in comparison."[1]

Much of the advocacy of the commission as the ideal type of agency for administrative regulation is based on the expectation that a group of commissioners will be better equipped than a single administrator to make sound decisions, interpret the public interest faithfully, develop staff expertness, and remain independent of both partisan politics and the regulated interests. These alleged advantages of regulation by commission depend heavily on the prospects of obtaining well-qualified commissioners and keeping them in office long enough so that they can

[1] Board of Investigation and Research, *Practices and Procedures of Governmental Control*, House Document No. 678, 1944, 78th Congress, 2nd session, p. 166. The Transportation Act of 1940 provided for the appointment by the president of a three-man Board of Investigation and Research to study the transportation problem. It followed several earlier attempts to resolve issues of transportation policy through the creation of special offices and committees of inquiry, including the Federal Coordinator of Transportation, 1933-1936; the Interstate Commerce Committee of Three, 1938; the President's Committee of Six, 1938; the Byrd Committee, 1936-1938; and the National Resources Planning Board study of transportation, 1941-1942.

make a maximum contribution to the regulatory process. The record indicates that the hopes for the commission have not been fulfilled in this regard.

## Characteristics of Federal Commissioners

Several studies of commissioners have been made, including those by Mansfield, Herring, and the Hoover Commission Task Force on Regulatory Commissions.[2] Evidence is overwhelming that many of the men appointed to the various commissions have tended to be mediocre and lacking in relevant training and experience.

### BIPARTISANSHIP

All commissions except the National Labor Relations Board are required to be bipartisan. There is little evidence that commissioners divide on major policy issues according to their party affiliations. In most respects bipartisanship appears to be an extraneous influence in the development of commissions. Herring recorded in his study of national commissioners in 1936 that party affiliation appears to have no fixed relation to social and economic views. The lack of a close correlation of party affiliation and regulatory views should not be surprising. Frequently the president, in designating a commissioner from the opposite party, will select a man who does not represent the dominant views of that party. Franklin Roosevelt often appointed Republicans who were closer to the policy of his administration than many Democrats were. Moreover, as commissioners share their regulatory experience and influence one another, party differences on general economic policies come to have less relevance to day-to-day problems.

### AGE

The age of commissioners at the time of their appoint-

2 Harvey Mansfield, *The Lake Cargo Rate Controversy*, chap, VI; E. P. Herring, *Federal Commissioners*, Harvard University Press, Cambridge, 1936; and Task Force on Regulatory Commissions of the Commission on Organization of the Executive Branch of the Government, *Task Force Report on Regulatory Commissions*, 1949, pp. 7-28.

ment varies considerably. The average age is approximately 50 years. If the members of the SEC, FCC, FTC, and NLRB are surveyed from the time the commissions were created up to 1948, it will be seen that the median age of commissioners at time of appointment was 47 to 48. Of approximately 80 commissioners serving on these 4 commissions up to 1948, 20% were under 40 at the time of their appointment, 38% were from 40 to 49, 29% were from 50 to 59, and 14% were 60 or over. There is some tendency to appoint younger men to relatively new commissions. For example, among the 12 commissioners of the NLRB from 1935 to 1948, 4 were under 40. However, of 26 commissioners serving on the FTC from 1915 to 1948, only 4 were under 40 at the time of their appointment, while 13, or fully one half of the total appointees, were 50 or over. In the SEC, which was created in 1934, 8 of the 21 commissioners from 1934 to 1948 were under 40 and only 5 of the appointees were over 50 at the time of appointment. Since the average tenure among commissioners is brief, their average age at any given moment is only slightly above the average age at the time of appointment.

TENURE

Herring noted in 1936 that one of the most significant characteristics of commissioners was the brevity of their tenure. In 1949 the Hoover Commission Task Force on Regulatory Commissions noted the rapid turnover of commissioners. As of 1949, the Task Force found that the average tenure of a commissioner in the SEC was three years; in the CAB it was three years; in the FCC, excluding two members who served eleven and nine years respectively, the average tenure was three and one-half years. On the other hand, the average tenure on the Interstate Commerce Commission was thirteen years. The Task Force concluded: "With rapid turn-over, many members do not remain long enough to master the problems of regulation and to perform their duties well, and new appointees are deprived of the opportunity of learning from experienced members with long service. With low salaries, men of ability tend to move on, leaving the less qualified in office. Of course, some men are willing to make the financial sacrifice in order to engage in public service, but inadequate compensation restricts too narrowly the possible range of selection."[3]

### TRAINING AND EXPERIENCE

About two out of three commissioners have been lawyers or law school professors. The remaining commissioners have generally been businessmen, bankers, legislators, engineers, editors, or publishers. Only a small proportion of commissioners have had previous experience in regulated industries.

On the basis of the recent researches covering personnel of commissions, there appears to be little reason for changing the general conclusion reached by Harvey Mansfield in his study of ICC commissioners in 1932: that partisan political considerations unfortunately have dominated the appointment of commissioners.[4]

The quality of commission appointments varies depending on the general reputation of the commission, its current stage of development, and the prevailing political climate. Ordinarily, there is greater likelihood of outstanding presidential appointments during the early years of a commission; conversely, once the commission has achieved maturity the competence of its leaders is likely to decline. On this score the Board of Investigation and Research in 1944 found the history of administrative appointments to the commissions not reassuring: "It is true that some of the most distinguished men who have served the Federal Government have been members of regulatory commissions, and it is not uncommon for new agencies to start with carefully selected and admirably qualified personnel. But as an agency's pioneering period passes, and it becomes accepted as part of the governmental establishment, the in-

---

[3] Task Force on Regulatory Commissions, *op.cit.*, p. 24.
[4] Mansfield, *op.cit.*, p. 193.

centive to make outstanding appointments dwindles, and the way opens for political considerations to claim a larger part."[5]

## CONTINUITY AND STABILITY

Long, staggered terms of commissioners were considered guarantees of continuity and stability in regulatory policy and administration. Under a system in which a president is unable to name a majority of the members of a commission within a four-year period, provided all commissioners fill out their full terms, it was anticipated that such a commission could formulate policy without too much regard for the policies of the administration in power. Shifting political tides were regarded as dangerous to regulatory administration. Complex regulatory matters were considered to be too delicate to survive the political turmoil of frequent changes in basic policy. The commission system was regarded as a bulwark against unwise changes in policy and a safeguard against partisan influences in administration. Undoubtedly, frequent changes in basic policy would undermine the stability and health of regulated enterprises, and to prevent or moderate sharp changes was one of the justifications of the commission. Continuity and stability were considered as positive values to be earnestly sought in regulatory affairs. As matters transpired, however, the vaunted continuity and stability afforded by the commission system failed to develop. The failure took two forms, both of which weakened the commission as an effective vehicle of governmental regulation of economic affairs. First, in most commissions the average tenure of the commissioners was about half the length of a full term. Thus a president in office for two terms, and perhaps even one term, might look forward to appointing a majority and sometimes all the members of a commission. Second, where tenure has been longest and a tradition of reappointment of commissioners has developed, the problem has been not

[5] Board of Investigation and Research, *op.cit.*, p. 27.

too little tenure but too much. In both the FTC and the ICC, for example, the long terms of office of most of the commissioners led not to continuity and stability but to inertia and paralysis. The experience of these two commissions indicates that continuity and stability are relative terms. One must ask, Continuity and stability for what policies and methods? Continuity and stability for weak, ineffectual policies and methods are scarcely administrative virtues.

In both the ICC and the FTC, long tenures and the tradition of reappointment have tended to make incumbent commissioners relatively insensitive to new industrial developments and rather hostile to new ideas about regulatory policy and administrative practice. A commissioner with twelve years of service who has just been reappointed is unlikely to be responsive to proposals for change in the regulatory program. Over-age commissioners tend to be obstreperous and unsympathetic with whatever new blood is introduced into the agency. A new commissioner is apt to become frustrated very quickly in meetings with long-term fellow commissioners, who are confirmed in their accustomed ways of doing public business.

Commissioners with long tenure may, in fact, undermine continuity of policy rather than promote it. In his discussion of the regulatory experience of the FTC, Herring found that continuity of policy was disrupted more by fundamental differences of opinion held by commissioners than by frequent changes in commissioners. According to Herring, "conflicting personalities and widely divergent viewpoints among the commissioners must be put down as a basic cause of weakness in the Federal Trade Commission."[6]

It is ironic that long, staggered terms of commissioners were designed to safeguard against frequent changes which might otherwise result from the normal political process. Presumably the president and Congress, as political parts

[6] E. P. Herring, *Public Administration and the Public Interest*, McGraw-Hill Book Co., New York, 1936, p. 114, 133.

of the government, were transitory in nature, here today but gone probably in two, four, or six years. However, the president and Congress have shown more staying capacity than have most commissioners. Continuity has been as much a product of the system of seniority which governs committee chairmanships in Congress as it is a result of the commission system itself and the long, staggered terms of commissioners. Generally, Congressional tenure has been greater than the average tenure of commissioners.

## Presidential Attitudes toward the Commissions

All presidents have tried in one way or another to influence the conduct of commissions, but the principal tool of presidential influence has been the appointing process. By nominating commissioners and by designating or recommending chairmen of the commissions, the presidents of both parties have been able to exercise a measure of control over their behavior. Presidential attitudes, however, have differed markedly. Some presidents have given considerable attention to commission affairs while others have been too preoccupied with other matters to deal with the problems of commission regulation. Herring concluded from his study of national commissioners that on the whole the process of presidential appointment, even though it was the most effective instrument of presidential influence over the commissions, was "almost casual in its lack of system." The appointing process has generally not been used to improve regulatory administration or to revive interest in regulatory matters. Instead, emphasis has been placed upon pleasing groups or sections that are politically powerful.[7] Nevertheless, the appointing process remains the major instrument of the president.[8]

The obstacles in the way of removing commissioners or

[7] Herring, *Federal Commissioners, op.cit.*, p. 96.

[8] See Emmette S. Redford, *Administration of National Economic Control*, The Macmillan Co., New York, 1952, p. 282; Robert E. Cushman, *The Independent Regulatory Commissions*, Oxford University Press, New York, 1941, p. 682.

in securing their resignations has had an adverse effect upon the appointing process. Lacking the control which they have over their own political appointees, presidents have sometimes been reluctant to appoint men known for their independence. They tend to be wary of getting strong-minded, competent men who have a reputation for independent action and stand outside the normal channels of presidential control and direction. Presidents have been somewhat fearful that under the direction of able commissioners, commissions might get out of hand and beyond the president's capacity to influence their regulatory conduct.[9]

In his study of the regulatory commissions, Cushman found that most presidents have from time to time felt that they should be able to control the policies of the commissions, and they were confident of the legality and propriety of doing so.[10] President Theodore Roosevelt, in 1908, urged Congress to place all commissions and independent bureaus under appropriate executive departments supervised by Cabinet secretaries. According to Cushman, Senator Carter Glass was the authority for the statement that Wilson threatened to remove all the members of the new Federal Reserve Board because the Board was itself threatening to eliminate four of the banks created by statute. Cushman writes: "There is no doubt that Wilson with his 'prime minister' theory of the nature of the Presidential office felt that he was entitled to impress his policies on the independent commissions and to expect their conformity to those policies. Presidents Harding and Coolidge made plain on repeated occasions that they believed Presidential domination of certain of the independent commissions to be essential. Harding . . . engaged in a long and bitter fight to secure control over the Shipping Board and the Fleet Corporation, and it was clear that President Coolidge agreed with his views in the matter. On at least two occasions President Hoover made public statements indicating how he thought the Interstate Commerce Commission

9 See Herring, *Federal Commissioners, op.cit.*, p. 88.
10 Cushman, *op.cit.*, p. 681.

ought to exercise certain of its powers, and the commission somewhat reluctantly yielded to that influence. A member of the Federal Communications Commission told the writer in 1936 that the commission had always complied with all orders and requests made of it by the President, and had never raised any question about its obligation to do so."[11]

President Franklin D. Roosevelt had to devise more ingenious methods to make the commissions more sympathetic to his political program. According to Herring: "The President got around this difficulty in his characteristically adroit fashion. Placing his keymen in the departments was a simple matter, but bringing the independent organization within his control required more ingenuity. The judicial calm of the Interstate Commerce Commission was left undisturbed, but the most able and aggressive commissioner was created Federal Coordinator of Transportation. The United States Tariff Commission was reduced to a harmless condition through the passage of the Reciprocal Tariff act. The Federal Radio Commission was abolished outright and a New Deal commission took its place. The President secured the resignation of Hoover's chairman of the Federal Power Commission and added two appointees of his own."[12]

Roosevelt used his power of appointment freely to influence the choice of chairmen and the policies of commissions. He maintained close liaison with most commission chairmen and regarded the chairmen as spokesmen for their commissions and as the point of contact with the White House.[13] While President Truman used his appointing power to influence the regulatory commissions, he did not

[11] *ibid.*, pp. 681-682.

[12] Herring, *Public Administration*, *op.cit.*, pp. 222-223. Quoted also in Cushman, *op.cit.*, p. 682.

[13] The best source of information about presidential attempts to influence regulatory commissions is the series of reports prepared by the Hoover Commission Task Force on the Regulatory Commissions. The mimeographed reports are available in the National Archives and in some of the government libraries, including the library of the Bureau of the Budget. Relevant excerpts from these reports have been collected in footnotes in Redford, *op.cit.*, pp. 279-282.

maintain the same measure of interest in commissions displayed by President Roosevelt.[14]

The appointment of commissioners has been considered a crucial element in the development of a commission's independence from executive control and the ability to remain free from political forces in the adjudication of controversies and the formulation of regulatory policy. The achievement of a high degree of expertness in the staff of a commission depends heavily, in commission theory, upon the naming of "impartial," objective, independent-minded commissioners. Some commissioners have been distinguished public servants, and several have made creditable careers as commissioners. But on the whole commissioners have not inspired confidence as outstanding public servants and vigorous defenders and promoters of the public interest. There are indications that appointments of commissioners fall somewhat below the general standard of presidential appointments. The fact that a single commission has several members means that there are considerable pressures to name commissioners to represent certain geographical sections, professional groups, or kinds of industrial experience. In an appointment to one of five or seven positions, the president may name an otherwise unacceptable individual in order to placate key members of Congress, take care of certain administration supporters, or give freer rein to personal preferences. The president may be more willing to come to terms with vigorously pressed political considerations in the appointment of commissioners than in the appointment of other government officials. The lack of direct answerability of commissioners to the president allows him the dubious luxury of nominating individuals whom he could not tolerate if he were held immediately responsible for their administrative and political acts. Some of the casualness in the appointing process noted by Herring seems to stem from the view that single commis-

14 This is Redford's conclusion, based on an analysis of the Hoover Commission Task Force reports. See his *Administration of National Economic Control*, p. 283.

sioners are not very important or at least not as important as the heads of agencies and departments responsible directly to the president.

Partly because of the nonpolitical goal of the advocates of regulation by commission, the president may also be willing to name as commissioners individuals who have little capacity for strengthening his political position or for improving the commissions' relationship with Congress. Appointment of commissioners on the basis of merit alone overlooks the imperative that the head or heads of an agency win popular support for the agency's policies and programs. This is a legitimate and necessary political role which must be fulfilled by an agency head. He cannot afford to rely exclusively on expert knowledge of complex situations and the devising of objective solutions to regulatory problems. Since the requisites for the role of an expert commissioner may seem to the president to be less exacting than the qualifications needed by the political head of an executive department, he may be more casual in his nomination of the former.

### The Problem of Expertness in Regulatory Commissions

One of the reputed advantages of the independent commission is its facility for recruiting a staff of experts to handle the day-to-day tasks of administrative regulation. It is commonly believed that a commission, which would be independent of the troublesome and shifting sands of political fortune, would be more successful than executive departments in attracting highly qualified employees and officials and would be able to command their services and loyalty over a longer period of time. Reformers who looked upon the independent commission as a major instrument of regulatory reform regarded the political process as incompatible with the growth of expertness and professional skill in governmental administration. Herbert Croly understood that "The irresponsible partisan executive did not want expert officials, because his success in office did not depend upon the carrying out of an administrative or legislative policy. It depended on his ability to satisfy his partisan superiors and associates without an excessively flagrant betrayal of the public service." As Croly suggested, the presence of experts in administrative agencies under such circumstances was "superfluous" and "inconvenient."[15]

Expertness does not exist in a vacuum, nor does it exist as an independent entity. Expertness must be related to a particular process, subject, or purpose before it can be given any significance. The first question that must be asked about expertness is, Expertness for what? What functions, purposes, processes, etc. are served best by the expert staffs of the regulatory commissions? Does the expertness of a commission help it make policy where a high degree of discretion is involved? Does it enable the commission to formulate a comprehensive concept of the public welfare, plan regulatory programs, and carry out judicial duties?

First, in situations where the scope of discretion is great and the complexity of the problems is considerable, the contribution of experts to the process of policy formation is severely limited. Experts tend to be influenced heavily by the precedents built up through the exercise of professional judgment and, therefore, to be less sensitive to subtle changes in the context and nature of regulatory problems. The technical competence and skill of government employees is adapted best to the application of accepted policy to relatively uncomplicated situations rather than to the formulation of policy itself. At best, the special training and ability of the recognized administrative expert equip him to deal not necessarily with broad considerations of public policy but rather with the application of settled policy to delicate, complex situations. His expertness does not make available any special competence to exercise the

[15] Herbert Croly, *Progressive Democracy*, The Macmillan Co., New York, 1914, p. 357.

discretion required for the formulation of regulatory policies.

William Carey has suggested the nature of the impact of the professional expert on the regulatory process: "Regulation in the public interest has cultivated a whole new breed of lawyers who specialize in administrative practice. Within the regulatory commissions the ascendancy of the lawyer class is often paramount and unassailable. The mass of their product is so great, particularly over decades of effort, that it bends the process of policy-making (and particularly policy-changing) to its own ends. It becomes a burden upon the policy-makers."[16]

The ability of the expert to utilize his knowledge and skill varies with the type of administrative situation or problem. Generally, the wider the scope of a problem and the broader the implications of policy for the public welfare, the narrower the opportunities for the application of the special skills of the expert. As Appleby states, the more political a problem becomes, the less its solution depends upon expert analysis.[17]

Second, the expertness of a commission does not lead automatically to the development of a comprehensive view of the public interest in regulation of economic affairs. Unless, as Croly suggests, the expert is committed to support of the regulatory statute and the purposes which it seeks, unless he is willing to be "a promoter and propagandist" for the regulatory program, his concept of the public interest in regulation will have little relevance to public needs and desires.[18] Herring makes the same point in his discussion of the trials and tribulations of the Federal Radio Commission: " 'Expertise' can apply only to scientific problems and, while it ensures a grasp of technical limitations and possibilities, it does not contribute to a positive elucidation of the public welfare. Here even the

16 William D. Carey, "The Federal Regulatory Commissions," lecture delivered at Princeton University, April 4, 1952, mimeo., p. 3.
17 Paul Appleby, *Policy and Administration*, University of Alabama Press, University, Alabama, 1949, p. 62.
18 Croly, *op.cit.*, p. 361.

expert must rely upon his fallible judgment and his integrity."[19]

Third, does the expertness of commissions improve the planning of the regulatory programs? The evidence suggests not. Some of the closest observers of commission regulation and even some distinguished commissioners have recognized that the commissions lack the capacity for planning their regulatory programs. In a discussion of planning in commissions, Cushman concluded that "the independent regulatory commissions cannot carry on continuous long-time policy planning and they ought not to be asked to do so." The commissions may be competent to prepare plans and proposals dealing with narrow and specific problems within the areas of their experience, but they should not be burdened with responsibilities beyond their competence.[20] In his final report as Coordinator of Transportation, Eastman wrote: "Students of government relations to transportation have often pointed out a defect in our system of regulation, and that is the absence of any sufficient provision for planning and prevention. . . . Anyone who has served on the [Interstate Commerce] Commission knows that it is not well adapted to such work."[21]

Fourth, is the expertness of a commission well adapted to the discharge of its judicial functions? The usual view is that commissions are weak in the handling of normal administrative duties and strong in the adjudication of cases brought before them. But Robson, the distinguished analyst of the administrative tribunals in Great Britain, finds that the narrow specialization of those tribunals operates disadvantageously. "While technical knowledge is often needed for the adjudication of disputes, there are grave objections to giving judicial power into the hands of specialists whose outlook is confined to a single field. The worst defect of our domestic tribunals . . . is the oppor-

19 Herring, *Public Administration*, *op.cit.*, p. 166.

20 Cushman, *op.cit.*, p. 740.

21 Federal Coordinator of Transportation, *Fourth Report*, House Document No. 394, January 21, 1936, 74th Congress, 2nd session, p. 42.

tunity they provide for narrow professional instincts and group habits to assert themselves without let or hindrance; and the main disadvantage of such tribunals is the domination of the judicial process by petty loyalties and outworn traditions which predetermine the conclusion and render an impartial investigation impossible."[22]

Expertness in commissions appears to be most valuable and acceptable when the following conditions are approximated: (a) the scope of the problem is narrow; (b) the task of collecting data and analyzing facts is difficult and complex; (c) discretion is severely limited; (d) the task involves the application of settled policy to regulatory situations and does not concern the formulation of basic regulatory policy; and (e) Congress has defined the public interest with sufficient clarity to guide the direction and content of public policy. The work situation in commissions rarely fulfills these conditions. Normally the regulatory process there is characterized by the following: (a) a high degree of discretion is involved; (b) the emphasis is on the formulation of policy; (c) while their jurisdiction is narrowly confined to certain industrial fields or practices, the responsibilities of commissions within these fields are intensive and detailed; (d) a commission has a broad mandate for interpreting the public interest in the light of vague statutory standards and goals; (e) commissions are insulated from the political strength of the president and generally lack sympathetic support in Congress; (f) commissions are subject to the pressures of private interests under circumstances which leave considerable room for the play of clientele influences.

These latter conditions suggest a number of obstacles confronting the development of a satisfactory place for expertness in a commission. Experts tend to develop myopia in interpreting the public welfare. The lack of effective coordination of regulatory and national economic policies

[22] William A. Robson, *Justice and Administrative Law*, 3rd edn., Stevens and Sons, Ltd., London, 1951, p. 600.

strengthens the parochial influence of expertness within each commission. Expertness plays into the hands of the regulated interests. The alleged incompatibility of politics and expertness cuts the commission's staff off from popular contacts and political strength and makes them more subservient to the demands of the regulated groups. Dislike of and disdain for politics encourage the growth of passivity in the regulatory process. As professional groups become entrenched in a commission, opportunity lessens for the administrative generalist to counterbalance narrow professional views with the infusion of a broader perspective. It becomes more difficult to devise instruments of internal coordination. Finally, expertness becomes transformed into a strong-minded professionalism that narrows the concept of the public interest, promotes traditionalism, encourages long delays in the dispatch of regulatory business, and makes for inflexibility and stolidity in regulation.

One of the baffling problems results from the tendency of various professional groups to conceive of regulatory problems entirely within the frame of reference of their expertness and specialized skill. Lawyers, economists, and engineers vie with one another for domination of commission staffs. Ordinarily a problem involving important legal, economic, and engineering considerations will be analyzed by each group independently. Particularistic views tend to fractionize the approach toward regulatory problems and raise to the level of top policy the disputes about the status of various professional staff groups. The struggle between lawyers and economists has become classic in the experience of regulatory commissions. Lawyers are perhaps guiltier than other professional groups of judging regulatory matters within the framework of their own narrow experience. Counsel with respect to the legality or legal soundness of proposed regulatory action spills over into control and direction concerning regulatory matters. Economists may be just as guilty as lawyers in universalizing their regulatory experience, but they have been somewhat less successful than the lawyers in molding the regulatory approach and in entrenching themselves as controllers at key points in regulatory administration.

Lawyers generally tend to be the stoutest advocates of "keeping regulation out of politics" and of relying most heavily on the *expertise* of nonpolitical officials, especially lawyers. One of the typical "lawyer" views is that of James Landis, who wrote in his study of administrative adjudication in commissions: ". . . as an agency of government confined to a fairly narrow field, [the commission's] singleness of concern quickly develops a professionalism of spirit —an attitude that perhaps more than rules affords assurance of informed and balanced judgments."[23] Landis was not making a case for an administrative elite of experts. His high regard for the superior expertness of commission staffs was essentially an argument for increasing the independence of the commissions from inexpert judges. But he carries his argument too far. Singleness of concern and the development of a professional spirit have led not to balanced judgment ordinarily, but to excessive emphasis on narrow, technical considerations and to struggles between professional groups for status in influencing and determining the course of regulatory policy.

The impact of professionalism on the process of public administration has received only limited attention despite its significance. On the basis of his close observations of regulatory commissions for a number of years, William Carey has concluded that professionalism in administration "is not exclusively a problem of the lawyers, nor of the regulatory commissions. It ripples out into all facets of Government, and it includes the scientist, the economist, and even the administrative technician. Professionalism is fundamentally destructive of good administration, because it is a special kind of class system which views public policy through blinders. I think we are only beginning to be aware

[23] James M. Landis, *The Administrative Process*, Yale University Press, New Haven, 1938, p. 99.

of this as a tumorous disease, but we had better look to its treatment before the malignancy catches up with us."[24]

## The Limitations of the Expert

In 1931 Harold Laski challenged the view that experts were best able to interpret the needs of the community. He concluded that the expert can supply citizens and rulers with the raw materials necessary for making a final decision, but he cannot do the thinking for them. In a democratic society the citizen cannot abdicate his responsibility for making political judgments on the basis of relevant facts. Neither can he afford to permit democracy to suffer in ignorance because of the failure to utilize the knowledge and skills of the specialists. But Laski was fearful that democracy would transform itself into tyranny if experts were allowed to run society. "We must ceaselessly remember," he wrote, "that no body of experts is wise enough, or good enough, to be charged with the destiny of mankind."[25]

Laski's reservations about the uses and abuses of *expertise* have been shared by Lord Lindsay, who has written perhaps the most distinguished treatise in democratic theory since Laski's *Grammar of Politics* was published in 1925.[26] Like Laski, Lindsay would prefer to see the expert on tap but not on top. According to Lindsay, experts "do not like being told that the shoes they so beautifully make do not fit. They are apt to blame it on the distorted and misshapen toes of the people who have to wear their shoes." Lindsay quickly adds that "sound judgment" and "common sense" are not the "products of ignorance" and that ordinary people do not have access to a source of certain wisdom which is denied to the expert. But Laski and Lindsay agree that a democratic society cannot run the risk of permitting the expert's judgment to be final.

24 Carey, *op.cit.*, p. 3.
25 Harold Laski, "The Limitations of the Expert," Fabian Tract No. 235 (1931).
26 A. D. Lindsay, *The Modern Democratic State*, vol. I, Oxford University Press, New York, 1943, esp. pp. 267-281.

"Expertise," according to Laski, ". . . sacrifices the insight of common sense to intensity of experience. It breeds an inability to accept new views from the very depth of its preoccupation with its own conclusions. It too often fails to see round its subject. It sees its results out of perspective by making them the center of relevance to which all other results must be related. Too often, also, it lacks humility; and this breeds in its possessors a failure in proportion which makes them fail to see the obvious which is before their very noses. It has, also, a certain caste-spirit about it, so that experts tend to neglect all evidence which does not come from those who belong to their own ranks. . . . [The expert] tends to confuse the importance of his facts with the importance of what he proposes to do about them." Laski adds, "There is, in fact, no expert group which does not tend to deny that truth may possibly be found outside the boundary of its private Pyrenees."

Laski visualized the expert as one who becomes immersed in routine and therefore "tends to lack flexibility of mind once he approaches the margins of his special theme. He is incapable of rapid adaptation to novel situations. He unduly discounts experience which does not tally with his own. . . . Specialism seems to breed a horror of unwonted experiment, a weakness in achieving adaptability, both of which make the expert of dubious value when he is in supreme command of a situation."

The great failure of the expert, Laski stated, is his inability to understand "the plain man." "What he knows, he knows so thoroughly that he is impatient with the men to whom it has to be explained. Because he practises a mystery, he tends to assume that, within his allotted field, men must accept without question the conclusions at which he has arrived. He too often lacks that emollient quality which makes him see that conclusions to which men assent are far better than conclusions which they are bidden, without persuasion, to decline at their peril."

Laski concludes that the expert "remains expert upon the condition that he does not seek to co-ordinate his specialism with the total sum of human knowledge. The moment that he seeks that co-ordination he ceases to be an expert. . . . The wisdom that is needed for the direction of affairs is not an expert technic but a balanced equilibrium." The expert's difficulty is that he lives as an expert in a very small division of human knowledge and tends to make the principles of that discipline a cosmic framework for yielding answers and solutions to all problems and questions.[27]

The formulation of policy and the administration of public affairs require a sense of proportion which the expert all too often lacks. Experts who are preoccupied in their specialism have an "intensity of experience" which destroys their sense of proportion. In his account of the work of the Tennessee Valley Authority, David Lilienthal describes the various experts needed for the operation of the TVA: geologists, agronomists, chemists, architects, wood technicians, lawyers, accountants, etc. "TVA for example once had on its staff a dendrologist, a man who had spent most of his adult life as an expert in the reading of tree rings. By examination of the rings of ancient trees he was able to throw some useful light on rainfall cycles and extreme floods far beyond the humanly recorded data on these matters. This expert saw the whole world in tree rings, almost literally."

Lilienthal recognized that one of the TVA's problems was to find experts who were willing to work as part of a team and not in professional isolation. He wrote:

". . . even at best it is not easy for each specialist to appraise the relative importance of his own task as part of the whole picture, or its importance as compared with the tasks in some other technical branch. In fact, the desperate part of the problem, as many people have observed, is the realization of how rarely these different groups of specialists seem to care about anything beyond their own specialties.

". . . It is an ironic fact that the very technical skills which are ostensibly employed to further the progress of

[27] Laski, *op.cit.*

men, by the intensity of their specialization, create dis-
unity rather than order and imperil the whole process of
their common objective."[28] One of the problems which
administrators face is to decide what expert advice to take
and what to reject. Lilienthal suggests the problems which
the Board of the TVA faces when a dam is to be built and
the waters of a man-made lake are to cover thousands of
acres of land. How much land should the TVA purchase?
The engineer indicates what land will actually be under
water when the dam is closed. But should the land along
the shoreline be purchased? The agricultural experts argue
that farm land should not be flooded but used for growing
crops. The recreation expert wants a strip of land along
the entire shoreline to be used for parks and playgrounds.
The malaria-control expert wants water kept out of low
areas to reduce mosquito breeding. The highway engineer
wants to purchase lands which contain important access
highways to the new dam and lake area. The power experts
urge economy to protect the investment in electric power.
The navigation expert wants land areas reserved for termi-
nal and harbor facilities. And sometimes the archeologist
wants to preserve prehistoric remains in reservoir areas,
and the finance expert is concerned about removing land
parcels from the tax lists of local government units.

The problem faced by the TVA Board in this instance is
not merely to compromise the views of the various experts
but to look at the situation as a whole and to decide "what
course of action would yield the best results *as judged by
the common purpose*, the goal of the whole undertaking—
the well-being of the people of the region."[29] Indeed, one
of the most essential tasks of any administrator is to educate
the various groups of experts on his staff as to the common
purpose of the organization and to coordinate their efforts
to achieve that common purpose. What the administrator

[28] David Lilienthal, *TVA, Democracy on the March*, Harper and
Brothers, New York, 1944, pp. 66-67.
[29] *ibid.*, p. 69.

123

requires is not the concept of administration as a special *expertise* but an ability to handle relationships in broad terms. Paul Appleby has called it the quality of philosophy which does not embrace a set of absolutes and a technical logic but which comprehends people's emotions as well as their rational judgments.[30] The administrator must supply that element which fuses the work of his expert staff into a coherent program in the public interest.

The expert in administration, like experts in other professions, tends to exaggerate the importance of his skills, the skills of management. He usually fails to note the limitations of his tools. He seeks to apply them in some uniform and impersonal fashion to matters which require variable treatment. He frequently strives to tailor the program of his agency to the set pattern of administration suggested by his inflexible tools and skills. He is apt to insist on organizational patterns which satisfy his expert judgment but which fail to facilitate the achievement of the organization's basic objectives. He is inclined to regard system and red tape as inviolate even though they may add little to or actually detract from the administrative process. He tends to emphasize administration as structure rather than process.

Some professions, such as law, medicine, engineering, public health, and social work, embody similar limitations that have important effects upon the administration of a public enterprise. The expert doctor does not become, by virtue of his expertness, a great source of wisdom about the public's requirements for medical care. Nor does the social worker, by virtue of *his* expertness, acquire a superior right to make final judgments about the proper elements of an adequate standard of living or about the architecture of a state institution for the feeble-minded.

The limitations of the expert are relevant to all public agencies. But they appear to apply with special force to independent commissions. In commissions the staff experts

[30] Paul Appleby, *Big Democracy*, Alfred A. Knopf, New York, 1945, p. 43.

are rarely balanced by commissioners who possess not the detailed knowledge of the experts but the aptitude for gauging the public mind and for integrating the points of view and proposals of the experts into a policy in the public interest.

# CHAPTER 5

# Independence, Responsibility, and the Public Interest

CERTAIN problems of political theory and practice are more or less common to national commissions and are among their most significant characteristics as governing institutions. In this chapter some of the problems with significant theoretical implications are reviewed, while some problems of practical operation are discussed in the next chapter.

## Obstacles to Formulation of a Theory of Regulation

From the point of view of political theory, there are a number of obstacles in the way of a theoretical analysis of the independent commission. Advocates of commissions have been victimized by a naïve notion of reform, by a lack of sophistication in political theory, and by a tendency to isolate regulatory matters from the general context of political and social problems.

Post-Civil War political thought was heavily biased toward the laissez-faire approach in economics and politics. In economic enterprise the general welfare was held to be the sum of the efforts of individual entrepreneurs in pursuit of their own private interests. Similarly, the public interest in regulation was usually conceived as the aggregate or balance of contending private interests. It was held that the public interest in regulation represented an equilibrium of "private" forces; therefore, it had no independent existence of its own and could not be discovered by an independent analysis of economic situations. The bias of political *laissez faire* led to the expectation that the public interest in regulation would be identified automatically as the residue of the struggle among the conflicting demands of rival private parties. Under this conception the creative search for the public interest by government officials became gratuitous. The public interest, or the proper balance among the private parties, would be produced automatically, provided the struggle was permitted to work itself out without governmental interference.

The powerful legal bias in American politics has contributed to the lack of realism in analyzing regulatory problems. Lawyers have insisted upon viewing the regulatory process as the adjudication of controversies by an administrative agency. Accepting the familiar judicial mode of procedure as the best manner of settling controversies among private parties, lawyers have held that regulatory agencies should behave as much like courts as possible. At the same time they have popularized the notion that the courts have a virtual monopoly over the dispensation of justice and that regulatory agencies have inherent tendencies toward arbitrary action. The legal bias in regulation of economic affairs has emphasized the need to safeguard individual rights and interests against governmental attack. It has given little attention to the assumption of responsibility by a commission for an objective analysis of regulatory problems in its field of jurisdiction. The independent commission, therefore, has been viewed not as a governing institution with positive responsibilities and powers, but as a body against which private parties required protection. Lawyers have been concerned more with minimizing the adverse effects of governmental regulation upon private interests than with maximizing the public interest.

The development of regulation of the American economy has been haphazard. Concentration upon relieving particular abusive business practices has turned attention away from long-term problems in government-business relations. It was much easier to secure the votes for enacting a regulatory statute aimed at eliminating certain detested business practices than it was to obtain agreement on the general line of development of governmental responsibilities in the economic sphere for the coming decades. Immediate, limited objectives seemed to be far more promis ing than long-term conceptual goals as bases for political action. The so-called pragmatic evolution of governmental regulation gave credence to the view that the piecemeal approach was not only realistic but right and natural.

Above all, American regulatory experience has been accompanied by a naïve view of the political process. Politics is seen as something which must somehow be avoided or minimized in order to overcome tendencies toward corruption, fraud, and misuse of public funds, the machinations of politicians, and pressures from self-seeking groups and individuals. "Keeping out of politics" became the ideal panacea for exercising governmental functions without incurring the liabilities of the political process. John M. Clark, in his pioneering work on social control of business, recognized the seriousness of the situation: "One disquieting symptom is the frequency with which, when a new reform is suggested, ways are sought to 'keep it out of politics.' Politics is the democratic way of governing; is it becoming necessary, then, to keep government itself out of politics?"[1]

The aim in keeping regulation out of politics was clear. It was to put regulation in the hands of experienced men who would carry out the public interest without regard for the pressures of the parties in interest and the professional politicians. The derogatory view of the professional politician and of the political process has had serious consequences for the development of the concept of the independent commission. Stability and continuity of policy have been held to be achievable only by a commission manned by experts and insulated from normal political pressures. It is commonly believed that it is more difficult to influence a board or commission than a bureau chief or Cabinet secretary. As the Byrd Committee report indicated in 1937, "It is probable that the independence of these authorities [i.e. the independent regulatory commissions] is necessary to give stability to long-range policies and rela-

[1] John Maurice Clark, *Social Control of Business*, 2nd edn., McGraw-Hill Book Co., New York, 1939, p. 490.

tive freedom from pressure groups."[2] The alleged non-political character of regulation has been assumed and asserted in most analyses of the independent commission. For example, the Board of Investigation and Research[3] reported in 1944 that the independent commission should be retained as the administrative agency for transportation regulation. "To place rate regulation in the hands of an executive officer would be to move . . . toward politics rather than away, to diminish that protection from partisanship which is desirable." The Board asserted that a major objective of reform in the regulation of the transportation industry was the "removal of economic regulatory activities as far as possible from spheres of political contest."[4]

Those who hoped to reform democracy by escaping from politics lacked an elementary comprehension of the theory of the democratic state. They failed to recognize that "The genius of democracy is in politics, not in sterilization of politics."[5]

Finally, a middle-class tradition of genteel reform has militated against realistic consideration of the regulatory commission as an instrument of regulation. From the days of the Populists and the Grangers down to those of the Progressives and the New Dealers, reformers hoped to modify basic economic institutions by tinkering with the machinery of government. Simple panaceas were relied upon to achieve far-reaching changes. Reformers had great confidence in

[2] *Report of the Government Activities in the Regulation of Private Business Enterprises*, prepared by the Brookings Institution, Report to the U.S. Congress, Senate, Select Committee to Investigate the Executive Agencies of the Government, Select Committee Print No. 10, 1937, 75th Congress, 1st session, p. 100.

[3] For a statement about the Board of Investigation and Research, see footnote 1 in Chapter 4.

[4] Board of Investigation and Research, *Practices and Procedures of Governmental Control*, House Document No. 678, 1944, 78th Congress, 2nd session, pp. 141, 178.

[5] Testimony of Paul Appleby in U.S. Congress, Senate, Committee on Labor and Public Welfare, *Hearings on the Establishment of a Commission on Ethics in Government*, June-July 1951, 82nd Congress, 1st session, p. 171.

their reforms; but when they eventually became disillusioned, they usually renounced reform as a bad mistake. They lacked staying power and the ability to maintain the interest of the public in their programs.

Because of the bias of political thought, the legal emphasis on formal adjudication as the focus of economic regulation, the traditional haphazard approach toward regulatory problems, the naïve view of the political process, and the genteel tradition of middle-class reform, the advocates of the independent commission wholly misconstrued the regulatory process. As a result they were unable to understand the nature of the major problem which the commissions had to face.

## Independence of Regulatory Commissions

The independence of regulatory commissions can be regarded more usefully as a concept than as an element capable of precise definition. "Independence" relates to one or more of the following conditions: location outside an executive department; some measure of independence from supervision by the president or by a Cabinet secretary; immunity from the president's discretionary power to remove members of independent commissions from office.

In his analysis of independence in state regulatory agencies, Fesler deals with the various meanings of the term "independence" and concludes that it "is devoid of meaning unless it be defined in terms of independence 'from something.' "[6] Congress usually thinks of independence as freedom from the control of the chief executive and bipartisanship in the membership of commissions. Bipartisanship requires that one political party be limited to three out of five, four out of seven, or six out of eleven members, as the case may be. Of the various meanings of independence, the one which has played a vital role in the controversy about the effectiveness and fairness of inde-

[6] James W. Fesler, *The Independence of State Regulatory Agencies*, Public Administration Service No. 85, Public Administration Service, Chicago, 1942, p. 13.

pendent commissions is freedom from executive control.[7] There are strong tendencies in Congress to hamper and undermine the independence of the commissions. Freedom from executive control is emphasized by stressing the dependence of commissions upon Congress and reminding the president to respect them as agents of Congress. Because commissions deal with economic matters of great importance to those subject to regulation, individual Congressmen are also subject to considerable pressure to aid constituents in their dealings with various commissions.[8]

## HOW THE PRESIDENT INFLUENCES COMMISSIONS

Independence of commissions from executive control has become highly qualified. Not only does the president appoint the members of commissions, but he can appoint a majority of them in three to eight years. Since 1950 the president has had authority to designate the chairmen of all commissions except the ICC. Most commissions rely heavily on the Department of Justice for formal prosecution of cases involving alleged violations of regulations. In employing their staffs, commissions are bound by normal Civil Service rules. With respect to budgets, the commissions' appropriation requests are channeled through the Bureau of the Budget, in the Executive Office of the President, which analyzes the requests in the same manner as it examines the budget estimates of the regular departments. The Budget Bureau studies the administrative operations of commissions and makes recommendations for organizational changes. The president may direct or request a commission to undertake a special study; and, in the case of the FTC, the president may direct the investigation of alleged violations of antitrust laws. CAB decisions in connection with certificates or permits for overseas or foreign air transportation by domestic or foreign carriers

[7] See Emmette S. Redford, *Administration of National Economic Control*, The Macmillan Co., New York, 1952, p. 275.

[8] See E. P. Herring, *Public Administration and the Public Interest*, McGraw-Hill Book Co., New York, 1936, pp. 115ff.

and SEC orders suspending trading on exchanges are subject to approval, modification, or rejection by the president.

In addition, the president may influence the work of commissions in informal ways. Through conferences with certain commissioners, he may recommend action he would like them to take in particular matters, and he may seek their advice on matters of public policy related to their field of regulation. Presidents Harding and Coolidge attempted to control commissions by requiring from certain commissioners signed, undated resignations at the time of their appointment.

Redford reports that since 1913 the presidents "have taken no narrow view of their functions."[9] According to Cushman, all presidents from Wilson on have attempted in one way or another to influence the activities and policies of the commissions.[10] Even before 1950, when the president lacked statutory power to choose the chairmen of the FTC, SEC, and FPC, his wishes concerning their designation by the commissions were generally respected.[11]

A more realistic appraisal of political relationships is revealed in Louis Brownlow's story about Senator Wagner of New York. According to the Senator, who was an advocate of the use of commissions even for ordinary administrative work, a constituent "came to him furiously demanding that the Senator go at once to the White House and insist that the President rescind an order made by the Interstate Commerce Commission. The Senator said that he explained over and over again to his irate visitor that the ICC was independent and that the President could not give it orders. The man listened unwillingly and then at the end leaned across the desk toward the Senator, brought down his fist in a terrific blow that shook the whole office,

9 Redford, *op.cit.*, p. 279.

10 Robert E. Cushman, *The Independent Regulatory Commissions*, Oxford University Press, New York, 1941, pp. 681-685.

11 Data about presidential influence exercised through the chairmen of the commissions is conveniently summarized in Redford, *op.cit.*, pp. 279-282.

and clinched the argument by yelling: 'But the President appoints them commissioners, don't he?' "[12]

LIMITS TO PRESIDENTIAL INFLUENCE

Although commissions are clearly within the scope of presidential influence and may even be dominated by the president on certain policy matters, there are limits beyond which the president may not go in attempting to bend them to his point of view. First of all, Congress continues to think of commissions as responsible solely to it. Congressional hearings on matters relating to the work of commissions are replete with illustrations of the lively Congressional tradition of regarding commissions as independent from executive control.[13] Second, groups subject to regulation

[12] Louis Brownlow, *The President and the Presidency*, Public Administration Service, Chicago, 1949, pp. 101-102.

[13] See, for example, the questioning of members of the Maritime Commission by various Congressional committees regarding the sale of tankers by the national government. The testimony is quoted in "The Sale of the Tankers," one of the cases in Harold Stein, ed., *Public Administration and Policy Development*, Harcourt, Brace and Co., New York, 1952, pp. 501-506. Senator Wherry of the Senate Small Business Committee asked Raymond McKeough, Vice Chairman of the Maritime Commission, to defend his support of foreign sale of tankers by the Commission:

McKEOUGH: Now, when the Cabinet asked us to make this sale, and I speak very frankly, I am on the team in the Commission. I was appointed by President Truman. I had a little trouble getting in, you may recall, but I finally made it.

WHERRY: You said you play on the team of the Cabinet, and the Cabinet is the one that said, "This is what you should do to help out the general oil supply." Is not Maritime an independent agency?

McKEOUGH: Yes.

WHERRY: Then is not your responsibility to Congress?

McKEOUGH: That is right.

WHERRY: Then we have a team, too.

McKEOUGH: That is right. I agree. I do not yield to anyone in my regard of the Congress.

WHERRY: Certainly, playing on the team with the Cabinet does not alter the requirements set by the statute.

McKEOUGH: No, not at all; but I differ as to whether or not we did violence to the statute.

This particular testimony is found in U.S. Congress, Senate, Special Committee to Study Problems of American Small Business, *Hearings*, part 23, November 14, 1947, p. 2592. It is quoted on pp. 505-506 of *Public Administration and Policy Development*.

can normally be depended upon by commissions to defend their independence from executive control. As Redford concludes: ". . . the commissions' close association with their clienteles and their cultivation of their own channels of contact with Congress have tended to insulate them against novel or disturbing influence from the chief executive."[14]

Third, the omnipresent example of the Interstate Commerce Commission as a self-styled impartial tribunal free from executive control has established a pattern of thinking about commissions. The prestige of the ICC has helped to glorify the notion that the executive is the source of evil partisan influences from which the commissions must be protected. While this habit of thinking does not square with the facts of the political process, it nevertheless remains traditional in public discussion and has helped to maintain a gulf between the president and the commissions which is wider than that between the president and the regular executive departments. The historical accident of the appointment of Judge Cooley as the first chairman of the ICC in 1887 helped to establish what later became the traditional emphasis of ICC upon the judicial, case-by-case approach to regulation without regard to the changing economic policies of the political party in power.

THE FAILURE OF THE PRESIDENT TO REORGANIZE THE ICC

In 1950 President Truman submitted to Congress a group of reorganization plans giving the president authority to designate the chairmen of all commissions and to vest in the chairmen broad administrative responsibility for directing the work of the commissions. Plan No. 7 of 1950[15] proposed that the president designate the chairman of the ICC and that there be transferred from the Commission to its chairman "the executive and administrative functions of the Commission, including functions of the Commission with respect to (1) the appointment and su-

14 Redford, *op.cit.*, pp. 276-277.
15 *House Document No. 511*, 81st Congress, 2nd session.

pervision of personnel employed under the Commission, (2) the distribution of business under such personnel and among administrative units of the Commission, and (3) the use and expenditure of funds."[16] These proposals were in general accord with the 1949 recommendations of the Hoover Commission.

In hearings before the House and Senate Committees on Expenditures in the Executive Departments,[17] representatives, senators, and spokesmen for management and labor groups in the transportation industries testified in opposition to the proposals on the ground that they would destroy the independence of the commissions and weaken the legislative branch. Senator Edwin C. Johnson of Colorado, Chairman of the Senate Committee on Interstate and Foreign Commerce, testified that the destruction of the independent commission was a step on the road to a streamlined dictatorship. His comments are worth quoting at length because they represent the prevailing, orthodox conception of the independent commission.

"It is the long-established congressional policy," he said, "that regulatory agencies must be independent and directly responsible to Congress.

"The necessity of maintaining the independency of the regulatory bodies was discussed during the Senate debate in 1938 on the Government departments reorganization bill, a legislative culmination of a professional study of government and how to reorganize it. In that debate former Senator Champ Clark, of Missouri, one of the Senate's greatest students of parliamentary history, now one of our really great judges on the Federal bench, pointed out that 'the principal functions of such commissions as the Interstate Commerce Commission, the Federal Trade Commis-

[16] *ibid.*, section 1.

[17] U.S. Congress, House, Committee on Expenditures in the Executive Departments, *Hearings on H. Res. 545*, Reorganization Plan No. 7 of 1950, April 24 and 25, 1950, 81st Congress, 2nd session; and U.S. Congress, Senate, Committee on Expenditures in the Executive Departments, *Hearings on S. Res. 253, 254, 255, and 256*, Reorganization Plans No. 7, 8, 9, and 11 of 1950, April 24, 25, and 26, 1950, 81st Congress, 2nd session.

sion, and the Communications Commission are as agencies of the legislative branch of the Government and as extensions of the legislative power' and that 'the important function which has been conferred on such commissions is the ascertainment of particular facts in order to carry out a policy of Congress enunciated in a statute' and 'they are legislative rather than executive or administrative in character.' "

Senator Johnson quoted Vice President Barkley, commenting when he was the majority leader of the Senate. The commissions, Barkley had said, "are quasi judicial and quasi legislative. They are quite different from a commission which is created merely to aid the President in determining how he shall perform his executive duty of appointing people to office, in the way of testing their qualifications (for instance, the Civil Service Commission). One is an executive function, the others are legislative and judicial,· and the only reason why the Interstate Commerce Commission was set up, and why the Federal Trade Commission, and the Power Commission, and the Communications Commission were set up under the authority to regulate commerce among the States and with foreign governments, was the knowledge that Congress itself could not do that."

Senator Johnson continued: "Already Congress has in the last two decades taken long steps down the road to abdication of constitutional powers. We must not and should not unwittingly tread farther down that road. If efficiency and streamlining is the goal, then the answer is the kind of government that Hitler and Mussolini tried and Stalin is employing now." Referring to the bipartisan character of the commissions, Johnson said: "These are safeguards against arbitrary rule by one man. To place control over the staff in the hands of the Chairman is to make them all-powerful and thus virtually make the other Commissioners figureheads. The Chairman, of course, is appointed directly by the President. These plans, therefore, would be a substantial step toward the elimination of the bipartisan and nonpolitical character intended for these commissions."[18]

Senator Johnson's views were echoed and amplified by representatives of the regulated groups and the commissioners themselves, with the exception of the members of the Federal Trade Commission, who took the view that the designation of its chairman by the president was relatively unimportant and would produce no significant change in the operation of the FTC. Groups which rallied to the "defense" of the ICC against presidential and alleged dictatorial influences included the Association of Interstate Commerce Practitioners, Transportation Association of America, Association of American Railroads, Railway Labor Executives' Association, Freight Forwarders Institute, National Industrial Traffic League, American Bar Association, American Short Line Railroad Association, Indiana State Chamber of Commerce, American Trucking Associations, Inc., National Council of Private Motor Truck Owners, and National Association of Motor Bus Operators. The alliance of the ICC with pressure groups representing its regulated clientele was sufficiently powerful to defeat Plan No. 7.

The capacity of the president to influence commissions depends largely upon his general political strength, especially in relations with Congress. A president elected with a decisive popular vote and having the support of a sympathetic majority in Congress is able to exercise considerable influence over commissions. However, even such a president, as Franklin Roosevelt discovered in 1938, cannot hope to maintain his strength in Congress for more than a few years at best.

### The Case for Independence

In his famous speech in 1944 responding to testimonials on his contribution to the development of administrative regulation, Joseph Eastman made the classic statement of

[18] These quotations are taken from the Senate *Hearings on S. Res. 253, 254, 255, and 256, op.cit.,* pp. 16-17.

the traditional view of the independent commission: "With the country as big and as complex as it is, administrative tribunals like the ICC are necessities. Probably we shall have more rather than less. To be successful, they must be masters of their own souls, and known to be such. It is the duty of the President to determine their personnel through the power of appointment, and it is the duty of Congress to determine by statute the policies which they are to administer; but in the administration of those policies, these tribunals must not be under the domination or influence of either the President or Congress or of anything else than their own independent judgment of the facts and the law. They must also be in position and ready to give free and untrammeled advice to both the President and Congress at any time upon request. Political domination will ruin such a tribunal."[19]

Independence from presidential control has been favored consistently by advocates of regulatory reform as well as by the regulated interests themselves. Herbert Emmerich states that the roots of independence are to be found in "the efforts of groups to insure the responsiveness of these agencies to their interests rather than to over-all government purposes."[20] As a device to protect and promote the interests of regulated groups, the independence of commissions takes on a more realistic meaning. It becomes easier to understand why the independence of regulatory commissions has come to acquire a sacred inviolability. According to William Carey, the prime purpose of independence "is to free commissions from the insidious influences of politics. Even assuming this freedom to have been achieved, there are effects which are extremely serious. Cut

[19] Mr. Eastman made these remarks in his response on the occasion of the Silver Anniversary Dinner given to him at Washington on February 17, 1944. He delivered extemporaneously a primer of administrative regulation. The portion quoted is one of twelve points in the primer. The speech is reprinted in G. Lloyd Wilson, ed., *Selected Papers and Addresses of Joseph B. Eastman, 1942-1944*, Simmons-Boardman Publishing Co., New York, 1948, p. 375.

[20] Herbert Emmerich, *Essays on Federal Reorganization*, University of Alabama Press, University, Alabama, 1950, p. 36.

loose from presidential leadership and protection, the agencies must formulate policy in a political vacuum. Into this vacuum may move the regulated interests themselves, and by infiltration overcome the weak regulatory defenses to become the strongest influences upon the regulators."[21]

## THE HOOVER COMMISSION

On the other hand, the commissions have not lacked defenders against the charge that their independence from executive control has made them subservient to regulated groups. The Hoover Commission concluded that "the independent regulatory commissions have a proper place in the machinery of our Government, a place very like that originally conceived. . . ."[22] Its Task Force studying the activities of the various commissions made a much stronger statement:

"The independent regulatory commission is a useful and desirable agency where constant adaptation to changing conditions and delegation of wide discretion in administration are essential to effective regulation.

"The independent commission provides a means for insulating regulation from partisan influence or favoritism, for obtaining deliberation, expertness and continuity of attention, and for combining adaptability of regulation with consistency of policy so far as practical."[23]

The case for independence has been based on the claim that independence promotes and stimulates a number of desirable or essential attributes in the administration of regulatory statutes. What are the alleged advantages of independence? They can be identified by examining the claims made for independence by its advocates.

[21] William D. Carey, "The Federal Regulatory Commissions," lecture delivered at Princeton University, April 4, 1952, mimeo., p. 3.
[22] Commission on Organization of the Executive Branch of the Government, *Regulatory Commissions*, a Report to the Congress, 1949, p. 3.
[23] Task Force on Regulatory Commissions of the Commission on Organization of the Executive Branch of the Government, *Report on Regulatory Commissions*, 1949, p. viii.

THE CASE OF JAMES LANDIS

According to Landis, independence has two important effects upon regulatory commissions. First, regulatory policies are likely to be more permanent and more consistent to the extent that they are not too closely identified with particular presidential administrations. Second, independence enhances the professional qualities of the agency. He wrote: "It is difficult to appraise, even in general terms, the importance of making the administrative agency independent. . . . But such evidence as there is indicates that there have been gains. Railroad policies, for example, have achieved a degree of permanence and consistency that they might not have possessed had their formulation been too closely identified with the varying tempers of changing administrations. . . . On the other hand, professionalism in the nonindependent agencies has suffered on occasion at the hands of political superiors." Landis believed that the department head often subverted or adversely controlled his bureau chiefs and prevented them from maintaining direct contact with the public, whereas the commissioners of an independent agency did not have to depend upon the support and approval of a politically minded department head. He stated: "Powers of the head of a department are penetrating and pervasive. By a judicious selection of personnel, discrimination in promotions, a shifting of responsibilities, his views can only too easily control the staff. Interposing the head of a department between the active administrative official and the public means insulating the administrative head from the public and consequently depriving him of a sounding-board for his views. The chief of a bureau possesses no public position comparable to that of the head of an independent administrative agency. Support for his policy must derive from, or through, his chief and not directly from the public. To that degree he lacks the ability to withstand attack or to gather support for his views. And since the quality of his professional approach to his regulatory problems must filter through his superior, public appraisal of his performance is likely to rest upon a partial, incomplete, and perhaps unknown record."[24]

Landis was not concerned with the independence of regulatory agencies *in abstracto*. Rather he was arguing for their independence from the courts. Whatever may have been his specific purpose, his remarks would be more applicable to current administrative practice if they were stated in exactly opposite terms. The record of the commissions indicates that commissioners, on the whole, occupy a lower position in the administrative hierarchy in Washington than do the bureau chiefs in the executive departments. Bureau chiefs, moreover, are notoriously adept at resisting the efforts of department heads to integrate and coordinate the work of the bureaus of a department. Instead of insulating the bureaus from the public, the main task of a department head is to strengthen the political standing of the department and to win support for departmental programs. The deficiencies which Landis has ascribed to the bureau chiefs might more appropriately describe the role and position of the commissioners of an independent commission.

## OTHER ARGUMENTS

Although Joseph Eastman, as a member of the ICC, actively supported the proposal to unite all transportation regulation in a single agency, he did not deviate from his lifelong devotion to the idea of the independent commission. As a commissioner, as Federal Coordinator of Transportation, and as wartime Director of Defense Transportation, Eastman insisted that public regulation of transportation "must be administered by a permanent, independent, and nonpolitical body having a continuing and dependable policy." Eastman wanted a commission as

[24] James M. Landis, *The Administrative Process*, Yale University Press, New Haven, 1938, pp. 113-115.

"removed from influence by the President, Congress, or any political agency as the Supreme Court itself."[25]

In its study of regulatory administration in 1944, the Board of Investigation and Research appreciated, more than most special investigating bodies have, the complex nature of independence in the regulatory commissions. It recognized the importance of presidential support in the development of vigorous regulation in the public interest. However, it accepted the popular faith in independence from political forces as a guarantor of administration in the public interest. It included the following as advantages which independence confers: "Primarily these are relief from political pressure and greatly improved opportunities for maintaining consistency of policy. An administrative agency must from time to time, depending upon the nature of its work, make determinations on matters which involve political issues of considerable importance. If Executive powers or the great influence of the Executive are used to promote a particular decision, the standing and authority of the agency are at once endangered. More impartial action, and wider popular acceptance of the result, will be assured if the agency is both in fact and in reputation largely independent of the Executive. Continuity of policy, which is likewise served by such independence, is a factor of extreme importance to the businesses and industries subject to regulatory action. Executive control certainly could not assure such continuity beyond the tenure of the same Chief Executive, and even within a single administration sudden shifts and reversals of policies may occur, which, if reflected in regulatory decisions, would have destructive consequences. It is difficult to see how Executive control of administrative processes, in any explicit or detailed sense, can be beneficial in large areas of governmental regulation."[26] The Board thus concluded that the advantages of independence were relief from political pressures,

[25] Federal Coordinator of Transportation, *Third Report*, House Document No. 89, 1935, 74th Congress, 1st session, p. 15.
[26] Board of Investigation and Research, *op.cit.*, p. 21.

consistency of policy, impartiality, wider popular support, and continuity of policy.

Some of the argument in favor of the independence of regulatory commissions has been a reaction to rather dogmatic assertion of certain "principles" of administrative organization. The rather immoderate language of the President's Committee on Administrative Management in characterizing independent commissions as the "headless fourth branch of the government" and the growing acceptance of executive integration as a major goal of administrative reorganization encouraged some students of public administration to be skeptical about the benefits allegedly derived from reorganizations that strengthened the position of the president as the manager-in-chief of the executive branch of the government. Harvey Pinney, for example, refused to accept the dogmas of administrative reorganization and argued instead for independence of commissions. His basic argument was that the problems of a particular regulated industry represented a fundamental unity which required a corresponding unity in the government's handling of the problems.[27] Pinney seemed to be reacting to the claims being made by public administration specialists for the principle of executive integration. He denied that independence led to organizational chaos or irresponsible autonomy.

EVALUATION OF THE CASE FOR INDEPENDENCE

Has the case for the independence of the regulatory commissions been justified by the experience of the commissions? Has the commission, because of its independence, achieved impartiality, continuity and consistency of policy, and public acceptance of regulation? Has independence freed the regulatory process from insidious political influences and from the effects of changing political programs? In 1942 Fesler reported that independence, as applied to the state regulatory agencies, "is more myth than reality.

[27] Harvey Pinney, "The Case for Independence of Administrative Agencies," *Annals*, vol. 221, May 1942, pp. 40-48.

And like many other myths it has a sinister effect, for it lulls the public into a false confidence in the Olympian judgments of the 'independent' agencies, and diverts attention from the influences that are constantly at work." Fesler concluded that "full independence is an illusory will-o'-the-wisp."[28] This finding applies fully to the national commissions.

In 1950 the Bureau of the Budget conducted a survey of the operations of independent regulatory commissions.[29] The Bureau found independence to be a major source of weakness and ineffectiveness in the commissions. "Moreover, the controversial policy areas in which they operate are replete with major policy conflicts which cannot easily be resolved. The absence of organized public support for regulatory policies places a premium on the ability of the commissions to live with the industries and trades subject to regulation. These factors help to explain the tendency of the commissions to become timid in defending the public interest and developing regulatory programs. The commissions tend to become passive in their search for the public interest and to take refuge in a case-by-case approach to their regulatory problems. Over the years, they become weighted down by the paraphernalia of due process of law, and tend to look backward instead of ahead. This weakens their capacity for analyzing economic regulatory problems and formulating planned programs to resolve them satisfactorily."[30]

The conclusions of the Budget Bureau study coincide with Fesler's analysis of the "price of independence" of regulatory commissions: First, the belief that independence

[28] Fesler, *op.cit.*, pp. 61, 63.

[29] The author was associated with this project as a consultant to the Estimates Division of the Bureau of the Budget and prepared studies of safety administration, enforcement activities, and problems of adjudication in a number of the commissions. The conclusions of the study represent the judgment of the task force of the Budget Bureau and do not necessarily represent the conclusions of the Director of the Budget.

[30] United States Bureau of the Budget, "Project Summary, Survey of Regulatory Commissions," 1950, dittoed, p. 3.

insures "judge-like wisdom, balance, and insight" in the regulatory process is a dangerous popular illusion. It "pretends that we can preserve democracy and still vest economic powers in a governmental agency that is not clearly subject to officials who in turn are responsible to the people." Second, independence, according to Fesler, stands in the way of badly needed coordination of policy. ". . . the existence of commissions with great regulatory powers claiming virtual independence of the chief executive seriously handicaps attempts to approximate even a rough-hewn sort of coordination." Third, independent commissions have a tendency to lapse into lethargy. Fourth, in an era of positive government, the requirements of effective action include responsible and efficient management and adequate direction of governmental affairs. "Over the long run of the years ahead, it seems very doubtful that the people will return to a negative concept of government's role in the economy. It is therefore hardly conceivable that they will long tolerate an arrangement whereby the most important instruments for guidance of the economy are independent commissions without close ties linking them to one another and to either the legislature or the executive." Fifth, Fesler found that the independent commission "is notably lacking in the vigor essential to advancing toward the goals the legislative and executive branches had in mind in adopting the basic [regulatory] statutes." Lack of stimulation in the independent commissions was traced to "general inertia," "overemphasis on the judicial approach," and "excessive exposure to the views and influence of the regulated interests, without compensating exposure to governmental and private views expressive of the public interest."[31]

## The Implications of "Independence"

Although regulatory commissions have been called inde-

[31] James W. Fesler, "Independent Regulatory Establishments," in F. M. Marx, ed., *Elements of Public Administration*, Prentice-Hall, Inc., New York, 1946, pp. 207-235. The quotations here are from pp. 227-230.

145

pendent, their relationship to the president differs in degree rather than kind from that of a regular department. It has already been noted that independence is in any case relative, in view of the president's power to appoint commissioners and in the light of the influences of presidential requests, party loyalties, and Congressional desires. Single-headed departments and agencies or their subdivisions, such as the Bureau of Mines in the Department of the Interior, may in fact be substantially independent of presidential direction when a highly organized interest group exercises strong clientele influence over the agency or bureau. At a particular moment, presidential concern with the activities of the independent commissions may exceed his interest in one or more of the Cabinet departments. Heads of departments and bureau chiefs have also become very adept at pursuing their own programs and justifying appropriations despite presidential directives to support only programs included in the president's budget estimate as submitted to Congress.

While "independence" may not distinguish a regulatory commission markedly from other departments and agencies, maintenance of the myth of commission independence represents a conscious effort by regulated groups to confine regulatory authority to an agency that is somewhat more susceptible than an executive department to influence, persuasion, and, eventually, capture and control. David Truman noted that an independent agency, more than one clearly a part of the executive branch, will more readily reflect the relative standing of the organized and unorganized interests concerned with legislation.[32]

Perhaps the most serious implication of the theory of the independent commission is a dangerously naïve concept of democracy as a scheme of government to which political responsibility has no necessary relevance. Straightforward analysis of the requirements of democratic government has been supplanted by a so-called pragmatic, or practical, out-

[32] David B. Truman, *The Governmental Process*, Alfred A. Knopf, New York, 1951, p. 419.

look which achieves the highly impractical result, from the point of view of the public interest, of discrediting the political process.

Unsatisfactory integration of policy and defective co-ordination of administrative activity have become major obstacles to effective regulation and effective administration in general. In an age which throws upon the president an unmanageable burden of political leadership and administrative management, the survival of islands of administrative independence, however qualified, only serves to increase the difficulties of integration.

Independence deprives a commission of the opportunity to profit by the regulatory experiences of other commissions and agencies. By isolating it from the executive branch, independence depreciates the value of the regulatory experience of each commission. Regulatory agencies look inwardly for stimulation, novel ideas, imaginative approaches, and useful techniques. As a result, a commission becomes unwilling to relate its program to other programs of economic regulation and promotion. It develops an air of self-importance and resists overtures from other agencies to formulate programs in consultation with them. Consequently, a commission's resources for improvement and advancement are negligible and subject to continuing attrition.

Independence also has serious budgetary implications. The small staff and budget of commissions mean that little attention is given to these agencies by the Bureau of the Budget and Congressional appropriations committees. The relatively low level of managerial skill in the commissions discourages preparation of carefully drawn budget justifications. In a commendable attempt at self-analysis, the Budget Bureau in 1950 examined its method of treating the commissions' budget requests and found that the budget process had contributed little to the improved management in commissions. It found that "the very independence of these agencies leaves them without Cabinet or other top-level representation to plead their cases in relation to defense or other crucial needs of the day." According to the Bureau, "the relatively small amounts of money involved in the agency budgets encourage superficial analysis of their budgets." Budget review policies tended to be restrictive because of "the many obvious deficiencies of the agencies."[33]

Independence seems to have some implications for the appointing process. The casualness of presidential appointments to commissions can be traced in part to the belief that the president should not be too concerned with the work of the commissions. Presidents may be wary of naming highly qualified commissioners for fear that they will not be amenable to presidential requests and advice concerning regulatory action. The size of the commissions gives a president an apparent opportunity to nominate persons who would not normally be acceptable to him as directors of single-headed agencies.

Independence is closely related to ideas of expertness and judicialization. Taken as a group, these notions are mutually reinforcing. The judiciary is recognized as a model of independence, and serves as a potent example for organizing and conducting the activity of a commission. Independence also implies dissatisfaction with the political process, and for that reason is consistent with the view that regulatory administration must be in the hands of qualified experts operating in an atmosphere free from political influence.

Although logically the case for independence rests on unsound grounds, the political justification for it remains strong. Legislative histories of several commissions suggest that their enabling statutes might not have been enacted if Congress had not been able to delegate regulatory duties to agencies somewhat removed from continuing presidential guidance. However desirable the integration of

33 United States Bureau of the Budget, op.cit., p. 3. For a history of ICC appropriations since 1940, see ICC Practitioners' Journal, vol. 19, June 1952, p. 878. For the ICC's comments on its budgetary deterioration, see ICC, 68th Annual Report, pp. 130-136; reprinted in ICC Practitioners' Journal, vol. 19, February 1952, pp. 463-469.

INDEPENDENCE, RESPONSIBILITY, PUBLIC INTEREST

regulatory policy with national economic policy, and however unfortunate the Congressional suspicion of the president, it remains that, politically speaking, some regulatory agencies would probably not exist at all if they were not independent.

## The Responsibility of Regulatory Commissions

In a democratic society, political institutions are expected to be responsible. Their responsibility has both internal and external aspects. Internally, a political institution operates in a responsible fashion so long as it executes its statutory duties effectively, adheres to an acceptable code of conduct and behavior, and defines its functions in a manner consistent with applicable statutes and executive directives. Externally, a political institution acts in a responsible manner when it complies with legal and financial requirements established by the legislative and executive branches to insure honesty and effectiveness in performance of its duties, and in fact is held legally accountable to Congress for the expenditure of funds and the administration of its program.

The accountability and responsibility of a regulatory commission are affected by several conditions which are more or less unique with them. First, it is more difficult to fix responsibility for administrative direction and managerial decisions on a multiple executive. Second, commissions operate in storm centers of politics where pressures are great and attempts to influence the course of administrative action are considered normal and even essential. Third, there is a common belief that responsibility can be more clearly and firmly fixed in small agencies with limited functions than in large agencies with broader ones. Responsibility allegedly can be pinpointed by localizing it in a regulatory commission. For example, Landis stated that the existence of a large number of regulatory bodies tends to promote more effective public responsibility: "Placing responsibility directly upon a specific group means that a finger can be publicly pointed at a particular man or men who are charged with the solution of a particular question. This localization of responsibility gives, in turn, to these positions a real attraction for men whose sole urge for public service is the opportunity it affords for the satisfactions of achievement." He found that the responsibility of a Cabinet secretary for a particular statute was likely to be obscured in the light of his many other duties: "On the other hand, where the administration of one phase of [the National Industrial Recovery] Act—in the petroleum industry—was turned over to the Secretary of the Interior, the sharp pointing of responsibility was dulled, for administration had become virtually anonymous amid the other heterogeneous duties of the departmental head."[34]

Similarly, the Board of Investigation and Research regarded the independent commission as ideal for the focusing of responsibility: ". . . substantial independence makes an agency more authoritative and better placed to work out successful policies; it also centers responsibility upon it, and this may help to assure more impartial and efficient performance of its work. . . ."[35]

The belief that responsibility can be promoted by placing administrative authority in a large number of agencies outside the supervisory jurisdiction of a Cabinet official is a curious American concept. It assumes that the president is the least responsible political official in the national government, whereas a far better case could be made for the position that the president is the most responsible national official. The belief that responsibility is strengthened by fragmentizing authority and control is partly a reaction to extravagant claims made by proponents of reorganization that a particular formula for reorganization would be sufficient to bring about great economy and a higher level of efficiency in government.

RESPONSIBILITY TO CONGRESS AND THE PRESIDENT

The pattern of responsibility of the commissions to Con-

[34] Landis, *op.cit.*, pp. 28, 29.
[35] Board of Investigation and Research, *op.cit.*, p. 14.

gress is well known. Congressional controls that apply to executive departments apply as well to the independent commissions. Through informal contacts between commissions and individual members of Congress, the appropriation process, Congressional investigations, and legislative consideration of changes in and amendments to enabling legislation, Congress can exercise the same amount of control over independent commissions as it exercises over other administrative agencies. The difference lies not in the tools used by Congress to enforce accountability but in the approach of Congress to the commissions. Congress conceives of commissions as agents of Congress rather than of the executive. It regards them as a device for opposing centralization of presidential authority. Thus Congress places commissions in the unenviable position of opposing the president even though much of their political strength in Congress is dependent upon him.

While the tools for establishing lines of accountability for commissions are the conventional ones, Congress is usually more abusive in investigations and committee hearings concerning commissions. The reason for this is apparent. The controversial character of regulatory policy cannot normally be resolved by Congress, which cannot risk the setting of a national policy that will antagonize important sources of political support. Commissions must make policy that Congress was unable or unwilling to formulate. This situation has unfortunate consequences for the establishment of political responsibility. Commissions receive only minimum positive guidance on controversial issues from Congress and therefore do not know in clear terms what Congress would like them to do. Congressional investigations tend toward the harsh side, with little clarification of basic regulatory policy.

The weakness of the Congressional system of government seems most apparent in the sphere of regulatory legislation. The chairmen of the key committees that have jurisdiction over regulatory commissions, especially the House and Senate Committees on Interstate and Foreign Commerce, have extraordinary power. The committees themselves can hold their chairmen accountable only with considerable difficulty, and there are few means for keeping the committees responsible to Congress itself. The failure of both houses of Congress to establish codes of procedure to govern the process of committee investigations and hearings leaves each committee to its own devices. Beset with urgent pressures by private economic interests and sometimes spurred on by the personal convictions of committee chairmen and key committee members, committees that deal with economic regulation have relatively few defenses against abusive investigative tendencies and the will of a strong-minded chairman. Since the committees themselves are not clearly responsible to Congress, it is difficult for them to establish clear lines of responsibility for commissions on other than the personal terms set by committee chairmen.

Relations between the president and commissions are crucial to the maintenance of the political responsibility of commissions; but the obstacles to creation of effective relations are great. Congress tends to define responsibility in terms of subservience to undefined Congressional policies and freedom from presidential influence. Commissions cannot make their way against unfriendly Congressional committees without strong support from the president. However, commissions must operate in such a way that they merit presidential support. The president must be able to afford to support the commissions. They must be sufficiently effective and resourceful not to leave the president exposed politically in an unfortunate position.

The Humphrey case[36] and the attention given to it have rather distorted the relationship between the president and independent commissions. The case has led to an overemphasis upon the power of the president to influence regulatory policy by removing unfriendly commissioners. As a result there has been little study of other manners in

[36] Humphrey's Executor v. United States, 295 U.S. 602 (1935).

which presidents have attempted to influence the course of action taken by a commission.[37] Ordinarily, the objective of the president is to place regulatory policy in the context of broad national economic policies so that a commission may have the needed perspective in its search for the public interest and in its formulation of regulatory policies. The president's "intervention" may be essential in order to safeguard the public interest from utter bankruptcy or surrender to private pressures.

The key to the weakness of the political accountability of the commission lies in the inability of Congress to define the content of the public interest in matters of public regulation of economic affairs. Congress normally cannot define regulatory policy and is unwilling to let the president do so. Congressional insistence on regarding the commission as an agent of Congress responsible solely to it and not wholly or partially responsible to the president turns a commission into an organizational device for restricting the power of the president. Congress shifts responsibility for policy formulation to commissions under conditions which weaken them as administrative agents. Thus the standard of responsibility is vague and the means for maintaining responsibility are inadequate. Paradoxically, the political responsibility of the commission may be asserted only when the president undertakes the task of defining public regulatory policy and urges its adoption by Congress.

Responsibility is closely related to the degree of discretion which can be exercised by an administrative agency. Independent commissions normally exercise a broad measure of discretion. Ordinarily, the broader the discretion, the greater the need for firm lines of responsibility in order to insure that the commission does not abuse its discretionary authority. Lines of responsibility are needed not only to prevent unfairness but to strengthen the resolve of the commission to carry out the public interest. Responsibility is necessary to maintain integrity of purpose as well

---

[37] On this point, see the summary in Redford, *op.cit.*, pp. 275-283.

as honesty and fair dealing. Unfortunately, the commissions operate under conditions which appear to maximize the obstacles to the achievement of democratic political responsibility.

## Search for the Public Interest

Discussions of the "public interest" that commissions are supposed to seek frequently seem unreal. Usually, the public interest is conceived as a balancing by a commission of the interests involved in regulation. In its search for an equilibrium among the interested parties, it is assumed that a commission will be guided by its legislative mandate. Unreality begins to creep in, however, as soon as it appears that the commission's enabling statute may in fact provide only the most general guide to the goals of regulatory policy. Left largely to its own resources, which are apt to be weak relative to the strengths of the organized parties, a commission will probably be guided by dominant interests in the regulated industry in its formulation of the public interest. Thus the public interest may become more private than public.

Ideally, the public interest is derived from the regulatory objective of Congress, so far as it is possible to ascertain this objective. The Congressional objective may be derived not only from the language of the statutes but also from specific activities related to the appropriations process, confirmation of presidential nominations, and reports of committees. Because of the reluctance or inability of Congress to commit itself on regulatory objectives and policies, the ideal base for formulation by a commission of regulatory policies may be conspicuous by its absence. At best, it is difficult for a commission to maintain the integrity of the regulatory process even when it is guided firmly by clear Congressional objectives. Difficulties are magnified enormously when the legislative formulation of the public interest is vague or is lacking altogether.

Whatever objectives and policies are set forth by Congress, the overriding task of policy formation in the independent commission is the search for the public interest, that is, the determination of the goal of public policy and the way in which the goal can be achieved. The agency's attitude toward the discovery of the public interest in regulatory policy is largely determined by its sense of mission. If it has a strong drive to serve the public, if it consciously embraces the task of determining the best way in which it can contribute to the welfare of the public interpreted in the light of democratic political values, it goes far toward meeting the responsibility laid upon it by its enabling statute. On the other hand, if it does not exert positive efforts to make objective analyses of its regulatory problems and if it does not assume the initiative in identifying the major regulatory problems in its area of jurisdiction, it will tend to accept the definition of the public interest made by the dominant parties in interest.

The independent commission cannot escape the search for the public interest if it has a sense of mission and a feeling of responsibility for carrying out the objectives of its statute. Nevertheless, the roadblocks in this search are formidable. The commission must ascertain the nature of the problem facing the public in a particular regulatory situation, and it must identify the means by which the goal of serving the public interest can be achieved with the least cost to the private parties affected consistent with its concept of the public interest.

## ADJUSTMENT BY THE COMMISSION TO THE REGULATED PARTIES

How shall the commission define the public interest in the light of dominant factors in a regulatory situation? The private parties compete for the right to identify their respective interests as the public interest. The commission must determine the weight which should be given to the rival demands and the extent to which governmental power and authority should be used to modify relationships among the major groups in a regulated industry. Lacking effective and continuing political support and faced with the organized opposition of the parties in interest, a commission finds its survival as a regulating body dependent heavily on its facility in reaching a *modus operandi* with the regulated groups. The principal condition of its survival may be its willingness to accept the statement of the parties in interest concerning the nature of the regulatory problem and the way in which the demands of the rival parties should be resolved. The limits of regulatory policy tend to be set by the acceptability of regulatory policies to the dominant parties in interest.

In determining the content of the public interest, the commission has the obligation to discover the *general* public interest as distinguished from the interests of the parties immediately involved in the regulated industry. But the public interest must usually be identified without the constructive assistance of an organization representing the public. The organized public which eventually secures the passage of regulatory legislation quickly evaporates, leaving only an inchoate, unorganized mass.

A regulatory situation is apt to be highly complex and very controversial. Complicated data must be analyzed, the testimony of the regulated parties must be carefully checked, and independent administrative investigation must be made. Regulations may have serious repercussions upon an industry and upon the economy as a whole. The commission tends to approach its task with considerable caution and with respect for the strength of the parties. Without a strong sense of mission and public responsibility and a willingness to pursue the public interest in an adventurous spirit, it tends to resolve delicate regulatory questions in favor of the position taken by the major parties before it.

What means are available to the commission for identifying and defining the public interest in regulation? Unfortunately, commissions have restricted their ability to discover the public interest by drastically limiting the nature of their activities and techniques. In the light of the burden delegated to them by Congress, commissions have sought escape from politics and controversy through judicial-like detachment. Instead of searching diligently for the public interest, commissioners prefer to sit calmly as if in judicial robes and elicit the nature of the public interest from the arguments made in formal hearings by the private parties.

## CLOSE CONTACTS BETWEEN REGULATOR AND REGULATED

The history of federal commissions documents the forlornness of the hope that the public interest can be discovered best when a regulatory commission concentrates its attention upon the affairs of a single industry or a group of closely related industries. Although specialization was supported partly in the hope that it would facilitate the search for the public interest, it has normally reduced the capacity of a commission to discover and implement that interest. A commission specializes not only in terms of the industry or industrial practices which it regulates but also in terms of the procedures and methods it employs. It tends to emphasize the adjudication of individual cases in the hope that the public interest will somehow emerge from the case-by-case disposition of regulatory controversies.

The theory of the commission assumes that the public interest can be discovered best in an office detached from the executive branch. Independence from the political strength and support of the president provides for maximum exposure of a regulatory commission to the most effectively organized parties in interest. Cut off from continuing presidential support and forced to reach a working agreement with the regulated parties, a commission develops a passive outlook with respect to the nature of the public interest. It gradually permits the private parties to define the public interest for it, and its own search gives way to indolence and passivity.

Close contacts between a commission and regulated groups dull the perspective of the agency. Senator Aiken of Vermont and Louis Brownlow recently discussed the problem in Congressional hearings:

SENATOR AIKEN: Is not most of our trouble in the regulatory commissions due to the fact that the members are thrown in a constant association with the people they are supposed to regulate, rather than the public which they are supposed to represent and protect? It takes almost superhuman powers on the part of a regulatory commissioner, after he has been in office for a certain length of time, not to promote the business he is supposed to regulate instead of regulating it. I find that in the States as well as in the Federal Government. I have seen it.

MR. BROWNLOW: I believe it thoroughly. The first time I heard that theory expressed was by Commissioner Prouty of the ICC.

SENATOR AIKEN: He was from my State.

MR. BROWNLOW: He was from your State. He was a hard-boiled Vermonter, and he was on the Commission a long time, and I came to know him very well almost 50 years ago. He said, "We don't see anybody but the railroads and the shippers. We don't see any other lawyers but railroad and shipping lawyers. We naturally get interested in the railroad business. It is a big business. It is difficult not to become absorbed in one subject."[38]

The weak defenses of a regulatory commission against attack by the regulated groups are illustrated in the following exchange of comments in the same Congressional hearings:

SENATOR DOUGLAS: I have just one question I would like to ask. I have noticed that the members of regulatory commissions, such as FCC, FTC, Federal Power Commission, and so forth, are in a very exposed position if they are militant in defending what they believe to be the public interest. If there are not appreciable groups

[38] U.S. Congress, Senate, Committee on Labor and Public Welfare, *Hearings on the Establishment of a Commission on Ethics in Government,* June-July 1951, 82nd Congress, 1st session, p. 213.

of consumers or general public who stand behind them to protect them, they do not get much popular support.

On the other hand, the interests which are affected adversely by their position open up a drumfire of criticism against them, not merely in the trade journals, but by whispering and in Congress, and frequently that becomes a campaign of public vilification. I think certain members of the FCC in the past experienced that.

Mr. Coy (*Chairman of the FCC*): Do not count me out.

Senator Douglas: . . . That puts them in the position where they know they are in for a lot of trouble, and they will not get much support.

Is this observation of mine strained, or is it fairly accurate as a reflection of what happens?

Mr. Coy: I think it is quite an accurate reflection. It is a very accurate description of what we face.

Senator Douglas: Therefore, a man has to be of heroic mold, so to speak, once he gets on the commissions, to be militant in defense of the general interest. Since by definition the number of heroes is limited, does not that put the public at something of a disadvantage?

Mr. Coy: I do not think that it is such a burden as you might imply from your statement. As a matter of fact, I find it rather easy dealing with most of the problems that we have to deal with. The only problem that I have to keep reminding myself of, as a means of making the problem somewhat easy, is that I live in a very small community, and that people can really understand these issues, and that I have to be able to explain the problem to them, and if I cannot explain it to them, then I have arrived at probably the wrong conclusion about the matter.

I grew up in a small town in Indiana of 6,500 people. Everything that a public official did there was in a gold fish bowl. We live in that in the Federal Communications Commission. If I keep thinking about where I grew up or if I can solve a problem or vote on a problem in a way that I could explain to the people that I

159

grew up with, I am more concerned about that than
I am about the people who go yapping about you.

SENATOR DOUGLAS: I think that your illustration is interesting, but I do not think it is appropriate. In your
community in Indiana, the general interest was dominant. The people in the main were taxpayers, consumers, and what not, and you therefore could always
appeal not only to their knowledge but to their interest, but I suppose you say now that you live in a small
community industrially, in the communications industry, but they have very definite interests which are
not necessarily the interests of the community as a
whole, and frequently are not the interest of the community as a whole, and you might be "approved" by
the industry, and yet not be serving the general interest.[39]

## THE PROBLEM OF PERSPECTIVE

The determination of the public interest requires perspective and judgment derived from wide experience in
handling technical problems as well as from considerations
of public policy. The commission's search for the public
interest is limited by the narrow experience afforded by its
regulatory jurisdiction. As an agency detached from the
main currents of political life and economic experience, it
profits little by the experience of other government commissions and offices. It has no method for feeding back into
the general stream of administrative regulation the lessons
drawn from its own experience.

The expertness of commissions tends to be matched by
specialization of Congressional committees dealing with
regulatory matters. As a result, broad public considerations
tend to be interpreted in the light of special knowledge
and special interests. Considerations of the public interest
receive little attention apart from the special circumstances
of particular regulatory situations. As Paul Appleby has
noted, specialized agencies work with specialized commit-

[39] *ibid.,* pp. 336-337.

tees in Congress and they cooperate somewhat to make determinations in terms of specialized interests. If Congress and the executive branch could bring problems of policy into broader focus and overcome traditional parochialism, the public interest would receive more attention.[40]

Last, the commission movement has assumed that experts who are withdrawn from political life and who concentrate their expertness upon the problems of a particular industry or industrial practice can be expert in determining what is best for the public. It is still relevant to question, as Herring does, whether independent agencies working in their limited areas can achieve a coherent and responsible view of the public welfare.[41]

With respect to the public interest, the theory of the commission holds that the determination of that interest is fully consistent with the nonpolitical view of the regulatory process. However, the nonpolitical approach and a commitment to the public interest can be consistent only if the public interest is nonpolitical. It should no longer be necessary to assert that, in a democratic society, one of the most legitimate political concerns is the public welfare. Only in a totalitarian society is the general welfare a matter of private, nonpolitical concern. Herring has stated the dichotomy in a restrained manner: "Any administrative agency should, of course, remain free from petty favoritism in dealing with private parties. But whether such a commission can give substance and form to the 'public interest' and remain detached from the conflict of special interests before it, is another question. Basically the function of the commission is to *favor* one interest as against another, the standard of judgment being the abstract concept of the public welfare in the minds of the administrators."[42]

Under prevailing conditions a regulatory commission's view of the public welfare is inevitably limited to its own sphere of experience. Parceling out regulatory tasks to a

40 Testimony of Paul Appleby in *ibid.*, p. 176.
41 Herring, *op.cit.*, p. 138.
42 *ibid.*, pp. 133-134.

number of independent commissions makes administration in the public interest extremely hazardous if not impossible. As long as each agency administers its regulations without regard for the programs of other agencies, the welfare of the regulated industry becomes a standard of reference for determining the public interest. This is "an unduly narrow basis for administration in the public interest."[43]

In the complex government of departments, bureaus, agencies, and offices, the commission does not stand near the top of the administrative hierarchy. Commission decisions are made within a limited frame of reference by officials who are not constrained to win the support of a wide public. As public business moves up the hierarchy from bureau to department to the office of the president, the considerations that go into the making of policy tend to become more general and more political. They tend to lose their specialized substantive character.[44] Appleby notes the reasons for this process. "The movement of business upward within a hierarchy and laterally between hierarchies is a movement toward a greater and broader consensus. In arriving at this consensus, parts are played by more information, more points of view, more functional prerogatives and responsibilities and exposure to more popular forces."[45] One of the significant limitations of the commission in its search for the public interest is inherent in its independent status. In settling its problems on its relatively low level in the administrative hierarchy, it is insulated against public pressures which would normally be considered at higher levels in the hierarchy. As Appleby has stated: "The higher one is placed in the hierarchy, the wider the citizen exposure and responsibility are, and the more desire to be liked and applauded extends to larger publics."[46]

[43] *ibid.*, p. 214.
[44] See Paul Appleby, *Policy and Administration*, University of Alabama Press, University, Alabama, 1949, p. 53.
[45] *ibid.*, p. 79.        [46] *ibid.*, p. 88.

## THE NEED FOR EXECUTIVE COORDINATION

The public interest can scarcely be identified and defined short of effective coordination of the various regulatory programs with each other and with national economic policy. As regulatory policies are fitted into a coherent program of national regulation of economic affairs, the nature of the public interest becomes less abstract and less dependent upon the limited experience of the individual commission.

Executive coordination should supplement, not substitute for, Congressional formulation of objectives and general policies. But the need to develop a coherent program of national regulation of economic affairs highlights present obstacles to the coordination of regulatory programs and national economic policies. Does there exist coherent and coordinated economic planning with reference to which the regulatory agencies are out of line? On the whole such central planning and supervision are not found in the national government. The real difficulty lies not in fitting the programs of independent commissions into national economic policy but rather in developing national economic policy itself. The finding of the Hoover Commission's Task Force on Regulatory Commissions that coordination of commission activities with the activities of the executive branch has not been a serious problem does not reflect effective executive coordination or the willingness of commissions to be coordinated. It merely illustrates the planlessness of the economy and the general disorder of which the independence of regulatory commissions is merely a part.

CHAPTER 6

# Some Problems
# of Regulatory Practice

## Policy Integration

WHEN the independent commission was established in 1887, it occupied the center of the governmental stage. As more commissions were established in subsequent decades, the role of government in economic affairs continued to expand. Regulatory tasks were frequently assigned to other agencies, and new functions in the fields of fiscal and monetary policy were added to the traditional activities of executive departments. Soon commissions were administering controls which were important but no longer the most central governmental functions dealing with economic life. The independence of commissions created no special problems of policy integration as long as regulatory activity did not expand greatly and as long as the government did not undertake broad functions in the area of economic affairs. In response to the Great Depression, however, the government embarked on a comprehensive policy of relief and economic recovery. Later, as war deepened and eventually involved the full-scale mobilization of the United States in the early 1940's, the government assumed even greater responsibility for making strategic decisions with respect to the use and expansion of our productive facilities and the availability of goods and services for purchase by consumers. After World War II, the enactment of the Employment Act of 1946 widened the scope of governmental responsibility for the prosperous and stable operation of the economy in the national interest.

In the light of the expansion of governmental duties in the economic sphere, regulatory commissions no longer occupy a dominant position in the relations of government and business. It is no longer possible to avoid integrating the regulatory policies of commissions with the broad national economic policies of economic stability, mobilization for defense and war, the control of competition and monopoly in business enterprise, and the elimination of poverty. Regulatory policy can no longer be interpreted solely in the light of the peculiar problems of special industries. If regulatory policy is to contribute in a maximum way to the creation of a stable and prosperous economy operating for the public welfare, commissions must fit their regulatory policies into the general framework of national economic policy.

The integration of economic policy can be approached in several ways. Within commissions, policies affecting the industries subject to regulation must be coordinated. Second, policies of regulation and promotion within a single agency and between agencies must be fitted into a coherent pattern. Third, so-called policy-making activity as distinguished from administrative duties must be carried out so that the two types of activity supplement each other. Finally, integration refers to the coordination of the policies of a regulatory commission with the overriding national economic policies discussed in the previous paragraph.

Policy integration is not a formula for obtaining structural neatness or organizational clarity, neither of which is necessarily virtuous or advantageous. Rather, it is an indispensable requirement for the definition of the public interest by commissions. Given the wide measure of discretion delegated to commissions by Congress and the vague statutory mandates accompanying these delegations, commissions need help in interpreting the nature and specific content of the public welfare.

Hindrances to policy integration operate except during the early months in the tenure of a strong president elected with a powerful popular mandate. Normally, centrifugal forces in American political institutions discourage and discredit presidential efforts in the direction of integration. Congress holds out the commission as a device for "supplementing legislative action without greatly increasing Executive power."[1] The weakness of responsible political institutions undermines our political capacity for dealing democratically with basic issues of public policy.[2] The hostility between the president and Congress, which we have come to accept as normal, turns the regulatory commission into a political trophy to be won by the dominant political branch rather than a device for securing the public interest. In any case, policy integration is very difficult to achieve even when the major administrative agencies are under the direction of the president and his Cabinet secretaries. Interagency relations are typically sporadic and unsystematic. The head of a department has scarcely won acceptance as the political representative of the president, charged with the duty of fighting the political battles of the agency in a manner which strengthens the position of the agency and the president. Coordination of the activities of the many national agencies comes hard, and integration in broad policy areas is rarely adequate. The particularism of Congressional committees strengthens the centrifugal forces within the administration. Congress is not organized to focus its resources and attention on broad policy issues; it prefers to consider economic policy questions in bits and pieces.

Policy integration becomes relevant only in terms of a particular policy or set of policies. Integration is not significant except in terms of stated goals of policy and normally cannot be achieved until basic goals and objectives have been hammered out and a consensus has been reached. It has never been an important concern of the advocates of

[1] Board of Investigation and Research, *Practices and Procedures of Governmental Control*, House Document No. 678, 1944, 78th Congress, 2nd session, p. 22. See also James M. Landis, *The Administrative Process*, Yale University Press, New Haven, 1938, p. 46: "The administrative process is, in essence, our generation's answer to the inadequacy of the judicial and the legislative processes. It represents our effort to find an answer to those inadequacies by some other method than merely increasing executive power."

[2] See George A. Graham, *Morality in American Politics*, Random House, New York, 1952, esp. pp. 116-189.

regulation by commission. The promoters of independent regulatory commissions have preferred to consider the regulatory problems of a particular industry in relative isolation from other economic problems of the government. The Congressional mandate passes to the commissions the unenviable task of formulating basic goals for regulatory policy without a clear line of direction from Congress. Policy integration, in this situation, has little meaning for commissioners preoccupied with their own difficult problems. The task of fitting the regulatory policies of one commission into the framework of national economic policy has not appealed to commissioners as realistic or necessary. Even if commissioners recognize the need for policy integration in the economic sphere, there have been few periods in the history of the commissions which have offered opportunities for integration.

Policy integration is not merely a problem of presidential capacity to coordinate the related work of several agencies. It is a problem of obtaining sufficient perspective to make regulation effective and consistent with major goals of national economic policy. It involves the discovery of ways to feed the regulatory experience of the independent commissions back into the setting of national economic policy and vice versa. It is a problem of getting the most dividends for the public welfare out of regulation by commission.

Integration of policy is closely related to the function of planning in regulatory commissions and in the government as a whole. Ideally, integration implies the prior existence of a standard of public interest and a set of goals for national economic policy. It requires a mechanism to maintain adequate communications in the administrative branch and qualities of alertness and imagination in considering national economic problems. It must be based on a sound system of economic analysis and economic intelligence. It must be genuinely motivated by a will to act in a democratic manner to achieve democratic goals. It must accept politics as a legitimate process for the improvement of the public welfare.

Under prevailing political conditions, national policy integration is difficult to achieve anywhere in the government. But it is especially difficult to arrive at in the areas of activity occupied by independent commissions. Integration cannot be achieved merely by locating a commission within an executive department under the nominal direction of a Cabinet secretary. Organizational change may be helpful in creating conditions which are more favorable to departmental and presidential coordination, but a redrawing of the organizational chart in itself accomplishes nothing constructive. The consequences of the failure to integrate regulatory and other economic policies are apparent. The search for the public interest continues to work itself out in an environment which is favorable to private interests and uncongenial to the broader interest of the country. The relative independence of the commission from presidential "interference" gives credence to the dangerous antidemocratic myth of keeping political matters out of politics. Above all, commissions forgo the most promising source of political strength which might equip them morally and politically to maintain a youthful and crusading spirit for many years. As Ellen Wilkinson, a distinguished Labor member of Parliament, said in her final comment as a member of the famous Committee on Ministers' Powers in 1932: "Nothing is so dangerous in a democracy as a safeguard which appears to be adequate but is really a façade."[3]

In view of the strength of centrifugal forces in American politics, the organizational problem of independence of commissions is relatively minor. Independence is a symptom rather than a cause of the diffusion of executive responsibility. As such, the problems that stem from the independence of the commissions will be resolved not by redrawing organizational charts but by striking at the centrifugal forces. Independence reflects such basic political factors as Congressional-presidential rivalries, the decen-

[3] Statement of Ellen Wilkinson, Committee on Ministers' Powers, *Report*, Annex VI, Cmd. 4060, 1932, p. 138.

tralization of political parties, the absence of party government, and the prevailing particularistic interests of Americans. Independence is unlikely to be modified until these factors are altered.

### Bias v. Impartiality

Regulatory commissions are commonly charged with bias in the adjudication of disputes and the determination of regulatory policy. On the whole, commissions have not acted in an unfair or arbitrary manner toward private parties. Charges of bias tend to reflect not unsatisfactory procedures or arbitrary action by commissions but rather the opposition of regulated groups to regulatory policy. Such charges usually indicate the unacceptability of regulation to the regulated groups.

A charge of bias leveled at commissioners is designed usually to make them timid or neutral toward the regulatory objectives set forth in the enabling legislation. Regulated groups prefer a commissioner who accepts their formulation of regulatory goals. Efforts of commissioners to make more objective determinations in the light of legislative mandates are met by cries of partisanship, bias, and unfairness.

One point is central to the analysis of the problem of bias in administrative regulation. It has been stated well by Louis Jaffe:

"Our tradition rightly interpreted is that the judge should be neutral toward the question of whether the specific defendant is guilty. It is a perversion of that tradition to demand that the judge be neutral toward the purposes of the law.

". . . It is a *sine qua non* of a good Administration that it believes in the rightness and worth of the laws which it is enforcing and that it be prepared to bring to the task zeal and astuteness in finding out and making effective those purposes."[4]

[4] Louis L. Jaffe, "The Reform of Federal Administrative Procedure," *Public Administration Review*, vol. 2, 1942, p. 149.

A regulatory commission cannot hope to carry out its responsibilities in a minimally satisfactory manner unless it assumes the obligation to enforce regulatory statutes and to support their aims and purposes. It cannot be neutral toward statutory objectives if it would act in the public welfare. It must be "biased" in the sense that it willingly accepts the statutory goal as the keystone of public policy and establishes criteria of regulatory policy fully consistent with its legislation. It must be partial to the regulatory mission, as defined in the statute, in the sense that it is responsive to its purposes.

Rather than having a tendency toward excessive zeal or bias, commissions can be justly charged with being inclined to accept a view of the public interest as defined by the dominant private parties. Favoritism toward regulated groups is overwhelmingly the principal form of bias to which commissions succumb. We often forget that one of the reasons for the creation of the independent commission was the desire to prevent emasculation of a regulatory statute through judicial amendment. Feller has noted that "the creation of the more controversial of these agencies was brought about by an explicit fear of the bias of the judiciary."[5] A distinguished British scholar reported that administrative agencies have been selected to interpret and administer regulatory statutes in preference to "persons who are . . . by their environment and their specialized training, or by the dictates of their technique, imbued with the idea that social legislation is pernicious."[6]

The tendency of commissions to be unresponsive to regulatory goals as outlined in a statute must be related to the original fear that the courts would not treat new regulatory legislation fairly. Regulated groups, hoping to maintain the dominant position of the courts in regulatory policy,

[5] Abraham Feller, "Administrative Law Investigation Comes of Age," *Columbia Law Review*, vol. 41, 1941, p. 589.

[6] W. Ivor Jennings, "Courts and Administrative Law—The Experience of English Housing Legislation," *Harvard Law Review*, vol. 49, 1936, p. 454.

proceeded to entangle new regulatory commissions with litigation and later succeeded in judicializing the procedures of commissions.

Fairness cannot be interpreted rightly as neutrality toward public purposes. As Kenneth Davis writes: "This is far from saying that law should be administered by zealots or crusaders who lack perspective or stability. Judgment must of course be guided by intellectual perception, not by emotion; performance of judicial tasks necessarily calls for integrity, character, and ability. The administrator's belief in the cause he is furthering, even though that cause has won legislative approval, must not overpower the recognition of competing interests. Sincere conviction should not be so steadfast as to shut out inquiry and re-examination. Belief must not be so unyielding as to smother the contributions that alert practical administration may make to the molding and remolding of policy. And yet a dominant point of view or bias may appropriately color all activities, including even the fact-finding function. Thoroughly conscientious men of strong conviction may sometimes interpret evidence to make findings which indifferent men would not make. The theoretically ideal administrator is one whose broad point of view is in general agreement with the policies he administers but who maintains sufficient balance to perceive and to avoid the degree of zeal which substantially impairs fairmindedness."[7]

The line which separates proper devotion to the public interest from excessive administrative zeal is not easy to define. Unfortunately, there has been little need to do so since the greater and more pressing problem from the point of view of democratic administration is how to make the commissioners more, rather than less, responsive to the public interest.

[7] Kenneth C. Davis, *Administrative Law*, West Publishing Co., St. Paul, 1951, p. 374.

## Problems of Internal Organization

MULTIPLE DIRECTION

Analysis does not lead to the conclusion that the administrative problems of regulation by commission can be cured by modifying the basic form of organization. On the other hand, certain aspects of the organization of a commission contribute to its ineffectiveness as a regulatory mechanism. The most obvious organizational characteristic of the independent regulatory commission is its multiple direction. It is headed not by a single executive but by a group of commissioners who share power and authority to direct its affairs. No single commissioner has final authority to act on a major problem of policy. The consequences of multiple direction in the commissions have been unfortunate from the point of view of managerial efficiency and operating effectiveness. Major policy decisions, and perhaps all decisions of any significance, are made formally by a corporate body under conditions which seem to enhance the element of bargaining and decrease the possibility of achieving internal consistency in complex decisions. While there may be some truth in the assertion that responsibility is pinpointed by delegating regulatory duties to an independent commission, it should be recognized that too often the assignment of a task to a board or commission is a scheme to delay action, to relieve tension by giving continuing study to a problem, and to encourage compromise in the formulation of policy.[8]

The deficiencies of boards are well known. They rarely are capable of dispatch and energy. They seem better fitted to maintain the *status quo* than to advance. Novel ideas are snuffed out by deep-seated differences among the members. The sharing of responsibility tends to diminish en-

[8] These points were made by Harold Stein during the conference at Princeton University on Theory of Organization, June 18-19, 1952. Stein was suggesting some generalizations which might be tentatively abstracted from the analysis of case studies in public administration as published in Harold Stein, ed., *Public Administration and Policy Development*, Harcourt, Brace and Co., New York, 1952.

thusiasm and vitality. Plurality removes the members from the harsh impact of public opinion.[9]

Multiple direction is usually accompanied in commissions by splintered management. Responsibility for management of the work load and staff is normally shared by commissioners who have little taste for it and whose attention is likely to be absorbed by formal proceedings. Recent efforts to strengthen the position of the chairman as the principal executive officer are designed to overcome the adverse consequences of splintered management. A Budget Bureau official who has followed the activities of the commissions closely for several years has stated: "In general, as the Hoover Commission pointed out, multi-headed agencies do not manage their affairs or program their work as well as single-headed agencies. This characteristic is magnified in the regulatory commissions because the members are preoccupied with disposing of formal proceedings. Too often, administrative responsibilities are parcelled out to all commission members, the chairman serving largely as the commission spokesman. Given a management-minded chairman as the commission's principal executive officer, it is possible so to organize and direct staff work that (1) continuing unified executive direction can be provided, (2) planning and policy formulation can be undertaken apart from specific cases, and (3) improvements can be made in the time-consuming quasi-judicial procedure. The so-called 'strong chairman' reorganization plans offer the basis for progress in this area, and where the chairman has taken hold, we have seen definite signs of improvement of internal commission management."[10]

Collective management tends to lower managerial capacity and make incisive policy-making difficult. These tendencies are magnified when individual commissioners direct specific segments of commission activity. In the ICC,

[9] See Emmette S. Redford, *Administration of National Economic Control*, The Macmillan Co., New York, 1952, p. 290.

[10] William D. Carey, "The Federal Regulatory Commissions," lecture delivered at Princeton University, April 4, 1952, mimeo., p. 5.

for example, where until 1953 the parceling out of managerial duties had gone furthest, individual commissioners were preoccupied with the duties of bureaus or units under their direction and became so involved with administrative detail that they had little time or inclination to consider the broader managerial aspects of supervision and direction in the commission as a whole.

Commissions tend to organize not for action but for adjudication. The staff is geared to cautious consideration of pending formal proceedings and not to taking speedy action. Flexibility in handling complex regulatory situations tends to give way to inflexible reliance on prescribed formal procedures. Little or no authority to make subsidiary decisions is delegated by commissioners to top staff officials. In his discussion of the unfortunate consequences of excessive formalism Davis concluded, "Many tasks call for round tables and unbuttoned vests, not for witness chairs and courtroom trappings."[11]

RELATIONSHIPS BETWEEN COMMISSIONERS AND STAFF

The relationships between the commissioners and the staff of a commission are virtually unique in American administrative experience. The number of officials below the rank of commissioner who can actually make a decision without prior approval by the commissioners is severely limited. Also, the staffs of the commissions are small in comparison with those of other types of agencies.[12]

As Hyneman has stated, referring to the FCC, the primary task of most commission employees is to help the commissioners make and publicize their decisions. According to him, the internal organization of the commission is arranged in accordance with its multiple direction: "First, the principal objective in organizing the working

[11] Davis, *op.cit.*, p. 183.

[12] On September 1, 1954 the largest commission, the ICC, had 1,868 employees; only two others employed as many as 1,000 (the NLRB, 1,183; the FCC, 1,110), and the average employment in the remaining four (the CAB, FPC, FTC, and SEC) was 621.

force must be to make sure that information and ideas will flow up from the staff to the commissioners; second, the organization which is developed must allow the flow of ideas and information to spread out at the top to as many points as there are commissioners who wish to talk to members of the staff." Commissioners, Hyneman writes, want to direct this flow and prevent staff officials from controlling the work of the commission. He believes that commissioners hope to create an administrative situation in which no official, other than themselves acting as a group, is able to coordinate the work of the agency and thereby control the ideas and data available for policy formulation. Keeping the staff in its place in this fashion becomes a major objective of commission organization as the commission grows older. As a result, the staff does not supply the managerial skill which the commissioners themselves ordinarily lack.

Hyneman also notes that commissioners like to feel free to confer at will with members of the staff. They tend to have little regard for administrative relationships between supervisory and other personnel. They want, instead, to be able to talk at length with the man who worked on a specific case or problem. Consequently, commissioners do not build up the prestige of the supervisory officials, and contacts between the commissioners and the staff are not conducive to the development of firm administrative relationships.[13]

The collective form of direction also has had serious implications for personnel and budgetary policies within the commissions. The weakness of management leaves the commissions with few friends in the managerial arms of the Executive Office of the President. The Bureau of the Budget tends to lose sympathy with commissions because of their haphazard administrative practices and apparent inability to make headway against mounting backlogs of work. With respect to personnel, staff members who most directly aid in the disposition of business before the com-

---

[13] Charles S. Hyneman, *Bureaucracy in a Democracy*, Harper and Brothers, New York, 1950, pp. 502, 512.

missioners are likely to be advanced faster than other staff members. Employees with managerial capacity are given little recognition and may even be regarded as suspect by commissioners who are anxious to maintain their authority to direct the affairs of the commission. They want little help from supervisory employees. "The members of a commission, like the head of any other agency, like to promote to a high position the individual who impresses them as having the best qualities for the job. The job, as the commissioners see it, is to make careful and penetrating analyses of the factors involved in complicated problems and to give the commissioners imaginative and thoughtful counsel on the probable consequences of alternative solutions for those problems. Therefore they tend to promote to the top position in each division the man whom they consider to be the most competent and the most dependable accountant or engineer or lawyer, as the case may be. And the man who excels in the qualities which the commissioners value most is likely not to be effective in directing the work of other people."[14]

### Planning

The quality of administration and organization of a regulatory commission can be evaluated by an analysis of the amount and kind of planning in which it engages. Planning is directly related to the basic approach which the commission uses in its regulatory work. It underlies its policy-making activities, relationships of commissioners to staff and of the commission to other agencies, and the emphasis the commission places on formal adjudication as distinguished from other types of activity. Planning can be defined simply as organized foresight in preparation for administrative action. It implies that the agency assumes some initiative in organizing its work and takes some responsibility for achieving certain goals.

The failure to utilize the planning process effectively has been one of the major defects of regulation by commission.

14 *ibid.*, p. 507.

Almost all observers of such regulation, including its defenders, have noted the inability of commissions to develop facilities for planning their activities and for adapting procedures and policies to emerging problems and situations. Eastman's comment as Coordinator of Transportation is typical: "Our regulation in the past has operated too much on the cure basis, dealing with complaints after they arise but not forestalling them. National planning has been conspicuous by its absence."[15] The absence of planning in the affairs of commissions is consistent with the nonpolitical view of the regulatory process[16] and the judicial approach to regulatory administration. A commission which does not engage in planning appears to develop more harmonious relations with regulated groups. The absence of planning facilitates the development of clientalism in the regulatory process. Planning is usually absent where the commission has already passed from the stage of youthful vigor to the passivity of maturity. In its absence the past guides administrative conduct by enthroning precedent.

The absence of planning in most commissions has been accounted for by many observers. Cushman traced the failure of the commissions as planning agencies to the following:

1. Lack of time and the great burden of day-to-day work.

2. Inadequate research staffs.

3. The incapacity of commissioners to plan their activities. Commissions "are not usually made up of the kind of men from whom broad policy planning could reasonably be expected."

4. The fact that planning often calls for the coordination

15 Joseph B. Eastman, address before the American Life Convention, Chicago, October 10, 1934, mimeo., p. 8.

16 For a strong statement of the traditional nonpolitical view of the regulatory process, see B. H. Meyer, "In the Public Interest," an address delivered before the Wisconsin Chapter of Phi Beta Kappa, May 17, 1928, and reprinted in part as "The ICC and Its Work," in *Railway Age*, June 2, 1928. It is quoted in I. L. Sharfman, *The Interstate Commerce Commission*, part 4, The Commonwealth Fund, New York, 1937, pp. 260-261. Meyer was a member of the ICC from December 31, 1910 to May 1, 1939.

177

of interests lying in the areas of several regulatory agencies.

5. The fact that commissions are composed of human beings, with impulses, interests, and foibles, who have a substantial stake in the *status quo* and who feel that wise planning should avoid radical changes. "One would hardly expect the Interstate Commerce Commission, even if it were a more useful planning agency than it is, to plan a broad transportation policy which did not have the continuance of that commission embedded in its provisions.[17]

In addition, it should be noted that the absence of planning is comfortable and convenient to commissioners who want to minimize conflicts with hostile regulated groups. The judicial approach, in which the commissioners wait for cases to be brought to them by private parties, provides a calm setting for the regulatory process. The absence of planning seems to make the process more gentle and gentlemanly. Moreover, the commissions were established originally not to formulate broad economic policies of regulation but to eliminate specific abuses.[18] They are best equipped to handle narrowly conceived problems. In the transportation field, for instance, the regulatory commissions are better adapted to the development and regulation of individual forms of transportation than to the development and regulation of a unified system of transportation. Research activity runs to statistical compilations rather than economic analysis and is somewhat out of place in most commissions. The Board of Investigation and Research found three important limitations to research in the regulatory commission: the pressure of daily work, the

[17] Robert E. Cushman, *The Independent Regulatory Commissions*, Oxford University Press, New York, 1941, pp. 729-733.

[18] Sharfman describes the traditional approach of the ICC in these words: "Not very frequently, considering the extensive record of administrative performance, has the Commission departed from the characteristic regulatory approach pursued in the vast bulk of its activities, which has consisted in effecting correctives for specific maladjustments as they emerge and in subjecting proposed courses of action of individual carriers to scrutiny and control. There has been little disposition to achieve complete transformations in the organization and functioning of the railroad industry." Sharfman, *op.cit.*, part 4, pp. 373-374.

difficulty in securing highly skilled personnel, and a disinclination to depart from traditional paths.[19] Research is usually regarded by commissions as somehow connected with controversial policy and therefore to be avoided.

It is difficult to exaggerate the significance of the relative inability of commissions to plan programs of regulatory activity. The persistence of antipathy toward planning regulatory policy suggests that the absence of planning is a congenital characteristic of regulation by commission. It may well be a fatal defect in the operation of the commissions in the public interest. Commissions cannot adequately serve the public welfare without the imagination and skill required for planning.

## Consequences of the Judicial Approach

The judicial approach is the other side of the coin. The administrative consequences of the judicial approach by regulatory commissions form the basis of many of the most serious operating problems of the commissions. They may be summarized briefly.

Major reliance is placed upon the private parties to develop the evidence which is used by a commission to make its decision. While it may occasionally undertake investigations on its own motion, it tends to sit back passively to await the development of the issues and the presentation of the relevant data by the parties.

The judicial approach may make regulation more secure in the sense that its survival is conditioned upon reaching a workable agreement with the regulated parties. From this limited point of view, the judicial approach is fully consistent with the view that a commission need not search for the public interest since the public interest will automatically emerge from the conflict of private interests in regulation. The passivity of the judicial approach lends a note of respectability and calmness to the regulatory process. But it may also yield the dangerous illusion that judicialization produces effective regulation.

[19] Board of Investigation and Research, *op.cit.*, p. 150.

To the extent that a commission adopts courtlike procedures and methods, it reduces attention devoted to the search for the public interest. The Board of Investigation and Research has applied this finding to the ICC: ". . . the Commission's role as 'guardian of the general public interest,' an unfailing champion of the public in proceedings which take place before it, is incompatible, at least in theory, with the judicial position of presiding with complete impartiality over a contest between individual litigants. . . . A strictly judicial conception of the Commission's functions would minimize the attention which the public interest should receive and emphasize the effect of the decision upon the parties."

The case-by-case procedure favored by the judicial approach helps to perpetuate indefinite and conflicting standards of regulation: "Indefinite or conflicting standards of decision are easily maintained so long as situations are dealt with separately; one case may be decided by a rule that points east, and the next by a rule that points west, which leaves those who look to the decisions for guidance without any rule on which they may confidently rely." Moreover, rules derived from individual proceedings deal with policy in a highly fragmentary fashion: ". . . individual proceedings, when based on complaints or applications which concern only a few parties, seldom if ever produce sufficiently comprehensive records for the adequate solution of questions of major importance." Issues can be postponed or delayed if "each decision is held narrowly to its particular facts."[20]

The judicial approach discourages the development of more satisfactory procedures of administrative regulation. Deviations in procedure from the accustomed judicial pattern are held suspect and probably unfair and arbitrary as well. Procedures which are countenanced are those which afford the greatest protection to the private parties by offering them opportunities for delaying, obstructing, and directing the course of adjudication. The procedures of

[20] *ibid.*, pp. 66, 82.

formal adjudication often "seem to favor indecision and obscure weakness in policy."[21]

The judicial model for regulatory administration places a damper on comprehensive policy making. A commission is so busy disposing of individual cases brought before it by the private parties that it has little time or taste and few resources for planning, research, and the other activities incidental to comprehensive industrial regulation. For example, the Board of Investigation and Research noted the implications of the case-by-case approach in the ICC: "Preoccupation with deciding individual controversies, as much as limitations on its resources, has turned the Commission away from broad research projects, although these activities are logically all but inseparable from that formulation of transportation policy which is a primary function of the Commission, whether performed through decisions, rule-making or legislative recommendations. . . . The method of proceeding case by case in the definition of policy has its advantages, as has been seen, but the Commission so closely follows the courts in this respect that the practice gives rise to misconceptions. Parties begin to see the Commission, not as an active regulating agent, but as a body which examines 'the law,' finds in that mysterious congeries the appropriate principle, and then 'applies it to the facts found.' This description, when given to the judicial process, at times somewhat taxes the imagination, but when the administrative process is so described it is difficult to recognize the reality behind the description. There are instances when the Commission must actually interpret a statute and apply it literally, but the usual determination of whether a specific rate is 'just and reasonable,' or a certain service is required by 'public convenience and necessity' is simply an act of administrative judgment such as the controlling statute not merely permits but obviously contemplates. The interests of sound regulation will be served if this is recognized. The illusion that there

[21] *ibid.,* p. 79.

is anything approaching a definite 'common law of transportation' to be found in the Commission's reports mis-
construes the Commission's functions and conceals its real
powers."[22]

Finally, the judicial pattern of operation appears to
sanctify passivity and "impartiality" and to condemn an
aggressive search for the public interest. It emphasizes the
value of independence of a commission from the policies
of the administration in power.

The effects of judicialization on the regulatory process
are not entirely adverse. The judicial approach may be
helpful where the commission's staff is small and is unable
to cope with the burden of cases. In this situation, reliance
on the parties for producing relevant evidence may be the
only method available for getting at the facts. The judicial
approach also produces a measure of public confidence in
the capacity of the regulatory commission to dispense
justice fairly and equitably. In the light of the distrust of
regulatory agencies and of governmental administration
in general, the judicial model may offer some semblance
of security and respectability to an embattled commission.

## Precision in Regulation

Some students of the regulatory process believe that it is
possible to eliminate political overtones and reduce the
controversial character of regulation by making the standard of regulatory action firm and precise. For example,
John Bauer, who has studied and analyzed public utility
regulation for many years, holds out the hope that regulation can be made truly effective provided exact rules and
requirements can be established to guide industrial conduct and administrative behavior. Effective regulation, according to Bauer, means "precise demarcation of relative
public and private rights, exact presentation of those rights
through accounts and records, regular protection of those
rights through systematic rate adjustments and financial
safeguards, and positive responsibility to promote the pub-

[22] ibid., pp. 65-66.

lic interest in harmony with private rights."[23] Recently, Bauer suggested remedies for the "lack of administrability" of public utility regulations due to undefined rights, uncertain facts, and unmanageable administration.[24] He would overcome indefiniteness in rate making by providing exact rules of conduct.

The desire to make the bases of regulatory decisions more explicit and more predictable is a worthy one. Bauer's principal goal, however, is to make the work of regulation "purely administrative" and presumably nonpolitical. His desire is fully consistent with the traditional American hope to take regulation "out of politics" and to reserve powers of decision in regulatory matters for experts free from the turmoil and invidious surroundings of politics.

While exactness and precision are desirable, along with flexibility and adaptability, in the regulatory process, they cannot define away political forces. Regulation is and always will be an intensely political process. Its success depends as heavily upon political leadership and widespread public support as it does upon sound techniques and administrative precision. As long as the American economy is dynamic and subject to continuing change in technology and organization, the goal of administrative precision can only be approximated. As long as policy considerations remain dominant in regulatory affairs, it will be impossible to define precisely the weight to be given to these considerations for any future period.

### The Problem of Ethics

The 1951 Senate investigation of the problem of ethics in government devoted some attention to the ethical considerations involved in regulatory administration. The subcommittee of the Senate Committee on Labor and Public Welfare, which undertook the investigation, was particu-

[23] John Bauer and Peter Costello, *Public Organization of Electric Power*, Harper and Brothers, New York, 1949, p. 33.
[24] John Bauer, *Transforming Public Utility Regulation*, Harper and Brothers, New York, 1950.

larly concerned that members of independent commissions, almost without protection against groups subject to regulation, might not be able to maintain the integrity of the regulatory process. The ethical problems reviewed by the subcommittee ranged from the acceptance by commissioners of small gifts from regulated parties to the capture of a commission by such parties.

The subcommittee found that the most serious ethical problems of public officials were the product of four factors: "(1) There is much at stake in public policies which directly affect the income and welfare of individuals, industries, and groups. (2) Members of Congress have almost free discretion in making these policies, and administrative officials have great discretion in administering them. (3) The great authority vested in elected officials is justified by the principle that they, as representatives of the public, will exercise their authority in the public interest and for public purposes; similarly, the discretionary authority delegated to administrators is based on the assumption that they will exercise it reasonably in accordance with public policies, and for the furtherance of public purposes. (4) Although the importance of the issues, the breadth of discretion involved, and the basic nature of responsible government make it necessary that so far as humanly possible issues shall be decided on their merits, interested parties are not willing to let the wheels of government turn unassisted, but in a great variety of ways bring pressure to bear upon legislators and administrators in order to secure favorable decisions."

The subcommittee discovered that a number of situations gave rise to ethical problems. First, the government needs mature men with experience in business affairs. However, "Can they be perfectly fair if cases come before them which directly or indirectly involve the company from which they came? Can they be completely objective in decisions which affect their industry, for example, where the industry favors a policy divergent from public policy or from proposed public policy? Can these men be completely detached in determining what the public interest requires?" The subcommittee's *Report* suggested that "The most difficult problem would seem to be that of an industry background which makes it difficult for a man who has grown up in a particular industry to make governmental decisions which touch that industry and yet give due weight to the public interest."

The second type of ethical situation concerns problems of subsequent employment. The subcommittee noted that suspicion attaches to employees who place contracts or make decisions affecting loans, subsidies, or rates and then take positions with companies they formerly dealt with on behalf of the government. The possibility of well-paid positions with private firms may influence government officials who deal with these firms. The subcommittee observed that regulatory commissions and lawyers who practice before them believe that the "possibility of more lucrative private employment adds so greatly to the attractiveness of public employment that restricting this opportunity would affect, for the worse, the quality of the Government regulatory personnel."

A third set of problems concerns the process of becoming unduly involved. "A recognized problem of long standing is that of public officials becoming unduly involved with persons, concerns, or industries which are affected by their decisions. There is a strong presumption that a substantial economic involvement will create either a bias or an emotional problem through fear of bias." What gifts, if any, may an official accept without creating suspicion that an improper relation exists between the donor and the government official? Involvements may be political, economic, or personal. Perhaps the most difficult situation of involvement arises when a public official has great discretionary power to decide cases which come before him. In these situations, "he must be on his guard against being unduly influenced. For example, a contracting officer and his family may be drawn into a social program of dinners, parties, golf, and other social engagements by a contractor or his agents. If this continues, it makes the contracting officer and the contractor members of the same social circle. Even if the engagements are purely social, the official may find it hard to be completely detached when it comes to handling official business with his new friend. If business matters are discussed during social engagements, complete objectivity becomes more difficult still."[25]

Certain questionable legislative practices also create ethical problems for administrators as well as legislators. Reference of certain matters from a Congressman to an official with a request for favorable action along indicated lines places pressure on the official that is difficult to resist.

The analysis of the factors and conditions which promote unethical behavior on the part of government officials applies with special force to the commissioners and staffs of the independent regulatory commissions. In the commissions, particular cases and issues of policy are extremely important to private interests, pressures upon the officials are intense, dependence upon the regulated interests is heavy, and administration is in the long run impossible without the willing compliance of the regulated with regulatory policies. The ability of officials and employees to resist unethical pressures and undue involvements is weakened. The ethical problems noted by the Senate subcommittee exist in all government branches and all administrative agencies, but they are especially applicable to independent regulatory commissions.

The line between ethical and unethical conduct is hard to draw because American society does not condemn much behavior that may fairly be construed as unethical. For example, should a commissioner accept free entertainment from the president of a regulated company? Is dinner acceptable, or lunch, or a case of whiskey? Are small gifts at

25 U.S. Congress, Senate, Subcommittee of the Committee on Labor and Public Welfare, *Report, Ethical Standards in Government*, 1951, 82nd Congress, 1st session, pp. 19, 20, 22, 26.

Christmastime permitted?[26] The ethical problems of commissions cannot be remedied merely by transferring their
regulatory jurisdiction to other types of agencies.

[26] See the discussion of these questions by a former chairman of the
CAB in U.S. Congress, Senate, Committee on Labor and Public Welfare,
*Hearings on the Establishment of a Commission on Ethics in Government,*
June-July 1951, 82nd Congress, 1st session, pp. 274-291.

## CHAPTER 7

# The Politics of Adjudication

THE literature of the regulatory process deals extensively with disposition of formal cases by commissions and with legal problems in rule making and in adjudication of disputes. Lawyers and law schools have succeeded in focusing concern upon problems of procedural due process, the extent to which the courts will review the decisions of the administrative agencies, and the possibilities of establishing a uniform code of procedure for all administrative agencies to follow in the course of their rule-making and adjudicatory activities. It is useful to review some of the more significant political and administrative aspects of the adjudicatory functions of commissions in order to place the legal studies of regulatory procedure in a broader perspective.

### Political Significance of the Movement to Reform Administrative Adjudication

Since 1933 the American Bar Association and other groups have been engaged in a powerful movement to modify the process by which a regulatory agency makes rules and decisions affecting the rights and duties of private parties. The attempt to reform the adjudicatory process[1] set off one of the most significant public debates in modern American political experience. While it captured the attention of only a limited number of interested persons, its implications for the future development of governmental affairs in the United States are critically important.[2]

[1] In the following discussion the convenient label "the adjudicatory process" is used to denote the formal rule-making and adjudicatory activities of the commissions.

[2] As yet there has been no complete study of the movement to reform the adjudicatory process, but a number of articles and short accounts are available, including the following: U.S. Congress, *Legislative History of the Administrative Procedure Act*, Senate Document No. 248, 79th Con-

Bitterness, invective, and extravagant statements have plagued public discussion of the process of adjudication. Advocates of procedural uniformity in the regulatory agencies anticipated that their proposed reforms would have a powerful influence in changing the substantive result of regulatory administration, while opponents usually regarded the efforts of the American Bar Association to require uniformity as a none too subtle method to reduce the effectiveness of governmental regulation and even to sabotage the regulatory process.[3] It is not difficult to account for the generation of heat rather than light by this debate. Administrative adjudication, after all, expanded and matured after the Great Depression had set in. It became closely identified with restrictions on property rights, with changes in the law of contract which reduced the protections previously accorded "private" economic transactions, and with the narrowing of the scope of personal business freedom. Adjudication and the growth of the discretionary power of the regulatory commissions were regarded by some as the tools of socialism and denial of individual freedom.

The movement to reform administrative adjudication was also part of the movement opposing "bureaucracy" and the expansion of governmental activity affecting the

---

gress, 2nd session, esp. pp. 60-71, 241-282; Arthur T. Vanderbilt, "Legislative Background of the Federal Administrative Procedure Act," in George Warren, ed., *The Federal Administrative Procedure Act and the Administrative Agencies*, New York University Law School, New York, 1947, pp. 1-15; Arthur W. Macmahon, "The Ordeal of Administrative Law," *Iowa Law Review*, vol. 25, 1940, pp. 423-456; Foster H. Sherwood, "The Federal Administrative Procedure Act," *American Political Science Review*, vol. 41, 1947, pp. 271-282; James Hart, *An Introduction to Administrative Law*, 2nd edn., Appleton-Century-Crofts, Inc., New York, 1950, pp. 624-636; Louis Jaffe, "Invective and Investigation in Administrative Law," *Harvard Law Review*, vol. 52, 1939, pp. 1201-1245; Louis Jaffe, "The Reform of Administrative Procedure," *Public Administration Review*, vol. 2, 1942, pp. 141-158; Kenneth C. Davis, *Administrative Law*, West Publishing Co., St. Paul, 1951, pp. 4-25; Abraham Feller, "Administrative Law Investigation Comes of Age," *Columbia Law Review*, vol. 41, 1941, pp. 589ff.

[3] For example, see Frederick F. Blachly, "Sabotage of the Administrative Process," *Public Administration Review*, vol. 6, 1946, pp. 213-227.

status of private business affairs. When the vast enlargement of the scope of governmental activity was subject to
attack during the 1930's and 1940's, regulation was set
aside for special denunciation. The bar, which had been
trained to accept the independent judiciary as the only
suitable agency for the disposition of cases affecting personal and private matters, looked upon commissions with
deep skepticism. Most lawyers and judges frankly doubted
the capacity of regulatory agencies to act "fairly" in making rules and adjudicating controversies. Accustomed to
the advocacy of individual rights, the bar interpreted fairness in the light of the interests of the parties it represented.
The regulatory agencies were suspect if their interpretation
of the public interest was disadvantageous to affected private interests. Newer commissions, in particular, were regarded as unfair because they weighed the claims and
demands of private interests in the light of such interpretation.

FROM JUDICIAL REVIEW TO DUE PROCESS

The reform movement spearheaded by the American
Bar Association had two important chronological phases.
At first an effort was made to enlarge the scope of judicial
review of administrative decisions and to establish a specialized administrative court with authority to review the
decisions of commissions. The administrative court proposal lost support after 1938. While it reappears from time
to time in the course of Congressional hearings and law
conferences, it has not been revived as a significant reform
device. In its second phase the reform movement proposed
a procedural code to govern the handling of cases by regulatory agencies so that the rights and interests of private
parties would be protected against arbitrary and unfair
disposition. Reform advocates continued to urge a wider
review by the courts of the findings and decisions of the
agencies, but their emphasis shifted gradually from judicial
review to a procedural uniformity that would overcome
the diversity, flexibility, and tendency to experiment that

survived in the newer commissions. The concern with procedure reflected the decline of the courts as interpreters of substantive due process in economic affairs. After the shift in the trend of Constitutional decisions in 1937, the courts could no longer be regarded as reliable defenders of private rights in the battle against expanding governmental controls. As judicial interpretation of *substantive* due process under the Fifth and Fourteenth Amendments dramatically changed after 1937, the reformers relied more heavily upon interpretations of *procedural* due process as a way of keeping governmental regulation within reasonable bounds and within the limits of fairness and equity to private parties.

Because of the commitments of private parties and their lawyers growing out of the economic stakes of regulation and the realities of the struggle for political power, the public debates concerning the reform of administrative adjudication abound in epithets, encomiums, and immoderate, unrestrained charges and countercharges. As Judge Augustus Hand suggested in 1948, "The subject of administrative procedure is relatively new and acutely contentious. Its development must be regarded with patience in the long struggle of ideas."[4]

The popularity of New Deal measures to promote economic recovery and eliminate poverty in the 1930's made outright opposition to many governmental regulatory programs rather hazardous. Reluctance to attack such basic policies as the right to bargain collectively was resolved by attacking the measures employed to translate these policies into administrative reality. The outcry against the procedure of adjudication frequently reflected a desire to alter radically the substance of administrative regulation.[5] President Roosevelt declared in his message vetoing the Walter-Logan bill in December 1940: "The bill that is now before

[4] Judge Augustus Hand, Foreword to Symposium on State Administrative Procedure, *Iowa Law Review*, vol. 33, 1948, p. 195.
[5] See James M. Landis, "Crucial Issues in Administrative Law," *Harvard Law Review*, vol. 53, 1940, pp. 1077-1102.

me is one of the repeated efforts by a combination of lawyers who desire to have all processes of government conducted through lawsuits and of interests which desire to
escape regulation."[6]

While the bar was skeptical about the consequences of
administrative adjudication, it was forced to recognize the
growth of administrative discretion in the regulation of
economic affairs and a proportionate decline in the role
of the courts. The bar gradually became somewhat reconciled to the inevitability of administrative regulation, which
became an important source of income and livelihood for
lawyers. While the legal profession was on the whole willing to come to terms with the rise of commissions, it was
unwilling to permit these agencies to develop procedures
of adjudication along unfamiliar or novel lines. Lawyers,
in effect, accepted the process of governmental regulation
by commission so long as the regulatory agencies behaved
as much like courts as possible.

## THE ADMINISTRATIVE PROCEDURE ACT

The major achievement of the reform movement was the
enactment of the Administrative Procedure Act in 1946.[7]
The Act was drawn up by groups whose special interests
lay in obtaining the maximum amount of judicialized procedure and control and of review by the courts. It revealed
an exaggerated belief in the significance of formal informa-
tional devices, such as publication of proposed and final
rules and regulations in the *Federal Register*. Extravagant
claims have been made by proponents. Arthur T. Vanderbilt, who later became chief justice of the New Jersey Supreme Court, hailed it in 1947 as marking "the beginning
of a new era in administrative law,"[8] and referred approv-
ingly to Senator McCarran's statement that the Act is "the
most important statute affecting the administration of
justice in the federal field since the passage of the Judiciary

6 House Document No. 986, 76th Congress, 3rd session, 1940.
7 60 Stat. 237 (1946).
8 Arthur T. Vanderbilt, Foreword, in Warren, ed., *op.cit.*, p. iv.

Act of 1789.''[9] In an exultant mood, the American Bar Association declared in 1946, "Probably no measure in the history of modern legislation has been considered as long and as carefully, by as many persons interested and qualified to advise and assist in its development."[10] One student of the Act has called it "one of the most dramatic legal developments of the past century" and a statute which "goes far toward reviving and revitalizing some of the more basic concepts of procedural due process in Anglo-American jurisprudence."[11]

Other comments on the Administrative Procedure Act have been more moderate and restrained. Charlesworth concluded that the Act has not discernibly changed the procedure of administrative adjudication although it probably has made administrators more careful and may have slowed the process of adjudication somewhat.[12] Hart's analysis is very restrained and tentative in the light of the limited experience under the Act.[13] And Reginald Parker states that the Act has had a minor effect but that it has not been altogether useless. He feels that it has yielded some clarifications in legislation and that the provision concerning the independent trial examiner constitutes a step forward in the development of fair procedure.[14]

The model for the Administrative Procedure Act was the ordinary judicial procedure in an adversary action in which the government has no more standing than a private party. As the fruition of the campaign to reform administrative adjudication, the Act attempts to reduce the public

[9] Senator Pat McCarran, "Three Years of the Federal Administrative Procedure Act," *Georgetown Law Journal*, vol. 38, 1950, pp. 574ff.

[10] "Administrative Procedure Act Is Passed Unanimously by Congress," *American Bar Association Journal*, vol. 32, 1946, p. 325.

[11] Victor S. Netterville, "The Administrative Procedure Act: A Study in Interpretation," *The George Washington Law Review*, vol. 20, 1951, pp. 1-2.

[12] James C. Charlesworth, *Governmental Administration*, Harper and Brothers, New York, 1951, p. 168.

[13] Hart, *op.cit.*, pp. 624-636.

[14] Reginald Parker, "The Administrative Procedure Act: A Study in Overestimation," *Yale Law Journal*, vol. 60, 1951, pp. 581-599.

interest to the status of an ordinary private interest. It is interesting to consider the legal effect of the personification of the corporation and the government. In the interpretation of the due process clauses of the Fifth and Fourteenth Amendments to the Constitution, the corporation was held to be a legal person and therefore entitled to the legal protections accorded to individuals by the Constitution. Personification had the effect of protecting the corporation against governmental action and of strengthening its status in American society. In the case of the government, on the other hand, personification has the object and the effect not of strengthening the government but of weakening it. The conception of the legislative mandate to the regulatory agency as qualified by the existence of private economic rights places the government on the defensive, at least psychologically, and makes the assumption of initiative and the development of an aggressive search for the public welfare in regulatory situations difficult and perhaps impossible.

Whether the Administrative Procedure Act does more than codify the best prevailing practices of administrative adjudication is still debated by students of administrative law. Its significance seems to this author to lie not so much in specific changes it has brought about in the procedure of adjudication as in the extent to which the Act represents an important stage in the unfolding of ideas and attitudes concerning the role of administrative discretion in modern governmental practice and the possibilities and probabilities of achieving a fair measure of equity in the dispensation of administrative justice. It is more important for its political implications than for its specific procedural requirements and definitions.

The Administrative Procedure Act symbolizes the hostility of the legal profession toward the process of administrative adjudication.[15] Although lawyers supported the idea

[15] See Robert H. Jackson, "The Administrative Process," *Journal of Social Philosophy*, vol. 5, 1940, p. 146: "From the very beginning the administrative tribunal has faced the hostility of the legal profession."

of the independent commission as the proper governmental instrument of regulation and extolled the commission's capacity for keeping out of politics, the actions of commissions in the making of rules and the adjudication of controversies have been highly suspect. Lawyers have characterized independent commissions as nonpolitical; but with reference to the process of administrative adjudication, they have usually insisted that the commissions could not be trusted to judge cases fairly and objectively. John Dickinson, who wrote one of the early classics in the field of administrative law, expressed the legal attitude concisely: "Administrative tribunals do not have that independence from government which is one of the traditionally prized guarantees of the justice administered by our common-law courts. Their adjudications, taking place as very part and parcel of the process of government, are exposed to the influence of all the political forces which act upon government."[16] The sharp inconsistency between the views that commissions are nonpolitical and that administrative adjudication is suspect because it is subject to political forces has never appeared to bother the legal profession. The fight of the American Bar Association to secure the enactment of the Administrative Procedure Act suggests that the bar is willing to tolerate or accept the process of administrative adjudication only if the process can be reduced to the familiar terms of the separation-of-powers theory, and even then only if its procedures are judicialized and the courts are able to review administrative decisions.

### Hearing Examiners under the Administrative Procedure Act

Eight years' experience under the Administrative Procedure Act does not challenge the conclusions that the Act "neither created nor substantially altered a single government agency" and that it "neither reduces the number of

16 John Dickinson, *Administrative Justice and the Supremacy of Law*, Harvard University Press, Cambridge, 1927, p. 36.

administrative agencies, nor prevents their growth, nor changes their powers materially, nor subjects them to the control of either the President or the Congress to a greater extent than heretofore."[17] On the other hand, the hearing examiner provisions of the Act have made important changes in the conduct of hearings in regulatory commissions and probably constitute the most important modifications in the adjudication process brought about by the Act.

### THE CIVIL SERVICE STATUS OF EXAMINERS

Section 11 of the Act attempts to improve the quality of hearing examiners and to enhance their independence within their agencies. It authorizes the Civil Service Commission to prescribe the qualifications of hearing examiners and to determine whether incumbent hearing examiners are qualified to retain their positions under the Act. When the hearing examiner provisions of the Act became effective in June 1947, nearly two hundred examiners were employed in positions subject to the Act. Under the Act these examiners, if qualified by the Civil Service Commission, were to have an independent status in the agencies which employed them. The Civil Service Commission was given authority to prescribe the grades and salaries of examiners and make decisions concerning their promotion. The examiners could be removed only for good cause after a full hearing by the Civil Service Commission. Cases were to be assigned to the examiners in their agencies on the basis of rotation in order to eliminate any influence the agency might exercise through the control of case assignments.

The effort of Congress to make the status of examiners as independent as possible met with little success. When the Civil Service Commission authorized the conditional reappointment of the incumbent examiners, Senator Wiley of the Senate Judiciary Committee wrote letters to the Commission criticizing it for appointing to hearing examiner positions men of leftist tendencies and individuals "having

---

[17] Parker, *op.cit.*, pp. 581, 584.

an approach inimical to the welfare of private enterprise."[18]
Under attack by the American Bar Association and key
Congressional leaders, the Civil Service Commission promulgated its regulations governing the appointment, compensation, and removal of hearing examiners in September
1947.[19] Under the regulations the Commission appointed a
Board of Examiners to conduct qualifying examinations
for incumbent examiners. Incumbent examiners with Civil
Service status had to obtain a minimum grade of 70 on a
noncompetitive examination in order to be eligible for
appointment under the Act, but the Board of Examiners
was authorized to qualify only those examiners deemed to
be "eminently qualified."[20] The members of the Board of
Examiners, as announced in January 1948, included two
state supreme court judges, one employee of the Civil
Service Commission, and three attorneys who had held
high positions in the American Bar Association.[21] Fuchs
wrote, "It was a disastrous impropriety for the Civil Service
Commission to create a Board of Examiners so strongly
colored by the asserted ideology of the Association."[22]

During 1948 the Board of Examiners investigated the
records and qualifications of incumbent examiners. Its
recommendations were sent to the Civil Service Commission, which "did not review the Board of Examiners' de-

[18] These letters are quoted in Ralph Fuchs, "The Hearing Examiner
Fiasco under the Administrative Procedure Act," *Harvard Law Review*,
vol. 63, 1950, p. 743.

[19] 12 Federal Register (1947), p. 6321.

[20] Civil Service Departmental Circular No. 592, Supplement 2, November
5, 1947, p. 2. For further details, see Morgan Thomas, "The Selection of
Federal Hearing Examiners: Pressure Groups and the Administrative
Process," *Yale Law Journal*, vol. 59, 1950, pp. 431-475.

[21] The supreme court justices, who had no previous federal experience,
were Douglas Edmonds of California and Laurance Hyde of Missouri. The
Commission employee was Wilson M. Matthews. The three attorneys were
Carl McFarland, perhaps the leading representative of the philosophy and
attitude of the American Bar Association in administrative law matters;
Joseph W. Henderson, President of the American Bar Association in 1943-
1944; and Willis Smith, President of the Association in 1945-1946 and later
Senator from North Carolina. See Thomas, *op.cit.*, p. 439, footnote 31, for
further data.

[22] Fuchs, *op.cit.*, p. 748.

cisions but merely translated them into its official action."[23] The results were announced finally in March 1949. Forty-two incumbent examiners with Civil Service status and twelve without such status were disqualified, making a total of 25% of the total number of incumbent examiners. Many were qualified for positions in grades lower than their present grades. Twenty-seven out of forty-one examiners in the National Labor Relations Board were, in effect, rated ineligible for employment under the Administrative Procedure Act. The examiners appealed the decisions to the Civil Service Commission, both the ICC and the NLRB protested, and the Association of ICC Practitioners urged Congress to make an investigation. During the appeal process the appellant examiners were denied elementary procedural safeguards. The Board, dominated by men closely tied to the American Bar Association and identified as strong advocates of judicialized procedure, in effect denied to the examiners the rights normally accorded by the regulatory agencies to private parties in cases of adjudication. The Commission was eventually forced to repudiate the work of the Board, which resigned in July 1949. By that time, almost all disqualifications of incumbent examiners had been voided. The opportunity for the Commission to replace relatively incompetent hearing examiners with more qualified examiners was lost. Although the work of the Civil Service Commission was designed, presumably, to provide a nonpolitical, independent, and objective corps of hearing examiners, the process of qualifying incumbent examiners was scarcely nonpolitical or objective. Fuchs concludes from his study of this episode that "what was wanted, consciously or unconsciously, were examiners who would be tender toward economic interests affected by regulation."[24]

[23] Thomas, *op.cit.*, p. 441.
[24] Fuchs, *op.cit.*, p. 749. For a detailed statement of the appeals process, see Thomas, *op.cit.*, pp. 444-458.

## SOME OPERATING PROBLEMS

After the debacle in connection with the Board of Examiners, the most important issues concerning the hearing examiners have been the degree to which the Civil Service Commission should control the promotion of examiners and how it should require that cases be assigned to examiners on a basis of rotation. The Commission could not decide what authority it had under Section 11 of the Administrative Procedure Act. Finally, it submitted its question concerning the scope of its authority to the Attorney General. The legal question was whether, under Section 11 of the Act, promotions of hearing examiners may be made by the employing agencies, subject to prior approval by the Civil Service Commission, on the basis of a noncompetitive examination, or whether Section 11 directly confers responsibility on the Commission for selecting examiners for promotion. The acting Attorney General held that the Commission was not limited to approval or disapproval of agency recommendations and that it had authority to determine which examiners shall be promoted to vacancies at higher grades.[25] In his opinion of February 1951 he noted: "One of the principal purposes of the Administrative Procedure Act was to render examining officers in administrative agencies separate, and genuinely independent of pressure, from the prosecuting officers or others in their agencies who might, directly or indirectly, influence their determinations. Consistent with this purpose, provision was made for the protection of examiners against arbitrary dismissal by their agencies. But the hope of promotion may motivate men as strongly as the fear of loss of their jobs. If salaries and promotions are subject to agency control, there is always danger that a subtle influence will be exerted upon the examiners to decide in accordance with agency wishes."[26]

[25] For the Attorney General's opinion and related documents, see *Hearing Examiner Regulations Promulgated under Section 11 of the Administrative Procedure Act*, Senate Document No. 82, 1951, 82nd Congress, 1st session.

[26] *ibid.*, p. 3.

Following the receipt of this opinion, the Civil Service Commission began to draft its regulations governing appointments and promotions under the Act. It met with representatives of the Federal Trial Examiners' Conference, the organization representing the hearing examiners employed under the Act in national regulatory agencies. In July 1951 the Commission submitted to Senator Pat McCarran, Chairman of the Senate Judiciary Committee, a copy of the proposed regulations governing promotion policies and procedures. In September McCarran informed the Commission of his opposition to the proposed regulations. He felt that they would establish a very slow, cumbersome procedure in which "Commission action would be predicated upon agency recommendation." McCarran took the occasion to give the Commission a stiff lecture on how it had neglected its responsibilities and failed to interpret the Act correctly. The idea of Section 11 of the Act, according to McCarran, "was not only to require the Commission and the agencies to seek fit persons but also to make examiners largely independent in matters of tenure and compensation. It required assignment by rotation not by classification. It intended to grant judicial independence which is not achieved by a system of promotional rewards subject to agency control. Indeed, such a system of promotional rewards is not conducive to this objective at all. Uniformity, stability, and independence were desired. It was not intended that these should be restricted by agency control of classification or compensation. . . . The Civil Service Commission has offered a nefarious promotion scheme which is neither conducive to harmony nor to judicial attitude [sic], for it leaves to the agency the initiative and the control." McCarran stated vigorously that "the Commission has demonstrated no special competence in selecting examiners or in affording them the security of tenure and fixed compensation which are prerequisite to judicial independence."[27]

27 *ibid.*, pp. 8-10.

After considering the views of the Chairman of the Senate Judiciary Committee, the Commission issued its regulations on September 21, 1951. The regulations provided for rotation of examiners within each agency "on cases of the level of difficulty for which they, the examiners, have qualified, rather than on all cases of varying levels of difficulty arising in an agency."[28] The Commission noted that the grades of examiners varied in the agencies because of variations in the level of difficulty of their work. Rotation meant rotation within a grade level and not across the board. The Commission denied that the regulations endangered the independence of the examiners.

The hearing examiners strongly favored the appointment of all examiners at the highest General Service grade levels for Civil Service appointments instead of a range of grades from GS-11 to GS-15. It was felt that a range of grades would also require the establishment of a system of promotion governing advancement from one grade to the next higher grade, and that the actions of the employing agencies and the Civil Service Commission in determining the promotional scheme and passing on individual cases of recommended promotions would reduce the status of the examiners in the agencies to that of regular Civil Service employees instead of maintaining their independent role as contemplated in the Administrative Procedure Act. As early as May 1947 the Federal Trial Examiners' Conference set forth its position on the issue of rotation, classification, and promotion. The Conference held that it was impossible to predetermine whether any case set down for hearing would be simple or complex. If the principle of rotation of assignments is to be followed, said the Conference, "every examiner must be of a caliber to hear and decide cases in every degree of complexity," and "the required caliber must be that which is called for by the most difficult and important case in the agency; under such conditions

[28] *ibid.*, p. 11.

there can be no gradations but all should be at the same and the highest permissible level."[29]

After the Civil Service Commission issued its regulations governing hearing examiners in September 1951, a group of twenty-five examiners, joined by the Federal Trial Examiners' Conference, brought suit in the Federal District Court of the District of Columbia to enjoin the Commission from enforcing its regulations.[30] On March 4, 1952, Judge Bolitha Laws handed down the decision of the court.[31] The Court ruled that the Commission's regulations were contrary to Section 11 of the Administrative Procedure Act, which did not contemplate distinctions between grades of examiners. The decision therefore declared invalid the attempt of the Commission to classify examiner positions; to control promotions from one grade to another; to require the assignment of cases to examiners on the basis of rotation, depending on the difficulty and importance of each case; and to authorize the separation of hearing examiners when the work load of the employing agency declines.

The Civil Service Commission appealed the decision of the District Court to the Court of Appeals for the District of Columbia, which affirmed the lower court's decision on July 16, 1952.[32] Both decisions appear to be based on the assumption that classification, rotation according to the difficulty of cases, and individual intraagency promotions give the agencies control over the examiners' compensation and otherwise destroy the independence of the examiners

[29] From Report of the Executive Committee of the Trial Examiners' Conference, May 23, 1947, quoted in "Résumé of Hearing Examiner Conference Activities Especially as Related to the Administrative Procedure Act," *ICC Practitioners' Journal*, vol. 19, 1952, p. 976.

[30] U.S.D.C., Dist. Col., Civil Action 5171-51. For a copy of the complaint, see *ICC Practitioners' Journal*, vol. 19, 1952, pp. 369-378.

[31] Federal Trial Examiners' Conference v. Ramspeck, 104 F. Supp. 734. Excerpts of the opinion are found in *ICC Practitioners' Journal*, vol. 19, 1952, pp. 648-649.

[32] Ramspeck v. Federal Trial Examiners' Conference, *U.S. Law Week*, vol. 21, p. 2046. See also *ICC Practitioners' Journal*, vol. 19, 1952, pp. 1042-1046.

from control by the employing agencies. In March 1953, however, the U.S. Supreme Court overruled the lower courts and upheld the regulations of the Civil Service Commission relating to the classification of examiners, the assignment of cases to examiners in rotation insofar as practicable, and the separation of examiners when their work load declines.[33]

The dispute over the Commission's regulations reveals the lack of mutual understanding among the Commission, Congress, the regulatory agencies, and the hearing examiners as to the administrative requirements of Section 11 of the Administrative Procedure Act. When the Commission sought to classify examiners according to the level and extent of their experience and the difficulty of the cases adjudicated, Congress charged that the Commission was giving too much control over examiners to the employing agencies. The examiners sought to eliminate the classification scheme in order to secure uniform compensation for all examiners at the highest possible Civil Service level. Throughout the discussion of the status of the examiners under the Commission's regulations, there was little understanding of the operating requirements facing the regulatory agency. Judge Bazelon, who dissented from the affirming opinion of the Court of Appeals, said: "Freezing all examiners within an agency into one grade and mechanical assignment of cases would go a long way toward dissipating the administrative expertise upon which courts now rely in giving deference to administrative judgments."[34]

In July 1952 Congress passed the Communications Act Amendments, 1952,[35] which contain an interesting section affecting the role of the hearing examiner in the Federal Communications Commission. Section 409 (a) provides that the FCC shall designate examiners to conduct hearings in cases of adjudication as defined by the Administrative Pro-

[33] Ramspeck v. Federal Trial Examiners' Conference, 345 U.S. 128 (1953).
[34] From excerpts reprinted in *ICC Practitioners' Journal*, vol. 19, 1952, pp. 1042-1046.
[35] Public Law 554, 82nd Congress, July 16, 1952, 66 Stat. 711.

cedure Act. The designation of the hearing examiner by the agency contrasts sharply with the view of Judge Laws that "There can be no question that if the regulations make possible the participation of a litigating agency in selecting or avoiding any trial examiner, they offend the [Administrative Procedure] Act. . . . The regulations themselves must be clear and definite in putting power of assignment beyond the control or suggestion of litigating agencies."[36] But as one experienced examiner has observed, Congress "has no hesitancy in permitting the F.C.C.—even in a prosecutory type of proceeding—to designate what F.C.C. examiner shall hear the proceeding."[37] However, Section 409 (a) cannot be interpreted as a weakening of the Congressional advocacy of the independence of examiners, for the legislation containing it also contains provisions requiring a separation of the functions of prosecutor and judge within the FCC which go well beyond the requirements for separation in the Administrative Procedure Act.[38]

### CONFLICT WITH EMPLOYEE LOYALTY PROGRAMS

The requirement of the Administrative Procedure Act that examiners appointed under the Act be removable only for good cause and after a hearing created a conflict with the federal loyalty program. On December 20, 1951, the Civil Service Commission asked Congress for legislation to make the examiners removable on grounds of disloyalty under the terms of the loyalty program. As set forth by President Truman's executive order on that program, the government's case in a loyalty proceeding before the Loyalty Review Board of the Civil Service Commission consists of confidential reports of the Federal Bureau of Investigation that are not made a part of the record in the case.

[36] Federal Trial Examiners' Conference v. Ramspeck, 104 F. Supp. 734, 740.

[37] Harold D. McCoy, "Communications Act Amendments, 1952, Certain Aspects of Interest to I.C.C.," *ICC Practitioners' Journal*, vol. 20, 1952, p. 20. McCoy is assistant chief examiner of the ICC.

[38] See Section 409 (c) (1), (2), and (3), 66 Stat. 721, and the discussion in McCoy, *op.cit.*, pp. 19-21.

The identity of the informants is withheld from the accused, who has no opportunity to cross-examine his accusers. On the other hand, the Administrative Procedure Act requires that a hearing examiner be given the opportunity to cross-examine witnesses in any hearing for the discharge of the examiner. In a letter to the President and Congress, the Commission reported its dilemma and asked for remedial legislation: "If the Administrative Procedure Act is not followed, any adjudication of disloyalty is sure to be reversed in a subsequent proceeding in court. If the Administrative Procedure Act is followed, the evidence that can be presented at the hearing is certain to be insufficient to justify adjudication of disloyalty. It would appear, therefore, that as the law now stands it will be almost impossible to remove a hearing examiner who is disloyal to the Government of the United States."[39] The Commission's dilemma was the result of complaints, which the Loyalty Review Board in the Commission had received, questioning the loyalty of about ten of the hearing examiners appointed under the Act.[40]

In the effort to secure the independence of the hearing examiner from his employing agency, Congress has encountered difficulties arising out of its attempt to treat the examiner as different from other federal employees, as one to whom the normal Civil Service regulations governing classification, dismissal on grounds of disloyalty, and promotion do not apply. Matters of administrative convenience and operating efficiency have been disregarded as insignificant in the light of the goal of independence for examiners.

CONGRESS CHANGES ITS MIND

The decision to apply or not to apply the hearing examiner requirements of the Administrative Procedure Act to adjudication proceedings in a particular agency is essentially political in nature and is influenced by Congres-

[39] Quoted in John D. Morris, "U.S. Examiner Held Immune to Ouster," *New York Times*, December 21, 1951.
[40] *ibid.*

sional attitudes toward a particular governmental function or government agency. While the rulings of the courts concerning the applicability of the Act have been significant, Congress has not been reluctant to revise the judicial opinion by enacting new legislation. The first important instance of Congressional revision of a court decision bringing additional hearing examiners under the Act occurred in connection with the conduct of deportation proceedings. In the case of Wong Yang Sung v. McGrath in 1950, the Supreme Court held that the Administrative Procedure Act was applicable to deportation proceedings conducted by the Immigration and Naturalization Service in the Department of Justice.[41] The decision had the effect of placing about 300 examiners under Section 11 of the Act and giving control over their appointment, classification, and promotion to the Civil Service Commission instead of the Department of Justice. Congress apparently did not consider that fairness toward aliens subject to deportation proceedings required that the hearings be conducted by examiners independent of the Department of Justice and subject to personnel controls of the Civil Service Commission instead. In the Supplemental Appropriation Act of 1951,[42] which Congress passed about eight months after this decision, deportation proceedings relating to the expulsion or exclusion of aliens were exempted from the hearing examiner provisions of the Administrative Procedure Act. The Department of Justice quickly established a new position of deportation examiner subject to Civil Service rules but not to the special rules governing hearing examiners under the Administrative Procedure Act.

Approximately one year later the Supreme Court had another occasion to consider the applicability of the hearing examiner provisions of the Administrative Procedure Act. In the Riss case, in a *per curiam* opinion, the Court in effect held that the Act was applicable to hearings conducted by examiners in the Bureau of Motor Vehicles of

41 Wong Yang Sung v. McGrath, 339 U.S. 33 (1950).
42 Public Law 843, 81st Congress, approved September 27, 1950.

the ICC on applications for certificates of convenience and necessity to operate as a common carrier by motor vehicle.[43] The decision affected sixty-five to eighty positions in the ICC. At the time of the decision the Bureau of Motor Vehicles employed sixty-five examiners in grades GS-11 to GS-15 and forty examiners in grade GS-9. Under the Civil Service regulations governing examiners pursuant to the Administrative Procedure Act, the lowest classification of a hearing examiner is GS-11. Therefore the Commission named the sixty-five incumbent examiners in grades GS-11 to GS-15 to examiner positions under the Act, while the examiners graded GS-9 lost their status as examiners qualified to conduct hearings on motor carrier operating applications.

The Riss decision threatened the validity of an estimated 5,000 rulings made by the Bureau of Motor Vehicles in proceedings on applications by motor carriers for operating certificates. In March 1952 the House of Representatives passed a bill to validate the motor carrier proceedings conducted without compliance with the hearing examiner provisions of the Administrative Procedure Act.[44] As of July 1954 no further action had been taken by Congress.[45]

The third action taken by Congress affecting the applicability of the hearing examiner provisions dealt with hearings on loyalty cases. In 1950, loyalty proceedings conducted under authority of the Internal Security Act of 1950 were made subject to the hearing examiner provisions of the Administrative Procedure Act.[46] Some examiner positions have been brought under the Administrative Procedure Act by administrative action. For example, during the 1951 fiscal year, two positions in the Post Office Department

[43] Riss and Co., Inc., v. United States, 341 U.S. 907 (1951).
[44] See U.S. Congress, House Report No. 1637, 82nd Congress, 2nd session, recommending passage of H.R. 5045.
[45] See the account in "House Passes Amendment to Administrative Procedure Act Intending to Meet Effect of Riss Decision," *ICC Practitioners' Journal*, vol. 19, 1952, pp. 703-706.
[46] Public Law 831, 81st Congress, section 16, enacted on September 9, 1950.

dealing with fraud-order cases and five positions in the Veterans' Education Appeals Board in the Veterans' Administration were included under the Act. On July 1, 1954, after seven years of experience, 278 examiners were employed by 16 agencies under the Administrative Procedure Act, as shown in Table 2.

TABLE 2. *Number of Hearing Examiners Employed in Federal Agencies under the Administrative Procedure Act, by General Service Grades, as of June 30, 1954*

| Agency | Total | GS-11 | GS-12 | GS-13 | GS-14 | GS-15 |
|---|---|---|---|---|---|---|
| Independent commissions | 213 | | | 50 | 50 | 113 |
| CAB | 21 | | | 8 | 4 | 9 |
| FCC | 17 | | | | | 17 |
| FPC | 11 | | | | 10 | 1 |
| FTC | 8 | | | | | 8 |
| ICC | 106 | | | 41 | 34 | 31 |
| NLRB | 47 | | | | | 47 |
| SEC | 3 | | | 1 | 2 | |
| Other departments and agencies | 65 | 8 | 1 | 42 | 4 | 10 |
| Treasury | | | | | | |
|     Alcohol Tax Unit | 3 | | | 3 | | |
|     Coast Guard | 15 | | | 15 | | |
| Health, Education, and Welfare | | | | | | |
|     Appeals Council | 20 | | | 20 | | |
|     Food and Drug Administration | 1 | | | 1 | | |
| Veterans' Administration | 1 | | | 1 | | |
| Interior | | | | | | |
|     Bureau of Land Management | 1 | | | 1 | | |
|     Bureau of Indian Affairs | 9 | 8 | 1 | | | |
| Agriculture | 5 | | | | | 5 |
| Commerce | | | | | | |
|     Federal Maritime Board | 5 | | | | | 5 |
| Labor | 2 | | | | 2 | |
| Post Office | 2 | | | 1 | 1 | |
| Civil Service Commission | 1 | | | | 1 | |
| Grand total | 278 | 8 | 1 | 92 | 54 | 123 |

Source: Letter from Civil Service Commission to author, October 12, 1954.

## Impact of the Administrative Procedure Act on the Regulatory Commissions

The effort to safeguard the independent status of the hearing examiners has brought the Civil Service Commission, the hearing examiners, and the employing agencies into conflict. Although the Commission has been given authority to regulate the employment, promotion, and removal of examiners under the Act, it obviously cannot overlook the exigencies of administrative operation. For instance, several examiners may be promotable in terms of experience and training, but the employing agency may not have sufficient funds or may not choose to make funds available for grade promotions. The Commission is not in a position to order the agency to promote the examiners. On the other hand, Congress may reduce the appropriation of a regulatory agency so substantially that a reduction in the number of hearing examiners appears necessary. However, under the regulations of the Civil Service Commission and the Act, examiners can be removed only for cause and hence appear to be protected against removal because of reduction in force. Similarly, the loyalty provisions apparently conflict with the rule that examiners may be removed only for cause and after a hearing. While disloyalty constitutes good cause for removal, the loyalty hearings do not make available the right to cross-examine witnesses and other rights normally accorded a defendant in a court trial, as required by the Administrative Procedure Act. These conflicts symbolize the preoccupation of the Act with formal requirements of adjudication and the neglect of operating considerations.

Despite the charge of "administrative absolutism" and countercharge of "judicialization of administrative adjudication," the Administrative Procedure Act has not noticeably affected adjudicative procedure in the regulatory commissions. Most of the agencies had already judicialized their procedures and in some cases were outdoing the courts in safeguarding the interests of individual respondents. Several provisions of the Act have neither streamlined the adjudicative process nor immobilized it. Opportunity to submit written evidence, for example, had existed in some agencies prior to the passage of the Act, and written evidence does not appear to be used more widely today than before the Act was passed. Similarly, placing the burden of proof on the proponent of a rule does not appear to slow the rule-making process or to make it more burdensome. The need to give licensees a second chance before revocation of licenses has been offset by the proviso in the Act that the second chance may be omitted when the violation has been willful or when the public safety or interest requires immediate action. Thus SEC suspends or revokes licenses without a second chance on the ground that a violation has been willful and continuing, while CAB suspends or revokes certain licenses without a second chance on the ground that the public safety is involved. Delays and obstructions in administrative regulation appear to be caused more by ingrained administrative habits of work and by enabling statutes than by the Administrative Procedure Act. For example, revocation of a motor carrier certificate or permit by the ICC is practically impossible because of the statutory requirement of the Interstate Commerce Act that a certificate holder or permittee be given an opportunity to comply after a hearing has been held to determine whether his certificate or permit should be revoked. Revocation cannot be ordered until a second hearing is held to determine whether the violator has abided by the terms of the warning which followed the first hearing.

The agencies appear to have gone beyond the terms of the Administrative Procedure Act in judicializing their adjudicative procedures. The real danger is that in outdoing the courts in providing judicialized procedure, the agencies have multiplied the respondent's opportunities to delay and postpone proceedings and to hold up final action. Many adjudicative proceedings are no longer characterized by the speed and certainty of action which were their principal advantages over judicial settlement of regulatory controversies. In some cases administrative adjudication has become more time-consuming than court cases. In the aviation field it is relatively easier for CAB to bring suit in federal court than to institute enforcement proceedings within CAB against an alleged violator. Similarly, it is somewhat easier for the Civil Aeronautics Administration to institute a proceeding before the CAB to revoke an airman's certificate than it is for the CAB to take an enforcement action before its own hearing examiners under the Administrative Procedure Act.

In many agencies, examiners only recommend decisions rather than make initial decisions. Recommended decisions are reviewed by the commissioners themselves sitting *en banc*, and they make the initial decisions. When the commission makes an initial decision, it is essential to look at the procedures followed at the commission level in order to evaluate the fairness of the regulatory procedure. On the whole there is a lack of balance between the procedures followed by commissioners and those followed by staffs. In contrast to the great concern for formalizing hearings conducted by hearing examiners, the procedure at the commission level appears to be rather casual and frequently unsystematic. Discussions at the meetings of commissioners seem to be very informal, and initial decisions may be made by members who have not read a substantial portion of the record or studied the documents prepared by the staff summarizing the issues and evidence.

The important point is that the extreme formalization of procedures of adjudication at the staff level in connection with hearings conducted by examiners is not matched usually by the observance of similar standards of due process at the level of the commission itself. There has been little exploration of the degree to which the standards ought to be the same or similar. The preoccupation of students of administration, the American Bar Association, Congressional committees, and practitioners with the hearing process has not been matched by a similar study of decision making at the commission level. The lack of systematic processes at that level may be more disadvantageous to the maintenance of vigorous, effective regulation than excessive formalization of procedures at the staff level.[47]

The deficiencies of due process in decision making at the commission level are interesting in view of the criticism that commissioners have become so preoccupied with the adjudication of cases that they have neglected long-range planning and control of operations. It seems appropriate to ask, What kind of adjudication? Is it adjudication based on close analysis of the record developed in the hearing and other staff documents? Or is it adjudication based merely on cursory consideration of the case? There is at present insufficient information to generalize about the character of adjudication by commissioners, sitting as a commission. Whatever the current trend is, it seems sound to work toward some measure of consistency with respect to adjudication at the staff level and at the commission level and to adopt procedures that do not require commissioners to act like judges but do insist upon maintaining fairness and equity toward the respondents.

## Regulatory v. Executive Functions

One of the central ideas about the process of adjudication in regulatory agencies is the incompatibility of adjudication with other types of administrative activities. There is widespread agreement that administrative adjudication can be fair and impartial only when the hearing examiner is insulated from contact with the investigating and prosecuting staffs and when the agency is not asked to undertake activities which are "executive" rather than "regulatory." Although it fully accepted the independent commissions as permanent and desirable features of American government, the Hoover Commission criticized them for their lack of

[47] There is a striking parallel between the process of adjudication in commissions and the appellate proceeding in state and federal courts. While there has been ample study of trial procedures and techniques in the regular trial courts, there has been little study of procedure at the level of the appellate court. We know very little about the procedures actually followed by appellate judges in reviewing the decisions of lower courts.

planning and slow disposition of regulatory business. It traced some operating inefficiencies of commissions to their accretion of so-called executive functions. "Purely executive functions too frequently have been entrusted to these independent regulatory commissions. The consequences have not been too happy, for a plural executive is not the best device for the performance of operational duties. Moreover, these duties commonly call for close integration with the broad programs of the executive branch. The quality of independence, desirable in the disposition of controversies, creates obstacles to the handling of an executive program." The Commission then recommended the following transfers from the regulatory commissions: power-planning functions of the Federal Power Commission to the Department of the Interior; functions of construction, operation, charter, and sale of ships of the U.S. Maritime Commission to the Department of Commerce; functions of equipment inspection, safety, and car service of the ICC to the Department of Commerce; promulgation of rules of safety for aircraft operation of the CAB to the Civil Aeronautics Administration with right of appeal to the CAB.[48]

In its report to the Hoover Commission, the Task Force on Regulatory Commissions made the same distinction between regulatory and executive-type work:

"In our judgment, the independent regulatory commissions should ordinarily be confined to regulatory activities and should not be entrusted with essentially executive and operating tasks except for compelling reasons.

"In one sense, the strictly regulatory work involves some executive activity, such as the administration of the necessary expert staff, the making of studies and investigations and initiation of proceedings and the like. But these functions are essential to the effective performance of the regulatory work and should be retained by the commissions. What we mean by executive and operating activities are

---

[48] Commission on Organization of the Executive Branch of the Government, *Regulatory Commissions*, 1949, pp. 11-13.

those like laying out and managing an airway or airport system, or constructing or operating merchant vessels. Such activities should not be given to the regulatory commissions in the absence of very special circumstances." The Task Force emphasized that "The very qualities which make these agencies valuable for regulation, especially group deliberation and discussion, make them unsuited for executive and operating activities."[49]

The distinction between regulatory and executive functions is, at best, approximate rather than precise, but it has been given the status of dogma in the field of regulatory administration. Neither the Task Force nor the Hoover Commission itself visualized the close relation between safety performance and economic regulation. Surely, the safety record of an aircraft or motor carrier is or should be a matter of interest to officials concerned with the performance of carriers operating under government licenses, permits, or certificates. For example, when a carrier with a poor safety record applies to the CAB or the ICC for additional operating authority, it seems reasonable, if not essential, to consider the safety performance of the carrier in determining its over-all fitness and capacity to operate in the public interest. Yet neither agency has developed a systematic method for examining and evaluating the safety record of a carrier in such a connection. In these commissions, safety considerations rarely enter into matters of economic regulation. On the other hand, economic considerations do intrude upon safety matters. Safety in railroad, aircraft, and motor vehicle operations is costly. The expense incurred by a transportation company through compliance with certain safety rules is an important factor in safety administration. A proposal that a railroad install certain automatic safety devices raises questions about installation costs and their effect upon total operating costs of the carrier, and therefore upon its rates and profits as

[49] Task Force on Regulatory Commissions of the Commission on Organization of the Executive Branch of the Government, *Task Force Report on Regulatory Commissions*, 1949, pp. 29, 30.

well. There are indications that the conservative character of safety administration in the CAB and the ICC can be traced partly to a reluctance on the part of the commissions to require that companies install expensive safety appliances and devices or develop costly practices in the interest of safety.

Safety administration also involves important rule-making functions which are regulatory in character. The ICC, for example, has broad statutory power to establish "just and reasonable" rules of safety deemed necessary or desirable in the public interest. It holds hearings in connection with the making of safety rules, accident investigations, and the revocation of a carrier's license for failure to comply with safety regulations. The determination of minimum safety requirements in railroad operation is substantially similar to the process by which the CAB determines the proper routing of aircraft.

Safety rules, it must be concluded, cannot be classified as either "regulatory" or "executive," as these terms are used by the Hoover Commission and its Task Force. Safety administration involves typical adjudicatory activities as well as the operating methods of the nonregulatory agency. Whether or not such administration is regulatory or executive, the safety performance of a carrier and the prescription of safety rules are directly relevant to the adjudicatory process in the transportation commissions. The fact that this relevance is overlooked by the commissions contributes to their operating deficiencies. It does not in itself justify further fragmentation of the regulatory process by the transfer of so-called executive activities of regulatory commissions, such as safety regulation, to an executive department.

The attempt to distinguish between so-called executive and regulatory activities is significant because it is a reaction to the preponderant evidence that commissions have been highly inefficient agencies. The desire to shift "executive" activities to other agencies represents an effort to reduce the managerial burden of a commission and to permit it to concentrate on activities for which it is said to be especially suited. In a similar vein, the proposal of the President's Committee on Administrative Management in 1937 to separate the adjudicatory and nonadjudicatory functions of commissions was based on the implicit conviction that they were inherently weak agencies for the planning of regulatory programs and the management of staff and work load. Unfortunately, the factors which make the commissions weak agents of administration also operate to make them rather ineffectual instruments of administrative adjudication.

The process of adjudication within commissions raises a number of important political and administrative questions. Adjudication has been treated almost exclusively in legal terms while its political significance has been neglected. The movement to reform the process of adjudication has been based on important political, as well as legal, considerations. The experience of the regulatory agencies under the Administrative Procedure Act tells us more about the political and administrative context of regulation than it does about the technicalities of adjudicative procedure. Finally, the effort to separate so-called executive functions from the regulatory commissions appears to be based on an inadequate understanding of the nature of the regulatory tasks of the commissions.

CHAPTER 8

# Enforcement of Regulations

PERHAPS the least explored area in governmental regulation of business is the enforcement of regulations. While attention has been devoted to the history and policies of commissions, to commissioners who have influenced the course of regulation, and to legal procedures of administrative regulation, only passing reference has been made to the tasks of winning support for regulations, securing compliance of regulated groups, and applying sanctions against those who continue to violate the regulations.

### Significance of Enforcement in the
### Regulatory Process

One of the crucial tests of the effectiveness of a regulatory commission is its capacity to obtain the compliance of persons subject to regulation and to enforce its regulations against violators. This capacity becomes, in the long run, a primary measuring rod of the ability of the agency to operate in the public interest. The need for public support of regulation as a prerequisite for enforcing economic controls seems obvious; yet commissions have characteristically failed to acknowledge its essentiality. The emphasis on expertness and the judicialization of adjudicatory procedures within commissions encourage them to concentrate on internal matters, overlooking the impact of their regulations on the public at large. Some commissions are so preoccupied with developing a regulatory scheme acceptable to the regulated groups that they ignore the larger public affected by their regulations. The regulated groups press their recommendations concerning policy and procedure upon the commissions; the general public anticipates that the hard-won regulatory statute will somehow be administered automatically, or it loses interest entirely after the act has been passed.

Public understanding of the goals of regulation and public support for basic regulatory policies are essential to effective regulation of economic affairs. The widespread refusal to comply with Prohibition regulations in the 1920's stands as a constant reminder that regulations that aim to control the behavior of a large number of people cannot succeed unless they are accepted as reasonable and workable and do not impose arbitrary and needlessly unpleasant rules of conduct. Regulatory agencies with a substantial clientele have the greatest need to develop and maintain public support. As the public affected by regulation becomes more comprehensive, conscious efforts to cultivate consent and support become unavoidable. On the other hand, commissions with limited, specialized, and well-organized clienteles are forced into close daily contact with the latter, who are usually unwilling to accept restrictive controls over their business behavior.

INCENTIVES FOR COMPLIANCE

Ordinarily, regulated groups do not comply voluntarily with regulations that require changes in managerial policies and methods of doing business unless the advantages of complying with the regulations seem to outweigh predicted disadvantages. Incentive is needed to secure voluntary compliance. The availability of a subsidy or government loan for those who abide by certain regulations may serve as a powerful incentive for regulated parties to comply. Regulations that lead demonstrably to sounder business and financial practices and therefore to more efficient operation and lower costs may induce regulated groups to comply voluntarily. An industry that has been plagued with scandals may accept regulation as an economical way of winning the respect and esteem of the public. Public support for regulation may be sufficiently extensive to motivate regulated enterprises to comply rather than run the risk of incurring active public disfavor. Again, a business firm might be required to demonstrate its compliance with certain regulations as a prerequisite for obtaining some government contract. For example, if child labor and other undesirable labor practices are prohibited by national law in certain business enterprises, their enforcement bcomes less difficult if government contracts are denied firms that violate the prohibitions. Similarly, the allocation of scarce strategic materials to a manufacturing plant for the production of military equipment may be made contingent upon past compliance with regulations governing the use of strategic materials.

Incentives to induce compliance may be financial, psychological, or emotional. They may offer certain rewards for compliance, or they may reduce noncompliance because of fear of punishment for violations. While both positive and negative incentives are available, they have not been used extensively, and regulatory agencies have had little interest in their development. The reasons are not difficult to find. Regulations administered by independent commissions attract little public attention. Consequently, commissions must reach an adjustment with regulated groups without effective support from an alert public. Regulations developed in this situation tend to be mild rather than restrictive and are usually keyed to acceptability by regulated groups. Incentives are needed most when regulations are regarded by affected firms as severe, distasteful, or economically disadvantageous.

Lack of interest in incentives for compliance is also related to the specialized clienteles of most regulatory agencies. Commissions normally have little concern with governmental matters outside their regulatory jurisdiction. For example, they rarely request Congress for authority to use tax penalties or tax benefits as devices to promote compliance with their regulations. If Congress provided that a firm which consistently and knowingly violates regulations would lose certain tax benefits or be punished by incurring additional tax liabilities, commissions would have a powerful incentive for securing compliance. Few mechanisms are available for securing close and continuing cooperation between an executive department and a commission, and

Congress is reluctant to regard economic controls as interdependent. Moreover, each agency tends to rely on its own resources as much as possible. The Department of the Treasury, which administers revenue laws, naturally would be reluctant to permit tax administration to become encumbered with nonrevenue policies, and a regulatory agency would prefer to depend on those incentives and sanctions over which it exercises direct control.

REQUISITES OF EFFECTIVE ENFORCEMENT

A commission cannot expect to secure compliance unless it is prepared to punish those who repeatedly and willfully violate its regulations. It must have available appropriate sanctions that can be applied, with reasonable firmness and speed, against groups in the industry that refuse to comply voluntarily. Willingness to apply sanctions against violators must be demonstrated early in the development of administrative regulation, so that those affected will be restrained from developing habits of noncompliance and will respect the determination of the agency to require observance of its regulations. A regulatory agency must have access to a judiciary which is not unsympathetic to the broad purposes and goals of the statute and regulations that have been violated.

Enforcement is usually the last regulatory function to be recognized organizationally and functionally. During periods when basic policy is evolving and commission attorneys are drafting regulations and defending their validity and reasonableness, enforcement matters appear to be peripheral and postponable. The lawyers tend to write regulations in technical, legalistic language which undermines their readability and enforceability. Enforcement aspects considered at this stage are apt to be those that relate to the legality and constitutionality of the regulations and the enabling statute.

The central problem of enforcement in a commission is to develop and maintain the support of the public and the regulated groups without compromising the public interest. The enforcement task is likely to be more manageable and more successful if the agency is able to economize in applying controls. Learning how to economize coercion is basic to regulatory success. If regulation is consistent with the values of the community and becomes established as reasonable and legitimate, the costs of compliance are reduced and a higher level of compliance will be achieved. If the community has some means of expressing informally its disapproval of noncompliant behavior, governmental enforcement is minimized. If suitable inducements can be devised, the range of violation of agency regulations is likely to diminish.

## The Interdependence of Regulatory Controls

Given the piecemeal development of governmental regulation in the United States, the interdependence of regulatory controls is commonly overlooked. Each regulatory program influences the environment in which economic activity takes place, and the total substance of governmental control of business affects the environment of each regulatory agency. If regulatory programs fit into a consistent pattern, the burden of enforcement is likely to be eased. For example, employers may comply more willingly with regulations that limit their freedom of decision when labor unions must also abide by restrictive regulations. But labor and employer restrictions are administered usually by separate agencies. If the two regulatory programs are not coordinated, enforcement problems will be more troublesome.

The burden of enforcement is eased if the regulations issued by one agency are related to and are consistent with those issued by other regulatory agencies and are coordinated with the broad economic policies of the government. Enforcement is promoted to the extent that regulations are accepted as part of the framework of national economic policy. If a commission contributes to the achievement of an objective common to several agencies, it is more likely to have their support in securing compliance with its regulations. Interagency assistance and cooperation make available the total resources of the government for enforcement of regulations. From an enforcement point of view, therefore, regulatory programs are interdependent. A commission that is forced to rely entirely on its own resources for enforcement of its regulations maximizes its burden and rarely develops a vigorous enforcement policy.

Commissions operate customarily with considerable autonomy and with marked independence from an obligation to make their programs consistent with national economic policy. For example, the CAB and the ICC make no effort to develop a common pattern of regulation in the transportation field. As a result, the government fails to offer to competing transportation media the incentive of fair treatment to all elements in that industry. Neither the CAB nor the ICC acquires strength that might be derived from a rationally conceived national transportation policy. Each transportation agency must stand on its own feet, as far as regulation is concerned, unsupported by overriding national objectives.

The most critical problem of the FTC enforcement program stems from national inability to fix a course of antimonopoly action. The FTC has inherited the national ambivalence toward antimonopoly and competition. Moreover, it must operate in an environment marked by notable legislative deviations from antimonopoly objectives. Under the impact of economic depression and mobilization for war and defense, the FTC's activity has been modified and almost suspended at various times since 1930. Its programs are complicated by the American habit of both respecting the accomplishments of bigness and fearing the political and economic consequences of increasing concentration of economic power. Its burden of enforcement is increased immeasurably by the lack of a clear commitment to antimonopoly policy throughout the government and the country generally.

The programs of the SEC are perhaps relatively self-contained. Yet its responsibilities related to the activities of public utility holding companies have national economic and political consequences. In addition, enforcement of its regulations covering stock exchanges and dealers in securities can be eased or worsened by the general state of the economy and by the specific actions of such agencies as the Board of Governors of the Federal Reserve System.

## The Concept of Enforcement

The vigor and general character of its enforcement program are derived from the commission's attitude toward the role of enforcement, investigation of cases of alleged violations, imposition of sanctions, and educational and publicity campaigns designed to promote voluntary compliance. More often than not, a tradition of relatively weak enforcement prevails. Cases prepared for prosecution in the courts are usually those in which guilt of the respondent has been completely proved. Cases with less than complete proof of guilt are litigated only if prosecuting authorities can be convinced that prosecution is important to the success of the program and chances of securing a conviction are good. Ordinarily, an agency will be more willing to crack down on willful violators if it has made genuine efforts to explain why the regulations have been issued and what regulated groups must do to comply. A commission that does not meet regularly with representatives of trade associations and other regulated groups and does not issue explanatory material describing its regulations cannot expect them to understand and comply with the regulations.

Compliance activities—that is, trade relations and other educational activities—are fully compatible with the enforcement process, defined as the investigation of cases of alleged violation and the application of administrative and judicial sanctions. Some commissions may never achieve a balance between compliance and enforcement activities. They may regard educational programs to promote compliance as endangering their expert, nonpolitical role. Commissions that do work out a balance between com-

223

pliance and enforcement normally pass through a period of trial and error in which enforcement attorneys vie with other operating officials for the right to control the enforcement and compliance programs.

Should the agency have a "tough" or a "mild" enforcement policy? Should it ask the judges for stiff fines and perhaps jail sentences in the most flagrant cases of violation? Should it prosecute violators or rely upon private parties injured by the activities of a violator to bring suit to recover damages? Is it prepared to take action quickly against violators, or is it content to permit endless delay in disposition of cases? Is it willing to settle cases out of court on the basis of a voluntary payment by the violator to the United States Treasury, or does it insist on a court trial when a serious violation has been committed? Is it willing to risk prosecution of cases in which it is convinced that serious and willful violations have been committed but in which sufficient evidence for conviction may not be readily available?

The attitude of a commission toward its enforcement responsibilities affects its entire regulatory program. Unless it demonstrates a capacity to enforce its regulations, they will be more honored in the breach than in the observance. Those who discover that violations go undetected and unpunished will have little respect for the commission and will violate regulations with impunity if it is to their financial or commercial advantage. While responsibility for enforcement must be allocated to designated officials within an agency, the entire supervisory staff must assume some responsibility for aiding in enforcement and securing a greater measure of compliance.

The general enforcement attitude of the SEC is vigorous, and its approach to enforcement problems tends to emphasize education and voluntary compliance. It relies heavily upon staff initiative in ferreting out and investigating possible violations of its regulations. It regards itself as fully responsible for securing compliance and has been imaginative in developing enforcement programs.

The CAB, on the other hand, has been preoccupied with the development of regulatory policies and the processing of applications for routes, mergers, mail pay, and similar matters. It was established in 1938 and had only two or three years of regulating experience before the outbreak of World War II. Its major programs were not resumed until 1945-1946, after the civil aviation industry had expanded nearly four times in terms of passengers and freight carried and miles flown. Given its concern with developmental work, the Board has subordinated and at times ignored enforcement considerations. It illustrates well the enforcement problem in a relatively young commission dealing with a dynamic industry. It has not been prepared to be aggressive in enforcing its regulations except against irregular air carriers and against violations of safety regulations that lead to serious accidents. The Board has tried to protect the status of certified carriers by preventing irregular carriers from providing the services of a regular carrier. In terms of staff assignments, appropriations, and enforcement actions, in recent years the CAB has emphasized the enforcement of safety rather than economic regulations.

Although the FTC's traditional attitude toward enforcement was passive and highly legalistic, it has slowly developed a more aggressive enforcement policy since the end of World War II. It has made several significant changes in procedure to expedite enforcement activity, but the results are not yet entirely clear.

Enforcement considerations have rarely been significant in the activity of the ICC. Enforcement is considered a responsibility of individual bureaus rather than the Commission as a whole. Interest as well as responsibility appears to stop at the bureau line. The lack of serious concern with enforcement illustrates the case-by-case approach and passive character of ICC regulation. It has depended less on its own resources than on carriers and shippers to promote the public interest.

225

## Development of Enforceable
## Regulations

In order to be enforceable, regulations must be understood by persons and firms subject to them. They must delineate clearly what the individual or firm must do in order to comply. Enforcement will be promoted if affected firms and individuals are required to perform a specific act in order to demonstrate compliance, such as filing a report, applying for a license, or keeping certain information on file. No aspect of enforcement is more frustrating than administrative persistence in drafting complex and lengthy regulations that are incomprehensible to all but legal specialists. Intelligibility and coherence of regulations are major factors in the enforcement process, particularly when large numbers of individuals and firms are affected. For example, understandability is more important in the motor carrier regulations of the ICC than in railroad regulations, since thousands of motor carriers as against relatively few railroads must master the regulations. Many motor carriers are small enterprises which do not regularly employ an attorney, while all railroad companies employ legal staffs.

The problem of understandability is particularly acute when new regulations are issued affecting hitherto unregulated persons. During World War II, for example, the Office of Price Administration was regulating firms and individuals throughout the country who had never been previously aware of national regulations. Service station operators, grocery clerks, and beauty operators were affected along with giant manufacturing plants and metropolitan department stores. The OPA could take nothing for granted concerning the capacity of its regulated clientele to understand and comply with regulations. Yet attorneys in the OPA continued to write regulations in an orthodox legal manner: tightly drawn provisions, internally consistent, replete with legalisms, and applicable to all situations which might conceivably arise under price control and rationing regulations. Some OPA officials stressed the difficulty of securing compliance with legalistic, complex regulations understood only by a lawyer after very careful analysis. More than a few judges found OPA prosecutions difficult to handle because of the extreme complexity of some regulations. Although some OPA officials made valiant efforts to simplify wording without sacrificing the firmness and comprehensiveness that could be achieved by using more legalistic language, the attempt to write understandable yet legally enforceable regulations failed, not because it proved unworkable, but because few lawyers were willing to try it.[1]

A delightful comment on the style and rhetoric of legal drafting was made by the Canadian Wartime Prices and Trade Board in 1942. It announced a new price regulation by hailing it as not even looking like a government order:

"Board officials insist, however, that the new order is not a 'whimsy.' It avoids formal language, lengthy definitions and complicated legal terms because, an official said, 'statutory language is not appropriate to reach the people.'

"While the order is frankly an experiment, Board officials

[1] The following rules, largely ignored in the OPA, would have helped to simplify regulations without sacrificing their standing in court: (1) What the regulation covers should be clearly indicated. (2) Legalistic words and phrases like "pursuant to," "whereas," and "appended hereto" should be avoided. (3) Short sentences should be used. (4) All provisions in the regulation which deal with a particular class of business should be brought together. (5) Clear directions should be given, and examples and illustrations, using the second person instead of the third person, should be cited whenever possible. Sentences should not be used to describe mathematical calculations. Instead of saying, "No person shall do so and so," the regulation should speak directly to the businessman concerned by stating simply, "If you carried on a business on a certain date, you must not do so and so without a permit." (6) Headings should be used frequently. They help to keep the reader's attention and remind him of what he is reading about.

On legal drafting, see Alfred F. Conard, "New Ways to Write Laws," *Yale Law Journal*, vol. 56, 1947, p. 458; R. Dickerson, "FPR No. 1, An Experiment in Standardized and Pre-Fabricated Law," *University of Chicago Law Review*, vol. 13, 1945, p. 90; Jacob Beuscher, "Law-Taught Attitudes and Consumer Rationing," *Wisconsin Law Review*, 1945, p. 63; Victor Thompson, *The Regulatory Process in OPA Rationing*, King's Crown Press, New York, 1950, pp. 377-423.

admit, they pointed out emphatically that it is enforceable. 'Enforceability is not incompatible with simplicity,' they state, thus using more big words than turn up in the order itself.

"Tossed out of the new order are such fine legal phrases as 'devolves or vests in a personal or fiduciary capacity.'

"Gone are the breathless sentences which run 250 words or more. Writers of the new order have rediscovered the period and use it often.

"The distaste for coming right out in the open and stating the date of the order has been overcome in the new draft. Old orders used the phrase 'after the effective date of this order' every time there was need to refer to it. The new order boldly states June 14 every time the matter crops up."[2]

Understandability of regulations is also affected by the frequency with which they are amended. Regulations that remain stable in their main provisions and minor requirements are easier to enforce because the burden of keeping the regulated parties informed about changes is reduced. From the point of view of enforcement, the advantages of amending a regulation need to be weighed against the disadvantages of changing the rules of business conduct. One of the annoying habits of drafters of regulations is the insertion of numerous cross references indicating that a particular section of the regulation must be read in conjunction with another section.

Another factor in the understandability of regulations is the manner in which they are made available to the affected parties. Publication in the *Federal Register* may be helpful to the firms, usually very large, which subscribe regularly to the document, but it does not aid the great majority of firms, which do not. Furthermore, it is difficult to clip applicable regulations from the *Register* and keep them in order. Some companies now publish so-called legal services which are loose-leaf in style, so that new pages can

[2] Canadian Government, Wartime Prices and Trade Board, Press Release 0535, June 14, 1942.

be inserted to take the place of old ones as regulations are added or amended, but they are expensive and practically unavailable to small businessmen. Regulatory agencies need to experiment with different methods of keeping their clienteles informed about regulations which affect them. Copies of regulations and explanatory materials should be available to all who request them, and it would be desirable for the agency to assume the initiative in reaching all parties affected. Direct mailing lists, publication of amendments to regulations in trade association journals, community meetings, and industry advisory committees are some of the media that are available to keep the regulated groups abreast of regulatory requirements.

The enforceability of regulations is affected by the ease with which violations can be detected and proved. In drafting regulations, provisions ought to be inserted which facilitate the discovery of noncompliance. Investigations are likely to be costly and time-consuming unless the investigator is able to determine readily whether a violation has been committed. Some external control, such as the filing of a specified report, permits him to check the actual behavior of the party against the formal requirement of the regulation.

Enforceability is also conditioned by the pervasiveness of controls established by regulation. For example, wholesale and retail price ceilings can be enforced more satisfactorily if effective controls are also placed on prices at the producer and processor levels. The control of prices at these levels may be crucial, since a violation at this stage normally generates intense economic pressure on wholesalers and retailers to violate the regulation. The chain reactions of violations underline the need to control prices at the critical points in the process of production and distribution. Failure to control prices at such points will create a sense of unfairness and inequity and will render regulation less acceptable. The OPA experience indicates that, under inflationary conditions, a regulation which does not extend to all substantial segments of an industry is more difficult to enforce because uncontrolled segments create irresistible pressures on controlled segments to violate. Moreover, labor groups may not be willing to accept wage controls as part of a national policy of economic stabilization unless price control affecting cost-of-living consumer items, such as rent, food, and apparel, is effective.[3]

For years the regulation of public utilities, particularly electric power companies, was bogged down by disputes over the legal basis of valuation of utility property. So much attention was given to the valuation problem that the proper rate of return on investment received little study. In some cases the valuation problem was settled while the question of the rate of return was never analyzed in detail. Lengthy studies of valuation lost significance because of the lack of comparable analysis of an acceptable level of profits for regulated utilities.

There has been almost no experimentation with techniques for making regulation more understandable, and enforcement considerations are generally neglected in drafting regulations. The problem of enforceability varies from commission to commission. The SEC regulates a specialized clientele which is rather readily identifiable. Railroad regulations of the ICC affect a still smaller number of firms. On the other hand, CAB regulations and complementary regulations of the Civil Aeronautics Administration concern several thousand individuals, and ICC regulations in the motor carrier industry, thousands of carriers and drivers. The lack of clarity of regulations is most serious when the number of persons subject to regulation is high. Therefore, both the CAB and the ICC need to give more attention to drafting easily understood regulations. The problem of the FTC is different. In general, the FTC enforces statutes and does not issue regulations. Its interpretive problems deal with statutory construction rather than administrative rules and regulations.

[3] For further material on the OPA, see Marshall B. Clinard, *The Black Market*, Rinehart and Co., New York, 1952, pp. 205-225.

## Compliance Activities

The need to win the sympathetic support or acquiescence of the regulated parties can scarcely be overstated. While a commission must be prepared to punish the fringe of willful and flagrant violators, it must rely, in the last analysis, upon the willingness of the vast majority of persons to comply voluntarily with its regulations. The importance of winning the consent of the regulated clientele in turn emphasizes the importance of developing compliance programs, that is, educational programs and trade relations activities. A commission can achieve a wider measure of public support and understanding if it undertakes vigorous campaigns to teach those subject to its regulations how to comply before it investigates violations for the purpose of imposing sanctions. The development of cooperative and friendly relations with a regulated industry is not an unmixed blessing. Because a spirit of friendliness between a commission and its regulated clientele makes the regulatory task more pleasant, the agency needs to be on guard lest it fail to take vigorous enforcement action for fear that such action would dispel friendly relations.

The conscious development of compliance programs in regulatory commissions is very difficult. In commissions with rather limited and highly organized clienteles, groups representing an industry deal directly with regulatory officials. By maintaining a continuous barrage of public criticism directed at the agency, regulated groups often succeed in keeping an agency on the defensive and unable to take initiative for a more vigorous program of regulation. In an older commission, respect for and confidence in the regulated groups may become institutionalized, with the result that the commission recognizes no need to prod them into improved practices and better public service.

The main ingredients of a compliance program include the following: (1) the conduct of trade relations, including personal contacts, trade conferences, correspondence, educational campaigns, and consultation with businessmen; (2) the education of persons or establishments concerning their obligations under applicable regulations; (3) the conduct of relations with advisory committees to enlist industry support in securing compliance; and (4) assistance to enforcement officials in developing enforcement programs, that is, outlining the areas in which violations are most numerous, devising techniques for conducting specialized investigations, and referring instances of violation to the enforcement officials.

The SEC has aggressively sought to win voluntary compliance with its regulations and has relied rather heavily on developing trade relations activities. The ICC, however, has taken a very passive attitude toward compliance programs and depends primarily on rival shippers and carriers to obtain compliance. Except in connection with safety activities, the CAB undertakes no compliance activities as such. The FTC does conduct conferences in order to prescribe trade practice rules for individual industries. These rules have been successful only when members of an industry desire protection against the practices of their competitors. With the exception of trade practice conferences, the FTC makes few attempts to educate businessmen concerning what is and what is not legal. FTC field offices are used almost solely for investigations and not to provide the FTC with representation at the community level.

In general, the commissions have been reluctant to organize compliance activities. They have frequently rationalized their attitude by noting an incompatibility between an administrative tribunal and such activities as trade relations, public information, and enforcement. The more passive a commission, the less likely it is to accept responsibility for securing the compliance of the regulated. Conversely, the lack of a vigorous compliance program probably reflects the lack of vigorous regulation in the public interest.

INDUSTRY ADVISORY COMMITTEES

A prominent instrument for promoting compliance with and understanding of government regulations is the industry advisory committee.[4] Its use is based on the hope that administrative regulation will be enriched by establishing a formal channel of communication with groups affected by regulation. Through advisory committees, regulated groups have an opportunity to participate in the regulatory process. The use of such committees raises a number of problems, however.[5] The first problem is to assign an appropriate area of responsibility to the committees. Administrators may try to limit the functions of committees to giving advice in matters where irreconcilable differences of opinion are lacking, while the committees usually resent any restriction of the area in which they are consulted. Administrators also tend to be wary of making committees permanent and fixing their membership. But a permanent committee will probably develop a fuller grasp of regulatory problems and a sense of responsibility. Members of advisory committees can be selected either by the public agency or by the organizations of interested economic groups. During World War II most of the economic mobilization agencies relied upon trade associations for filling posts on advisory committees. The OPA, however, preferred making its own selection of members to accepting the nominations of trade associations on the ground that the trade associations were not representative of the industry and would not be willing to urge compliance with policies which would be unpopular with association members.

One of the most difficult problems concerns the representativeness of advisory committees. There is a strong tendency for committees to represent only the larger and

---

[4] See Avery Leiserson, *Administrative Regulation*, University of Chicago Press, Chicago, 1942, chap. III; Carl Monsees, *Government-Industry Cooperation*, Public Affairs Press, Washington, 1944.

[5] See discussion in Emmette S. Redford, *Administration of National Economic Control*, The Macmillan Co., New York, 1952, pp. 258-264.

better-organized portions of an industry and those who can conveniently send people to meetings. The commission that hopes to use an industry advisory committee will have to find ways and means to prevent it from developing distorted views or special means of influencing administration. The danger lies in permitting a committee to compromise the government.[6]

## COMMUNITY PARTICIPATION IN REGULATORY ADMINISTRATION

Community participation is another technique used by some agencies to win a wider measure of support for regulatory policies and programs. Parent-teacher groups have strengthened community relations in the educational field for many years. In social work, selective service draft boards, and civil defense, the activity of volunteers is well known. But voluntary participation of citizens in the program of a regulatory agency is very rare. The only regulatory agency with large-scale experience in community participation was the OPA during World War II. It recruited volunteers from communities to help administer locally both rationing and price regulations. In addition, volunteers, mostly housewives, were asked to check prices in retail stores against the prescribed ceiling prices and to report instances of violation to the local price board for further investigation or settlement.

The OPA experience suggests that community participation, as a device for organizing citizen support for a governmental program, is fundamentally sound. As a technique for winning the consent of the public and regulated businesses, it is practical and perhaps essential. However, the administrative difficulties involved in utilizing the services of volunteers on a local basis in a relatively complex program may serve as a warning to administrators. Because of the scope of OPA activities in terms of geography, population, and economics, and the relative inexperience of its administrative staff, the volunteer activities of the OPA may

[6] See Arthur W. Macmahon, "Boards, Advisory," *Encyclopedia of the Social Sciences*, vol. 1, The Macmillan Co., New York, 1930, p. 611.

not be a fair test of the theory of community participation. Unfortunately, many participants in community volunteer activities on behalf of the OPA appreciated the democratic, grass roots nature of local participation in price control and rationing without comprehending the enormous administrative burden of management and supervision required by the program.

Community participation is not without other perils. The ordinary citizen may become a special pleader for local interests just as the advisory committee may take too narrow and selfish a view of its responsibilities. Moreover, as John Gaus has remarked, "There is a great deal of sentimental nonsense that gets spoken or published about the knowledge of the local community and its needs and resources by persons who happen to live there. As a matter of fact, far too few communities contain many such desirable citizens, for the average person knows too little about the public affairs of his community. . . . And yet this very fact makes the association of local citizens . . . desirable wherever possible, since such association is educative. . . ."[7]

## *Organization of Enforcement Activities*

The major organizational problem concerning enforcement in most commissions is the location of responsibility for enforcement and compliance activities. There is no satisfactory substitute for assigning the task of investigating alleged violations and of disposing of completed investigations to a specially designated unit of the agency. While concern for the enforcement of regulations should permeate the entire staff of a commission, the responsibility for enforcement action must be firmly fixed, preferably in a section of the commission without other program responsibilities. Enforcement activity is sufficiently specialized to require skills and techniques which are quite different from those of economists, engineers, and even most lawyers. The record of regulatory commissions indicates that en-

[7] John M. Gaus, *Reflections on Public Administration,* University of Alabama Press, University, Alabama, 1947, p. 102.

forcement tends to follow one of two lines of development. First, there may be a striking lack of agreement in the agency about the proper division between compliance and enforcement activities. Enforcement usually emerges as a recognized function rather late in the commission's development and after disputes about the proper relationship of enforcement and compliance activities have produced undesirable habits of thought and behavior respecting the two kinds of functions. In a second line of development, a commission may establish a small enforcement staff consisting of a handful of investigators or inspectors and attorneys with a small budget and then lose interest in its activities. If the environment is hostile to effective regulation in the public interest, weak enforcement activity may be accepted by an agency as a condition of its continued existence.

Ideally, the attorneys and investigators responsible for enforcement should work in close association. Investigations are usually more productive if investigators consciously search for the kind of evidence upon which an enforcement attorney can base a judicial proceeding or administrative sanction. Close association of attorneys and investigators is workable only where attorneys supply the necessary supervision. The difficulty is that attorneys tend to be preoccupied with specific cases and to have relatively less concern for broad enforcement policy and for directing the activities of investigators. They tend to become so absorbed in the technical and legal phases of enforcement that they devote little attention to administrative matters. When investigators are separated from attorneys and are uninformed about the final disposition of a case, there is a strong inclination to regard the investigation as an end in itself. Competent investigators may conduct an exhaustive investigation of alleged violations and prepare a voluminous report which yields more evidence than an attorney requires for successful prosecution and yet may omit several seemingly minor matters which are essential to prosecution.

The need for adequate supervision of investigators is paramount. Whatever relation exists between attorneys and investigators in a regulatory agency, there should be supervisory investigators to direct and analyze the work of the individual investigators and to control the process of investigation. There must be a constant search for efficient administrative procedures, productive investigative techniques, and methods for improving the performance of investigators.

Enforcement organization varies from commission to commission. In the ICC there appears to be a general reluctance to engage in vigorous enforcement activities. The Bureaus of Motor Carriers, Safety, and Locomotive Inspection are responsible for enforcing their own regulations while those concerned with the operations, financial structure, and rates of railroads, water carriers, and freight forwarders depend on a central enforcement organization comprised of the Bureaus of Inquiry, Law, and Formal Cases. Enforcement in the ICC is considered to be a bureau rather than a Commission-wide responsibility. Bureaus concerned with rates, financial controls, and certificates of convenience and necessity are not interested in enforcement matters. This passive approach to enforcement merely emphasizes the general trend in the ICC toward almost exclusive preoccupation with judicial-type duties and the neglect of planning, work programing, and regulatory purposes.

In the CAB, enforcement of economic regulations appears to be neglected or deferred. There seems to be no agency-wide responsibility for enforcement, and only a very small Office of Enforcement, which cannot match other bureaus in the CAB in status and power, deals regularly with such matters. On the other hand, the enforcement attitude of the SEC is vigorous and its activities are well integrated into the Commission's program. Its Division of Trading and Exchanges has the major responsibility for enforcement and maintains surveillance of the securities markets, inspects brokerage firms, and conducts fraud investigations.

The organization and use of investigators also vary

among commissions. In the ICC the Bureaus of Motor Carriers, Safety, and Locomotive Inspection have separate inspection staffs to investigate violations. Investigations of regulatory matters outside the jurisdiction of these Bureaus are handled by the Bureau of Inquiry, which has general responsibility for undertaking formal investigations of alleged violations in order to develop the evidence needed for prosecution and for preparing appropriate cases for prosecution. In 1950 the Bureau of Inquiry employed eleven inspectors, who were closely supervised by attorneys of the Bureau. Each case is reviewed by an attorney for special evidential problems before it is assigned to a special agent. With respect to its work load, the Bureau of Inquiry has been limited by the reluctance of other bureaus to refer cases for investigation and by the small size of its staff.

The Office of Enforcement in the CAB conducts investigations of violations with the help of a handful of investigators. The Office appears to be overwhelmed by unchecked violations.

In the SEC there have been in recent years about 140 inspectors in regional offices to check on the activity of registered brokers and dealers in securities and to investigate alleged frauds in the marketing of securities. Inspections have been conducted on a test check basis following prescribed procedures. The regional office selects the firm to be inspected, although it is guided by inspection goals set forth by the Division of Trading and Exchanges in the headquarters office. The staff appears to be alert to problems of investigation and has tried to improve investigatory techniques. The field inspectors have considerable knowledge of brokerage practices and seem to be highly regarded by the industry.

### Disposition of Cases and Application of Sanctions

Once investigations are completed, the agency must make satisfactory disposition of them. In general, three courses are open to it. It may settle the case informally—for example, by sending a warning letter to the violator, by conferring with him to request his compliance in the future, by accepting a payment to the United States Treasury as a token recognition of the violation, or by similar means. Second, in appropriate cases the agency may apply an administrative sanction. For example, it may conduct a hearing to determine whether a license, permit, or certificate should be suspended or revoked, or it may refer certain cases for action to the Federal Bureau of Investigation or to another federal law enforcement agency such as the Bureau of Narcotics or the Secret Service. Finally, the agency may elect to initiate a civil suit for damages, an injunction, or a criminal proceeding leading to fine and/or imprisonment. The choice of sanction and method of disposition depends largely on the statutory authority of the agency and on its imagination in developing administrative methods which are not prohibited by statute or declared illegal by the courts.

Regulatory agencies have not succeeded in passing to private citizens the burden of enforcing regulations. The authorization of suits for damages brought by consumers against violators of regulations of the ICC and the SEC has produced only a trickle of these suits. A distaste for "squealing" and a reluctance to become involved in costly judicial proceedings will deter most citizens from bringing private damage suits against violators of government regulations unless the violations arouse strong indignation. The average citizen appears to prefer that his government enforce regulations even though violations may injure him financially.

Once a regulatory agency has established an enforcement policy, it must set forth criteria to govern the selection of cases for investigation and the determination of sanctions to be applied to violations. It must decide the types of cases to be settled by informal methods, by application of administrative sanctions, and by civil suit or criminal prosecution in the courts. Unless there is substantial consistency in the disposition of cases and the application of sanctions, an agency will be subject to charges of discrimination against certain respondents. A vigorous agency will usually prefer to use to the fullest advantage the methods and sanctions over which it has control. For example, it may decide to settle a case informally through a voluntary contribution by the respondent to the Treasury rather than take the additional time and effort to enter a civil suit seeking an injunction or a fine. It usually prefers to utilize administrative sanctions rather than litigation. It may be possible for an agency to develop an administrative sanction which can be readily and fairly applied and will bring about speedy correction of serious violations.

Sanctions and penalties should be adjusted to the type of violation. Minor violations should be handled without delay and be disposed of by application of a relatively mild sanction. On the other hand, serious violations should be treated with more emphasis, and more severe correctives or penalties should be applied. A minor violation, for example, should ordinarily be corrected through a small fine, an injunction, or an informal settlement rather than through punishment with a heavy fine or jail sentence. One of the difficulties in enforcement of regulations is the relative unavailability of administrative or judicial sanctions which can be applied readily to cases of minor violations. Frequently, the only available sanction appears to penalize the respondent too severely. For instance, temporary suspension of the right of a licensee to operate his business might be an appropriate and effective sanction in a case in which revocation of the license would be too severe.

If an agency expects to use criminal prosecutions for punishing flagrant and willful violators, it will be essential to reach an early understanding with the Department of Justice and the United States attorneys. In many instances the Department also handles the civil cases of a regulatory agency. As the central law enforcement agency of the government, the Department has authority, in the absence of other legislation, to determine which cases of alleged violation referred to it by a regulatory agency should be prosecuted in the federal courts. It is natural and inevitable that a central law enforcement agency which has the duty of prosecuting cases on behalf of a large number of agencies, as well as the responsibility for direct enforcement of statutes under its own jurisdiction, should tend to regard a case referred to it by a regulatory agency as somewhat less important in the total governmental scheme than the agency itself does.

The Department of Justice is also concerned about the volume of cases referred for prosecution and insists that the number of referrals be kept to a minimum. Consequently, agencies may refer only the most outrageous violations, which have been proved so thoroughly that there can be little or no question about securing a conviction from the court. Frequently, the best investigators and enforcement attorneys will prepare a case for referral to the Department of Justice only to find that the Department is willing to seek an injunction against the violator but not to prosecute for a criminal violation. A major effect of the existing relationship between the Department and the regulatory agencies is to decrease both referrals and prosecutions.

Prosecution normally rests with the United States attorneys. When the Department approves a case for prosecution, it normally refers it to the appropriate U.S. attorney. Except in unusual circumstances, the final decision to prosecute rests with this attorney. The Department may establish broad policies to guide the U.S. attorneys, but it ordinarily does not order them to litigate particular cases. The lawyers of the regulatory agencies try to work closely with the U.S. attorneys, who lack detailed and specialized knowledge of regulatory statutes and regulations. A lawyer of the regulatory agency may act for the U.S. attorney in the litigation, although the latter retains nominal control.

Frequently, the U.S. attorneys are prominent political figures in their communities. They have some tendency to favor prosecution of dramatic cases which will arouse community interest. Violations of complex, technical regulations whose prosecution would be tedious and complicated may be passed over in favor of cases of greater local interest. On rare occasions a U.S. attorney or federal judge may express a strong lack of sympathy with certain regulatory programs and be unimpressed with the need to deter violators by imposing stiff sentences in flagrant cases.

Regulatory agencies like to publicize their record of prosecutions, noting the number of cases won, lost, and dismissed or dropped. A high percentage of cases won is usually regarded as a mark of high achievement by Congress, the Department of Justice, and the agencies. However, a high percentage of cases won out of the total number brought to trial may reflect reluctance to litigate a case in which the evidence of violation is not overwhelming and conclusive. The cases in which an agency is convinced that serious illegalities are being practiced may not be referred for prosecution because of the absence of conclusive proof. Commissions which judicialize their procedures and think of themselves as courts are anxious to earn a reputation for presenting for prosecution only clear-cut cases of violation. Federal judges may compliment the agency for the careful preparation of its cases, but they will often be unaware of the cases which the agency has not litigated because of fear of damaging its reputation with the courts.

Sanctions vary widely among commissions. For example, the ICC has available criminal prosecution, civil injunction, and civil penalty to enforce its regulations. A provision for a civil suit to recover three times the amount of money received as a shipping rebate has rarely been applied. Usually only the most conclusive cases with respect to evidence of violation are recommended for prosecution; the ICC normally will not run the risk of an adverse court decision. Relations with the U.S. attorneys and the Department of Justice remain good so long as the volume of cases is small and ICC lawyers provide the U.S. attorneys with the help they require. The great majority of court cases are settled without trial because the evidence of guilt is normally overwhelming. In practice, federal judges do not impose prison sentences in criminal cases. Administrative sanctions are not available.

The CAB has three sanctions to enforce its economic regulations. It may institute formal economic proceedings before the Bureau of Hearing Examiners, civil actions for injunction, or criminal prosecutions. Formal enforcement proceedings conducted by hearing examiners are costly and frequently are more time-consuming than court actions. The CAB has failed to achieve promptness, speed, and certainty, which are said to characterize administrative as opposed to judicial proceedings. Although the Civil Aeronautics Administration has authority to settle civil penalty cases out of court, the CAB lacks a civil penalty sanction. The Board approves the institution of all court proceedings. The number of court actions has been negligible, and U.S. attorneys have refused to prosecute criminally in some cases.

The SEC may, after notice and hearing, issue a stop order in connection with the sale of securities, revoke the registration of a broker-dealer or investment adviser, and deny the registration of applicants for licenses or permits. In addition, the SEC may refer to U.S. attorneys requests to institute criminal proceedings or civil injunction cases. SEC lawyers develop the court cases and usually attend the trial to advise the U.S. attorney on the conduct of the case.

The FTC institutes administrative hearings to consider the issuance of cease-and-desist orders. In 1950 the average hearing took thirty months to conclude. Certain antideceptive practice cases may be settled informally. Although respondents file reports of compliance within sixty days after a cease-and-desist order has been issued, these orders have been systematically reviewed and enforced only since 1954. The Commission has traditionally relied upon the respondent's competitors to notify it of future violations.

## Cross Sanctions

James Landis was one of the first students of the regulatory process to note the possibility of granting or withholding governmental privileges and benefits as a means to encourage compliance. As Landis observed: "Government as a source of credit, as a source of supply, as consumer, possesses powers which frequently are broader in their implications than those that it has in its capacity simply to inflict punishment. . . . The government as purchaser was far more effective in bringing about conformance with the codes of fair competition under the National Industrial Recovery Act than was the government as policeman. The discovery of the effectiveness of that sanction led, of course, to the Walsh-Healey Act, when the direct effort to control conditions of labor seemed to have met insurmountable constitutional obstacles."[8] The use of the powers of one agency to enforce the regulations of another has been rare in the United States, and the trend which Landis seemed to see in the 1930's has not been widely developed. During World War I the War Industries Board and the Price-Fixing Committee exercised price control powers without express statutory authority. In fact, the only clear legislative authorization for price control lay in the Food and Fuel Act with reference to coal and coke and in the Trading with the Enemy Act with reference to commodities manufactured through the use of enemy patents. Price-fixing agreements could be enforced only by the threat of using the power of various government agencies to commandeer supplies of coal and to deny the use of transportation facilities. The mere threat to use such collateral powers was a very effective sanction in enforcing price regulations.[9]

[8] James M. Landis, *The Administrative Process*, Yale University Press, New Haven, 1938, p. 119.
[9] Information on the enforcement of World War I regulations is sparse. See, for example, the files of the National Archives on the Price-Fixing Committee, War Industries Board, Priorities Board, Railroad Administration, and Food and Fuel Administration. The only references discovered in these files relating to enforcement were the following: Legal Section of

Because of the success of the War Industries Board in enforcing price-fixing agreements in World War I, the OPA tried to secure the cooperation of other economic mobilization agencies in enforcing price and rationing controls during the Second World War. However, the authority of the Office of Defense Transportation to grant priorities in railroad transportation, that of the War Food Administration to inspect and license slaughterhouses, that of the War Production Board to exercise broad powers of priority and allocation in the case of materials essential to the war effort, and that of the Petroleum Administration for War to control the production and distribution of gasoline and fuel oil were not made available to the OPA. The latter argued that the total resources of the civilian mobilization agencies should be used to fight inflation and maintain orderly distribution of scarce goods to consumers in order to promote compliance with regulations which were very difficult to enforce, and in order to pool the administrative experience of the various agencies with a view to developing a higher measure of effectiveness in the economic mobilization program.

Several factors account for the refusal to cooperate with the OPA enforcement program. Several agencies were devoted more to the interests of the producer than to those of the consumer. They were reluctant to consider the administrative requirements of effective price controls, which were regarded as retarding production and conflicting with the distribution of materials and goods. These agencies viewed price increases as a major incentive to greater production, which was their principal preoccupation. The legality of the cross sanction—that is, of the use of the powers of one agency to enforce the regulations of another

---

the War Industries Board to Mr. Brookings, Chairman of the Price-Fixing Committee, "Legal Methods of Price-Fixing," April 19, 1918; Legal Section of the War Industries Board to W. W. Phelps, Secretary, Price-Fixing Committee, "Authority of Price-Fixing Committees to Assist Arizona State Council of Defense in Checking Profiteering on Retail Sales in Arizona," November 14, 1918; *Report of the Director General of the Railroads to the President*, pp. 26-27.

—was questioned, especially by the War Production Board. On the advice of its General Counsel, the WPB consistently refused to permit the use of its priority and allocation powers to enforce OPA regulations on the ground that such use was not expressly authorized by statute and was therefore of doubtful legality; and the WPB, as a matter of general policy, was "opposed to using the priority and allocation powers as indirect methods of compulsion or as sanctions."[10] Opposition to the cross sanction was also based on the view that each regulatory agency ought to be strong enough "to stand on its own feet" and should in no way be dependent upon the powers and authority of other agencies, especially in the enforcement of regulations. Another contributing factor was perhaps the normal bureaucratic reluctance of one agency to assume any responsibility for the program of another. Finally, the cross sanction was opposed on the ground that it would have extremely serious economic repercussions upon the respondent.

The OPA experience raises the general question whether a regulatory agency should rely exclusively upon its own resources or whether it should seek Congressional authorization to utilize the resources of other agencies and the facilities of state and local governments. The OPA successfully used the cross sanction in the enforcement of price and rationing controls on meat. The Defense Supplies Corporation during 1944-1945 withheld subsidy payments from meat packers who had violated OPA meat regulations. The effectiveness of the cross sanction makes it imperative that it be used only under clearly defined conditions and for certain types of flagrant and otherwise serious violations. The use of the cross sanction cannot be secretive or unannounced.

The extension of this use appears unlikely. The myth of independence, the obstacles to policy integration, the weakness of central management facilities, and the opera-

10 John Lord O'Brian and Manly Fleischman, "The War Production Board Administrative Policies and Procedures," *George Washington Law Review*, vol. 13, 1944, p. 47.

tion of the traditional centrifugal forces in American politics establish a strong opposition to it. So long as the economy remains interdependent and does not become merely a cluster of unrelated economic enterprises, the lack of interdependence and cooperation of regulatory agencies will remain a formidable obstacle to more effective enforcement of government regulations. The failure to develop the cross sanction is a striking commentary on the haphazard development of administrative regulation and of the administrative apparatus of the national government.

## National-State-Local Cooperation

There is scarcely a field of economic regulation unrelated to state or local governmental activity. In the regulation of railroads, motor carriers, electric utilities, securities dealers, banks, airplanes, telephone companies, food, drug, and cosmetic manufacturers, and other industries, state and local governments as well as the national government have functions to perform. Cooperation between governments in enforcing regulations helps to plug loopholes in enforcement machinery and enables different governments to pool their information and sources of evidence about violations. The specific benefits of cooperative action vary from one regulatory field to another. Because of their wider jurisdiction and more intensive form of regulation, national agencies seem to have more to gain from intergovernmental cooperation than do state and local governments. Where national officials have carefully prepared the way, state-local cooperation has been forthcoming. Under conditions of emergency, such as war or economic depression, the benefits to state and local governments which are derived from cooperation with federal agencies are more clear-cut. For example, during World War II several states and municipalities enacted legislation adopting OPA price and rationing regulations as state and local regulations. Violations of OPA regulations thus became violations of state and local law, and the facilities of these governments became available to aid in the enforcement of what were now their regulations.[11]

One of the advantages of the adoption of OPA regulations by state and local governments was that the OPA was able to pass on to them some of the burden of handling cases of petty violations, which could not be permitted to continue without endangering the integrity of the entire OPA program. In procedures similar to those which prevail in local small-claims courts, the states and municipalities which adopted OPA regulations disposed of hundreds of cases of minor violations which the OPA was able to handle only at the expense of neglecting more serious instances of violation.

In regulatory programs affecting large numbers of people, there may be no satisfactory way of enforcing regulations short of relying on state and local officials to take appropriate action. For example, the ICC maintains a small force of inspectors in its motor carrier safety program which is able to examine only a tiny fraction of the total number of interstate motor carriers. It is unlikely that the ICC will be able to enforce its regulations in this field even with very sharp increases in staff. Unless states and cities can be persuaded to undertake the burden of regular inspection of the trucks of more than 20,000 registered interstate truckers for compliance with safety regulations, the ICC cannot expect to achieve even a minimally satisfactory safety program. Today many carriers do not know that they are subject to ICC regulations and some that do have never been visited by an ICC official. While some commissions have developed cordial relations with state and local governmental agencies, there has been little or no cooperative action with respect to enforcement.

11 See, for example, New York State War Council Emergency Act, section 7 (6), chap. 171, New York Stat., Laws of 1941, section 101 (a); Rhode Island Laws 1943, 51; Anti-Black Market Act, Wisconsin Statutes, 22.15. For a list of cities which adopted municipal ordinances, see *National Municipal Review*, vol. 33, 1944, pp. 358-359. See also Charles R. Erdman, Jr., "Shall Municipalities Be Required to Enforce OPA Regulations," *New Jersey Municipalities*, vol. 21, 1944, pp. 12ff.

The adoption of national regulations by state and local governments has usually been considered inappropriate or improper. Despite obvious political difficulties, the most promising proposal for strengthening enforcement, at least in the case of motor carrier safety regulations, is the development of a joint federal-state enforcement program based on uniform federal-state safety requirements.

## Conclusion

Enforcement activities of the regulatory commissions tend to be weak, poorly staffed, and inadequately supported. They are marked by over-all inadequacy and reluctance to experiment with new enforcement techniques. Incentives to induce compliance are rarely articulated, and deliberate planning of compliance programs is conspicuously absent. The interdependence of regulatory controls is ignored.

# CHAPTER 9

# An Approach to the Regulatory Process

DESPITE growing doubts and skepticism, the independent commission is still recognized as the type of government agency most appropriate to the exercise of regulatory responsibilities that call for expertness, freedom from political pressures, stability and continuity of policy, and judicialized procedures. The weight of evidence suggests strongly that the commission form has failed to develop its presumed advantages. Whether or not the commission is a suitable agent of administrative regulation can be determined best in the light of an approach that is based squarely on the realities of such regulation. This chapter attempts to set forth the major elements of such an approach.

## The Political and Social Setting of Regulation

In the American environment, regulation has been demanded by groups that seek the protection of public policy to prevent the continuation of harmful business practices. Regulatory policies adopted in response to these demands have modified the concept of private property; consequently, those who control the use of private property have often regarded regulation as an attack on the basic institutions of private economic enterprise. On the other hand, the effective demands for regulation of economic affairs have almost always come from groups which have been hailed as vital to the preservation of freedom and capitalism, namely, small businessmen, farmers, and middle-class groups generally. While the process of regulation has imposed obligations and conditions on the use of private property, it can best be understood as an effort of an industrial society to adjust human relationships that have been profoundly altered by industrialization and related developments. Regulation represents one way in which a democracy has attempted to modify economic relationships in a capitalist society without destroying capitalism itself. In terms of the long-run development of political and economic institutions, regulation is a conservative approach to the demands of political majorities both for protection of private interests and for promotion of the public interest. As William O. Douglas said about regulatory agencies when he was chairman of the SEC, "They have become more and more the outposts of capitalism; they have been given increasingly larger patrol duties, lest capitalism by its own greed, avarice, or myopia destroy itself."[1]

With the exception of industries like radio broadcasting, air transport, and trucking, which demanded regulation to restore order in a chaotic situation, groups subject to regulation have always fought against the adoption of public regulatory policies. Regulatory agencies have usually been established during periods in which the forces demanding regulation have had the support of a strong president and have been able to find sufficient allies to command a political majority. Political struggles over the enactment of regulatory legislation have usually generated deep antagonisms and pervasive hostilities among the parties in interest. The opposition of some business interests to a strong president can be traced frequently to his successful advocacy of public regulation. Certainly much of the antagonism of business groups to President Franklin Roosevelt can be traced to the regulatory policies of the New Deal.

The antagonisms that accompany regulation have probably been most intense in the case of the electrical utility industry. In its report on public regulation of that industry, the Power Committee of the Twentieth Century Fund wrote: ". . . it should be remembered that nearly all

[1] William O. Douglas, *Democracy and Finance,* Yale University Press, New Haven, 1940, p. 244. This book, which is referred to in other chapters, is significant because it reveals the regulatory experience of a chairman of a commission in its crusading youth.

the more important questions arising in this field are exceedingly controversial in character. Upon these, opinions are strongly held and supported by persuasive argument. The immediate interests of those affected by the recurrent controversies are often, at least in surface appearance, sharply divergent. Expression of opposed views has often been extreme and sometimes marked by resort to bitter personalities. In some of its phases, discussion of the problems here dealt with has been further complicated by their relation to fundamental differences in political philosophy which in normal times divide the whole country. While in principal focus the question of the utilities has turned about the control of an essentially noncompetitive industry by government as representing the consumer, the tremendous sweep of the financial operations of the industry, the resulting stake of the investor in its wise and profitable management, and the development and results of concentrated control through the holding company system have combined to bring new demands for action by the government."[2]

The hostility of the regulatory environment helps to account for the desires of reformers to escape from the bitterness accompanying the regulatory process by "taking regulation out of politics." On the other hand, the impossibility of separating regulation from the general political and social setting should have been apparent to those who had an awareness of the forces and social movements that were transforming American society. The historical record contains ample proof that enabling legislation in the field of regulation results from prolonged agitation for reform that is eventually supported by a political majority and dramatized by an effective president. With the advantages of hindsight, it seems almost incredible that the advocates of regulation demanded independence from the president, without whose support they would have failed.

[2] *Electric Power and Government Policy*, The Twentieth Century Fund, Inc., New York, 1948, pp. 740-741.

## The Scope of the Regulatory Process

Traditionally, regulation is conceived as a narrow, self-contained process clearly separable from the main drift of national economic policies. Since changes in industrial processes and economic organization are central factors in the evolution of the American capitalist society, the unreality of treating regulation as peripheral to the central core of governmental functions should have been comprehended by the forces behind the regulatory movement. One of their greatest failures was the inability to grasp the relationship between regulation and other activities of the government and the importance of regulation as a major vehicle of institutional change.

The broad scope of regulation might be summarized somewhat as follows. Regulation, first of all, alters the concept of property by establishing conditions and prerequisites regarding the use of property. It modifies existing legal relationships in society and affects the distribution of political power and the capacity, potential or real, to utilize governmental powers to promote private interests and the general welfare. It is only one phase in the continuing historical process of change in the concept of property.

Regulation frequently aims to control industrial practices which are central to the managerial function in business. The establishment of rates and the determination of conditions of service are among the most significant tasks of public utility regulation. Yet these are the tasks which impinge most directly upon the domain of management. For managers in regulated industries, regulation merges with private management in the formulation of strategic business policies and becomes part of the structure of the industry. It was recognition of this factor which led Herbert Croly to regard the regulatory process as dividing responsibility for management between public and private officials and which convinced Joseph Eastman, for a time, that the railroads should be nationalized and operated directly by the government.

The intermingling of public control and private management is inevitable so long as public regulation has any effect at all. Mosher and Crawford noted over twenty years ago that effective regulation cannot avoid interference with management.[3] Regulation by the government not only affects the functions of management but "approaches management in point of view as well," as Graham has stated. He also says that ". . . in regulation public action may be taken either before or after vital decisions are made. If the public intervenes to control decisions so that they will be made in accord with public policy, then administrative supervision of a continuing character is essential. Surveillance is necessary and public officials tend to have a part in the institutional life of the groups they are regulating. For example, the Interstate Commerce Commission is now a part of the railroad industry. If Congress abolished the commission, the industry would be maimed and would have to devise a crutch of some sort to do the work of the lost member. This administrative relationship leads to peculiar problems for public authorities who regulate specific industries or restricted and unified groups. The official tends to become responsible not only for regulation but for the industry."[4]

It is no longer possible to distinguish public regulation from promotion of particular industries or national action to maintain economic stability. Regulation of practices in one industry may seriously affect the conduct of others. Subsidies for one form of transportation may adversely affect media of transportation that are not eligible for public aid. What is regulatory in its impact on one industry may have the effect of promoting the interests of another. Regulations enforced by one agency may sub-

[3] William Mosher and Finla G. Crawford, *Public Utility Regulation*, Harper and Brothers, New York, 1933, p. 92.

[4] Reprinted with permission from George A. Graham, "Regulatory Administration," in George A. Graham and Henry F. Reining, Jr., *Regulatory Administration*, John Wiley and Sons, Inc., New York, 1943, p. 16.

stantially nullify the promotional activities of another agency.[5]

It has been suggested frequently that promotional activities in transportation should be combined in a Cabinet department while regulatory responsibility should be allocated, as at present, to several agencies in the transportation field. The comment of a former member of the U.S. Maritime Commission on this issue is pertinent:

"In my view, there can no longer be a logical differentiation between regulation and promotion. Wherever the dividing line may have been in the past, regulation, on the one hand, today is largely motivated by the conviction that *promotion* of the interests of established transportation services is a major, if not the major means of protecting the transportation user, and the national economy as a whole, whereas promotion, on the other hand, through the selection of individual transportation companies to be beneficiaries of promotional activities of the Federal Government, in effect *regulates* the admission or exclusion of competition in the transportation field.

"Today the Government regulates transportation by promoting transportation, and by promoting it, the Government actively regulates it. *The time has come to cease treating regulation and promotion as though they were separate and distinct.* I not only believe that they overlap, but that in fact it is impossible to tell where one begins and the other ends. Transportation facts and realities have wiped out the dividing line. We can continue, for convenience's sake, the loose use of the term *regulation* when we primarily think of *restricting* the activities of carriers, although restricting one carrier, or group of carriers, protects and promotes others; or when we think of *rate* regulation, although more often than not approval of high rates is intended to promote a carrier's financial status,

[5] For a discussion of conflicts between federal regulation and promotion in the transportation industries, see *A Report to the President from the Secretary of Commerce: Issues Involved in a Unified and Coordinated Federal Program for Transportation,* December 1, 1949, published in 1950, pp. 43-46.

[and] approval of low rates [is intended to promote] his competitive status. We may think of *promotion* as doing something for a *carrier*, such as the payment of subsidies; yet keeping competition from him by regulation may promote a carrier as much, or more, than a subsidy, while denying a carrier promotion through a subsidy may mean *restricting* him as effectively as through *regulation*."[6]

Regulation cannot be limited to adjudication of disputes and can scarcely be separated into two distinct categories labeled adjudication and management. Policy formulation through the disposition of individual cases is an executive function as well as a quasi-judicial function of applying a rule of law to the facts in a specific controversy. The basic task of a regulatory agency is to fulfill the mandate of its enabling legislation and design a program to promote the public interest. Regulation defies the effort to classify its various functions as adjudicatory or administrative, on the one hand, or as executive, legislative, or judicial, on the other. Strict separation into these or similar categories is "heedless of the requirements for effective functioning," would make the agency "more prosecutor-minded than policy-minded," and would "hinder the pooling of experience and expertise within the organization" in the disposition of its business.[7]

Businessmen are among the first to insist that regulatory agencies should make it possible for them to deal directly with the government. They are familiar with the processes of discussion, bargaining, and conferences, all of which are normal methods of doing business. Such methods contrast sharply with those employed by the businessman's lawyer, who is adept in handling highly formalized techniques of stating a position and requiring discussion on the record. The heart of effective regulation is found not in the formal procedures of adjudication, to which the bar

[6] From pp. 5-6 of the memorandum of Raymond S. McKeough commenting on *ibid*. Italics in original document.

[7] James Willard Hurst, *The Growth of American Law*, Little, Brown and Co., Boston, 1950, p. 430.

has usually limited its attention, but rather in informal activities and informal contacts between an agency and its regulated clientele. In the last analysis an agency stands or falls not so much on the disposition of individual controversies before it as on the formulation and execution of basic regulatory policies.

The interdependence of regulatory policies and national economic policies can no longer be ignored. It may well be that, in the future, regulatory policies will be significant because of their contribution to national economic policies rather than their surveillance of a particular industry or certain industrial practices. The dependence of industry on the general level of prosperity and on the general state of the union suggests that regulatory policies cannot be formulated wisely as long as consideration is limited to problems in individual industries. Regulatory agencies have found increasing difficulty in identifying and defining the public interest in a single field. The public interest can be identified best in terms of a comprehensive view of regulatory problems in the setting of national economic policy. The fragmented, narrow outlook of the commissions is best suited to the handling of problems and issues which are relatively self-contained and which have little relevance to or implication for the economy as a whole.

Regulatory policy must be adapted to dynamic changes in economic organization, industrial practices, and political ideas and social goals. The mere proscription of abuses in certain industries may have been adequate at one time; but in a highly developed economy with great productive capacity, the elimination of abuses is necessary but not a sufficient goal of public policy. In fact, there has been a marked tendency for regulatory policies to move beyond the role of punishing violators to undertake the more positive role of strengthening industries in order to maximize their contribution to the national welfare. As regulation takes on more of the character of prevention, rather than punishment, of industrial malpractices and as the government assumes a wider scope of responsibility for the conduct of an industry under private management, regulatory decisions become more significant. Action must be carefully planned and executed if only because of the critical significance of regulation in the operation of the national economy. Each agency must be able to profit by the experience of others, and each should be judged not merely by its contribution to the control and management of a particular industry but also by its contribution to the solution of the key economic issues facing American society.

## Regulation Is an Intensely Political Process

The process of regulation is unavoidably political. So long as regulation is conditioned by the general political and social environment and remains founded on the efforts of organized groups to utilize public power to promote either private ends or the public welfare, it will remain a major aspect of political life. It is political not in the invidious image of progressive reformers, that is, corrupt, fraudulent, dishonest, and motivated by desire for private gain. Politics refers rather to the emergence of public issues, formulation of public policies, and administration of governmental affairs. In a democratic society it implies that the citizen has obligations to participate creatively in public affairs if only to the extent of casting his ballot intelligently.

The political nature of regulation reflects the inadequacy of the tools of economic and political analysis in providing a sure line of direction for the formulation of regulatory objectives. The determination of regulatory goals does not result inevitably from the logical analysis of certain economic facts, nor is it automatically deduced from a set of propositions concerning the nature of the political state and the proper boundaries of political action in a democratic society. Economic analysis, for example, may help to formulate regulatory methods and policies in the light of certain goals and policies, but it cannot be expected to provide a guiding set of principles for the discovery of the public interest and the refinement of appropriate goals.

The political character of regulation can be demonstrated in several ways. The issue of regulation concerns the decision whether or not to apply a public rule of conduct to private economic activity. It involves the use of governmental power to guide personal or organizational conduct. Because it has the capacity to alter economic institutions and relations among the parties in interest, it is subject to attack and harassment. As Robert M. Cooper wrote: "From beginning to end, the regulatory process operates in an atmosphere of more or less intense antagonism. . . . The idea that one group of officials may be set up to check, supervise, and control the commercial operations of another group of individuals without encouraging subterfuge, evasion, sharp practices, and animosity is inconceivable under a system of capitalistic economy. Although this antagonistic attitude is frequently driven below the surface of observation, its presence is none the less real. . . . The essential purposes of the two groups are socially and economically incompatible if carried to their logical conclusion."[8] In his study of the regulatory commissions, Herring made the same observation.[9]

Regulation thrives when it is supported by public opinion. Active and articulate public support is a *sine qua non* of effective regulation in the public interest. But public support does not develop automatically. It must be mobilized and nurtured by the parties demanding regulation and must be integrated into a program of political action by a chief executive and legislature. "There must be a national leadership that rallies the public behind a general program and that stirs up opposition to selfish demands."[10] George Graham has characterized the prob-

[8] Robert M. Cooper, "Techniques of Public Control—An Appraisal of Methods," *Annals*, vol. 201, May 1939, p. 3.

[9] E. P. Herring, *Public Administration and the Public Interest*, McGraw-Hill Book Co., New York, 1936, p. 183. See quotation in Chapter 3, pages 79-80, above.

[10] *ibid.*, p. 213.

lem well: "In the field of regulation, maintaining public support becomes in fact the cornerstone of success in administration. Regulatory policies are never finally accepted by all of the public until the issue becomes archaic. There is a constant attack on regulation from forces opposed to public control. Some acute economic or social distress may precipitate regulatory legislation. But attack upon it begins immediately—challenging the law in the courts, opposing appropriations in the legislature, impugning responsible administrators in the press or over the radio. There is no rest for those in charge of a regulatory program if they would carry it through to success. Seduction as well as assault may have to be resisted. Protecting the integrity of a program and maintaining support for it are a constant struggle."[11]

Regulation must appeal both rationally and emotionally to be effective. It is not enough that experts satisfy themselves that a particular decision is fully justified by the facts. Regulation should also be designed to achieve statutory objectives. Unless the goals of regulation have a strong emotional appeal and are sustained by a sense of fair play and social purpose, the rational formulation of policies will not be sufficient to maintain public support.

The president and Congress have the inescapable tasks of resolving conflicts of policy in governmental regulation of business. Since action strong enough to eliminate alleged abuses and guide business conduct in the future will be stoutly resisted by the regulated groups, the function of political leadership is to maintain the vitality and integrity of regulation in the public interest. A regulatory agency cannot be expected to make its contribution to the public interest unless the president and Congress are able to establish general policies to direct and sustain it in the face of strong opposition and hostility.

The search for the public interest normally is carried on against great odds. Even in regulation of the securities

[11] George A. Graham, "Trends in Teaching of Public Administration," *Public Administration Review*, vol. x, 1950, p. 73.

markets, which was strengthened by public response to the stock market scandals of 1929-1931, the SEC had to make its way carefully in determining the nature of the public interest. Justice Douglas, as chairman of the SEC, commented thus on the obstacles confronting the public interest in securities legislation: "It is idle to say that the requirements of business are constantly going to be determined in the light of the requirements of the public interest. The history of business reveals no such paramount importance of the public interest. Concessions to the public interest are frequently made. But the immediate requirements of management will tend to bow to the larger public interest only when necessary and to the extent that is necessary. It would be against all experience with psychological facts to expect sudden and permanent conversion. This in turn means that the bare minimum required by recent legislation may be the maximum to be expected. This in turn means that once those bare minima are established they will tend to become a routine and hence a mere formality. They will serve as the offering at the altar of the public interest. Thus, once professional scriveners are developed, it would be no great step to be able to make disclosure of material facts so blurred and so obtuse as to carve the heart out of the Securities Act. That is to say, when disclosure of truth becomes an art and when avoidance of disclosure becomes a game, the essence and spirit of the new legislation will have become subverted although the formalities may have been fully satisfied."[12]

A regulatory agency cannot hope to hide behind a quasi-judicial curtain of expertness in order to escape the vicissitudes of political life. It must undertake to win friends and influence legislators in order to obtain the authority and sanctions necessary to regulatory success. It is unlikely that Congress will be able to give content to the public interest in regulation with sufficient clarity to enable an agency to concentrate its attention on the application of settled

12 Douglas, *op.cit.*, pp. 250-251.

policy. The traditional emphasis of Congress on relatively local matters as distinguished from matters of national policy and the preoccupation of members of the House of Representatives with the business of their constituents do not enable individual legislators to develop an understanding of issues of national welfare. Given the divergent groups within the major political parties, Congressional leaders may consider it inadvisable to establish a consensus in each party on regulatory issues for fear of making party unity more precarious than it usually is. Congress finds it less hazardous to delegate to regulatory agencies a large measure of discretion in defining the nature of the public interest. As an agency undertakes the tasks which Congress has been unable or unwilling to assume, the pressures on Congress are transferred to the agency. As Avery Leiserson has observed: ". . . when the legislature finds it inadvisable to define specifically for future situations the content of the 'public interest,' the political problem of achieving consent to the application of such standards is passed on to the administrative agency. Its failure to solve this problem results in its being forced into politics, either in the sense that political influence will be brought to bear upon it by the political executive or the legislature, or in that the latter will ultimately revise or amend the plan of regulation."[13]

Because of the complexity of regulation and the reluctance or inability of Congress to clarify regulatory goals, a regulatory agency must play the creative role of formulating major regulatory policies. It must define the content of the public interest and seek to develop it in the cases that come before it. If regulation is to avoid capitulation to affected groups, the task of defining and aggressively pursuing the public interest cannot be abjured. The agency's approach to the public interest should be neither neutral nor passive. Indeed, as Hyneman has stated, the regulatory cards ought to be stacked in favor of the public interest so long as the

[13] Avery Leiserson, "Interest Representation in Administrative Regulation," *Annals*, vol. 221, May 1942, p. 80.

purpose of public control of business is furthering that interest.[14] There is no more legitimate function in the political process than the responsible identification and definition of the public interest.

### Regulation as a Reflection of the Conflicting Demands of the Parties in Interest

Regulation of economic affairs sets up a cross fire of competing demands. In the unavoidable attempt to establish a pattern of regulation, a regulatory agency must weigh the positions taken by the various parties. But the agency cannot simply put the position of a party in interest alongside the statute to determine the element of public interest in that position. Nor can it apply simple criteria in litmus paper fashion to evaluate the advantages and disadvantages of pursuing alternative courses of policy.[15]

The major difficulty here is the absence of standards of regulation which are independent of the standards of the interested parties. A commission is not provided either in its enabling legislation or in the legislative history of regulation with generally accepted standards to govern the development of regulatory policy. Ordinarily, it assumes the burden of developing standards after public support has begun to decline and the regulated interests have turned from opposition to the task of influencing the regulatory process.

Congress has been of little help in providing criteria for the development of independent standards of the public interest. While the legislature cannot and should not attempt to define in exact terms the standard of fairness with respect to rates, services, and similar matters, it abdicates its legislative responsibility if it provides a regulatory agency merely with slogans rather than working criteria for defining the public interest. Legislative deficiency in

[14] See Charles S. Hyneman, "Administrative Adjudication: An Analysis," *Political Science Quarterly*, vol. 51, 1936, pp. 383-417, 516-537.

[15] Herring, *op.cit.*, pp. 133-134. See quotation in Chapter 5, page 161, above.

defining the goals of regulatory policy was noted in England by William Robson; his words are equally applicable to the American experience: ". . . the wrong method of control is to give jurisdiction to administrative tribunals in vague terms containing undefined or undefinable standards, and to expect that economic conflict will thereby be resolved. Methods easily get misapplied; and the method of official adjudication, if it is divorced from administrative provision, is unsuited to the social control of private enterprise."[16]

The strength and power of the parties in interest and their ingenuity and imagination in resisting regulatory reforms are crucial factors in the process of regulation.[17] The ability of conflicting parties to translate their demands into regulatory policy depends heavily on their capacity for disciplined organization and their strategic position in American society. Each group attempts to write into law the rules of conduct which are most beneficial to its interests. When regulated groups are no longer able to resist efforts to enact regulatory legislation, they turn quickly to the task of influencing the regulatory process. The attempt to convert governmental regulatory power into private advantage has been a central feature of national regulation since the railroad industry undertook to come to terms with the establishment of the ICC.

The early history of the ICC supplies an excellent illustration of the attempt of the private parties to utilize the regulatory process to advance their interests. President Cleveland had appointed Richard Olney, a prominent Boston corporation lawyer, as Attorney General during his second term. Before Olney took office President Perkins of the Chicago, Burlington, and Quincy Railroad sought his aid in persuading the new Cleveland administration to

16 William A. Robson, *Justice and Administrative Law*, 3rd edn., Stevens and Sons, Ltd., London, 1951, pp. 607-608.
17 This point is developed by Merle Fainsod in his essay on "The Nature of the Regulatory Process," in C. J. Friedrich and E. S. Mason, eds., *Public Policy 1940*, Harvard University Press, Cambridge, 1940, pp. 297-323.

abolish the ICC. Olney advised Perkins with the utmost candor, as follows: "My impression would be that, looking at the matter from a railroad point of view exclusively, [repeal of the Interstate Commerce Act] would not be a wise thing to undertake. . . . The attempt would not be likely to succeed; if it did not succeed, and were made on the ground of the inefficiency and uselessness of the Commission, the result would very probably be giving it the power it now lacks. The Commission, as its functions have now been limited by the courts, is, or can be made, of great use to the railroads. It satisfies the popular clamor for a government supervision of railroads, at the same time that that supervision is almost entirely nominal. Further, the older such a Commission gets to be, the more inclined it will be found to take the business and railroad view of things. It thus becomes a sort of barrier between the railroad corporations and the people and a sort of protection against hasty and crude legislation hostile to railroad interests. . . . The part of wisdom is not to destroy the Commission, but to utilize it."[18]

The conflicting demands of private interests do not necessarily reduce a regulatory agency to the status of a lackey of those interests. Each agency has some potential or real capacity for developing a creative role and rising above mere acceptance of the demands of dominant interest groups. It may have the ability to utilize the strengths of the parties in interest without accepting their definition of regulatory goals and standards. The area of freedom from the standards of the private parties depends heavily on the prestige and competence of the regulatory officials, the

[18] Olney's letter is found in the Richard Olney Papers, Letterbook, in the Library of Congress and is dated December 28, 1892. It was first quoted by Matthew Josephson in *The Politicos*, Harcourt, Brace and Co., New York, 1938, p. 526. Excerpts of the Olney letter have since been quoted in Senator Joseph C. O'Mahoney, "Collectivism and the Modern Lawyer," *Vital Speeches*, vol. 15, June 1, 1949, pp. 499-500; by Samuel P. Huntington in his doctoral dissertation. *Clientalism: A Study in Administrative Politics*, Harvard University Library, May 1950; and in Eric Goldman, *Rendezvous with Destiny*, Alfred A. Knopf, New York, 1952, p. 203.

prevailing political temper of the times, the capacity of the agency to find political support in the Presidency and Congress, the vitality of public opinion in favor of regulation, and the strength of the private parties themselves. Fainsod has summarized the point:

". . . the degree of manipulative power which commissions can achieve in defining public policy is in large part dependent upon the strength and clarity of the communal purpose which initiates and sustains them.

"In areas where the common purpose is clearly formulated and widely shared, regulatory agencies find their task lightened and the opposition of the particularistic interests is relatively easily overcome. At the opposite extreme there are other areas where a new thrust of government inevitably precipitates sharp clefts in the community. . . . The skill with which [the regulatory agencies] build on shared purpose will determine the degree of manipulative power which they can acquire."[19]

Regulated groups seek to insulate a commission from the wider political environment and from sources of popular political strength. The object is to make the survival of the agency dependent upon a working alliance with the regulated groups on terms dictated largely by these groups. When they are successful in molding an agency into a friendly protector of private interests rather than an aggressive agent of the public welfare, the regulatory agency provides the regulated groups with privileged access to government. For regulated groups the regulatory process may be one method of converting public power into private gain. The extent to which regulation becomes the handmaiden of private interests depends in large measure on the existing balance among interest groups and the success of these groups in joining forces with potential private allies and powerful political leaders. Whether or not the regulatory process serves this function in a particular industry, the direction and general tone of regulatory policy

[19] Fainsod, *op.cit.*, pp. 321-322.

and administration reflect the varying strengths of the affected groups.

## *Regulation as a Process of Adjustment*

From a public point of view a regulatory agency has a mandate from Congress that it must translate into public policy. According to William O. Douglas, the job of a regulatory agency like the SEC "is to administer these [regulatory] laws as they are written, not to nullify them by inaction nor to trade out at the conference table decisions made in legislative halls. This is the mandate required by the trusteeship of public office."[20] The process of carrying out the legislative mandate involves continuous adjustment to the strengths and activities of the parties in interest. We have already seen that this adjustment is related closely to the general political environment and to the capacity of the regulated parties for effective economic and political organization.

The independence of an agency from the aims and demands of the dominant parties in interest tends to be strengthened when the following conditions prevail: first, a political environment favorable to the development of vigorous regulatory policy, including widespread popular support for effective regulation, active Congressional backing for able regulatory administration, and effective political leadership, especially from the president; second, satisfactory development of administrative capacity, including adequate appropriations and competent and imaginative personnel from the top direction of the agency down to the junior professional staff; third, an approach by the courts which accepts the regulatory agencies as legitimate agents of public policy whose views and judgments are entitled to considerable weight; fourth, a high regard for public service as a career and a political climate of opinion which approves of the exercise of social control as a democratic method of enhancing the welfare of the community;

---

[20] Douglas, *op.cit.*, p. 246.

and fifth, the development of institutions of responsible government so that the regulatory agency may be held to account legally and morally for satisfactory execution of its legislative mandate. This last condition includes the achievement of a good measure of responsibility in the operation of the committee system in Congress so that a Congressional committee is restrained from overriding the statutory mandate of a regulatory agency and from waging guerilla warfare against the attempts of the agency to inch its way toward effective regulation.

The factors that restrict the independence of a regulatory agency in its adjustment to the parties in interest are readily apparent. Such elements as vague statutory mandates for regulation, unsettled national policy in economic affairs, lack of concern in Congress or in the White House with the progress of effective regulation, the lack of popular support for aggressive regulation, and the isolation of the agencies from centers of political strength weaken the capacity of the agency. Inadequate budgets, weak personnel, inappropriate methods, and excessive preoccupation with judicial methods and procedures make the agency more dependent upon achieving amicable relations with regulated groups. Other restrictive factors include excessive interference by the courts with the work of the regulatory agencies, symbols of prestige which favor private business achievement and depreciate public service, the lack of popular sentiment in behalf of social control as a method of public policy, and a lack of responsibility in the legislative and executive branches. Finally, complexity and detail in regulatory administration have the effect of increasing the dependence of an agency upon the regulated parties for data, information, and knowledge, and multiply the agency's difficulty in keeping up with technological developments. The greater the regulatory detail, the greater the tendency of the agency to become reliant on the regulated industry to fill its key positions and the greater the need for industry support in securing adequate appropriations for the agency.

The adjustment which a regulatory agency makes to the demands and activities of the organized groups affected by regulation is roughly a balance of the forces which affect its political environment, its internal operations, and prevailing attitudes toward public questions. Recognition of these factors of adjustment is not new. Most of them are referred to in Herring's analysis of administrative regulation, in specialized studies of public utility regulation, in Fesler's study of the state utility commissions, and in Fainsod's essay on the regulatory process.[21] Herring, for instance, noted that free cooperation of an agency with the regulated interests is compatible with the general welfare provided the regulatory official is instructed by a well-defined, accepted public policy. He cannot resist adverse pressures unless the regulatory policy is clear and his authority is sufficient to achieve the desired results. These conditions must be established by political leadership. In their absence the administrator becomes "the residuary legatee of those political pressures to which the legislator is the rightful heir." Herring was also the first to note the effect of regulatory detail on the relations between the regulator and the regulated: ". . . the greater the degree of detailed and technical control the government seeks to exert over industrial and commercial groups, the greater must be their degree of consent and active participation in the very process of regulation, if regulation is to be effective or successful."[22]

Recent interest in the analysis of political behavior and the role of organized groups in the political process has focused attention on the adjustment of public and private interests in the regulatory process. David Truman has noted that groups that have become reconciled to a regulatory statute consider the independent commission as the

[21] See, for example, Herring, *op.cit.*; Mosher and Crawford, *op.cit.*; James W. Fesler, *The Independence of State Regulatory Commissions*, Public Administration Service No. 85, Public Administration Service, Chicago, 1942; Fainsod, *op.cit.*

[22] Herring, *op.cit.*, pp. 157, 192.

least objectionable type of agency. Because the regulated groups are organized more cohesively than those demanding regulation, they are able to keep close watch on the activity of the commission. As a result, the commission will do little beyond what is acceptable to the regulated groups.[23] Regulated groups strive to make the regulatory agency as friendly as possible to their aims and objectives and seek to place it on the defensive so that its capacity for aggressive leadership is limited. Keeping the agency "in its proper place" involves questions of administrative organization and practice. The judicial pattern of operation tends to neutralize an agency's independent search for the public interest, while the commission form of organization tends to give defensive advantages to the regulated.

Where factors in the process of adjustment heavily favor the dependence of an agency on the support and consent of the regulated, the regulatory process becomes a method for institutionalizing public favoritism toward the regulated. The repeated identification of the public interest with a particular private interest has been called "clientalism." In his study of the ICC, Huntington has defined this as "sustained discretionary administrative behavior favorable to the interests of a private person or group."[24] Where the process of clientalism or favoritism is far advanced, the interests of an agency and the regulated group can scarcely be distinguished. The agency becomes a protector of the *status quo* and uses its public powers to maintain the interest of the regulated, which has now been defined as the public interest as well. Although an agency in this situation stresses its role of mediator and judge among conflicting group interests, its actual role is that of advocate and

23 See David B. Truman, *The Governmental Process*, Alfred A. Knopf, New York, 1951, p. 418.
24 Samuel P. Huntington, *Clientalism: A Study in Administrative Politics*, Ph.D. dissertation, Harvard University Library, 1950. See also Samuel P. Huntington, "The Marasmus of the ICC: The Commission, the Railroads, and the Public Interest," *Yale Law Journal*, vol. 61, April 1952, pp. 467-509.

partisan. Huntington concludes that regulation can be considered as a means by which a regulated group acquires a cliental agency, that is, an agency which will confer the status of law on private desires. Under these conditions the terms of adjustment are set by the regulated groups, and regulation becomes a tool for furthering private ends and defending minority interests.

### Regulation as Control of Human Behavior

Regulation can fruitfully be regarded as a process of influencing and controlling human behavior along defined lines of conduct. In this sense it can, perhaps, be described as "an adventure in applied social psychology."[25] Through informal activities, issuance of rules and regulations, adjudication of disputes, and enforcement of its regulations, a regulatory agency is engaged in the task of influencing and compelling human behavior. In directing the conduct of the regulated groups, an agency endeavors to induce them to comply voluntarily with its regulations. It usually encourages cooperation on the part of the regulated groups rather than defiance and resistance. Normally it will try to make noncompliance as difficult as possible and compliance as easy as possible consistent with the objectives of the regulatory legislation.

The inducement of compliant behavior can be very sophisticated and ingenious, or it can be unimaginative and routine. In order to succeed, an agency must offer a wide range of inducements if it hopes to secure the conformity of the regulated. Regulation should appeal to the regulated in the sense that it encourages cooperative responses rather than opposition. It should overcome the normal inertia which obstructs changes in human behavior. It should reduce "the costs of change" to the regulated groups by minimizing disturbances to prevailing industrial practices. It should make the person to whom it

[25] Victor A. Thompson, *The Regulatory Process in OPA Rationing*, King's Crown Press, New York, 1950, p. 424.

is directed feel that conformance is more to his advantage than nonconformance.[26]

Broadly speaking, failure to comply can be handled in three ways by the regulatory agency: by devising incentives to promote compliance, by putting obstacles in the way of nonconformist behavior, and by applying sanctions to those who violate the regulations. The offering of incentives to induce compliance is basic to the regulatory process. George Graham has placed the problem of incentives in its proper perspective: "Professional students of regulatory administration are forced to re-examine basic public policies in a search for incentives to bring the efforts of special interests in harmony with the public interest as established by law. In many fields where economic regulation is attempted, the public policy is so stated that the special interests affected are in some ways encouraged to resist rather than to cooperate. Achievement has been clearest where it has been possible to hold out some incentive to cooperation for the more progressive elements of the industry. When it is recalled that every new phase of economic regulation, no matter how well accepted today, has been opposed by most of the industry concerned in its early stages and when it is realized that little can be accomplished if an industry is solidly opposed to regulation, the importance of offering incentives to cooperation becomes clear. Students of administration are necessarily driven to analyze and understand substantive issues underlying public policy. This is now a frontier area."[27]

Consent can be won by a wide variety of methods, although their identification is frequently overlooked. Incentives need not be economic in character; they may also be based on social, ethical, or political considerations. Personal appeals directed at encouraging an individual to

[26] For a useful discussion of these matters, see Herbert A. Simon, Donald W. Smithburg, and Victor A. Thompson, *Public Administration*, Alfred A. Knopf, New York, 1950, pp. 451-487. This paragraph is based on those pages.
[27] Graham, "Trends in Teaching of Public Administration," *op.cit.* p. 73.

undertake certain action to protect his family's health and well-being have been successful in health education and may be applied to other areas in which government agencies seek to control human behavior in the public interest. Patriotic appeals are common in wartime, and recent experience with federal price controls in a period of defense mobilization short of full-scale war suggests strongly that any price regulation worthy of the name cannot succeed unless it appeals to the patriotism and civic-mindedness of the great majority of citizens.[28]

Thompson has described other efforts by a regulatory agency to make noncompliance difficult: "In the process of regulating human behavior, the technique of throwing discouraging obstacles in the path of 'undesirable' behavior will probably always be used, either consciously or unconsciously. These obstacles act as a dam to deflect the currents of behavior into desirable channels. Whenever there is a favor to be granted or a privilege to be conferred, the fact that people have to find out where to apply, have to go there to apply, have to apply by filling out a form (more often than not, long and complicated), tends to discourage many from seeking that favor or privilege. This is regulation by impedimenta." A related technique to influence human behavior is "rule-making for psychological effect." A rule issued for psychological effect is supposed to help "to create a general public attitude more harmonious with the basic objectives of a program." For example, Thompson notes the gasoline-rationing program of the Office of Price Administration during World War II, in which the OPA maintained an official attitude of pessimism regarding the supply of gasoline in order to induce people to accept the necessity of strict rationing. Similarly, an agency may influence behavior by requiring that applicants meet certain deadlines in order to qualify for favors or benefits or to be eligible for a license or permit. Frequently, the deadline merely suits the convenience of the

28 For a discussion of this, see Graham, "Regulatory Administration," *op.cit.*, pp. 18-20.

agency and can be described in this sense as a "method of influencing behavior by bluff."[29]

The third general method of influencing human behavior in the direction of compliance with public regulations is the development of programs for educating the regulated to comply and for punishing those who do not. Educational and trade relations activities are essential in a regulatory program which affects a large number of people. Educational programs in themselves will not be effective unless an agency has the will and the authority to apply sanctions against violators.

Each regulatory agency is presumably concerned with the problem of how to secure the desired behavior of regulated groups. The regulatory agency must make predictions as to the likelihood that a particular rule or method will induce such behavior. To this extent the regulatory process must be concerned both with goals and with techniques of securing cooperative responses along the desired lines from regulated groups.

## Regulation as an Area of Policy Making

From a functional point of view the regulatory process can be considered as a broad area of policy making. The several functional parts of the policy-determining process can be enumerated.

Goals and standards are indispensable requirements of an effective regulatory program. However, the problem of defining them remains one of the most complex and difficult tasks to be faced. Some of the difficulties have already been noted. Regulation often deals with matters about which there is no settled national policy and no stable communal consensus. A regulatory statute, more likely than not, represents a vaguely worded compromise of conflicting attitudes in Congress as well as the country. It is accepted as a basis for commencing regulation but does not furnish a workable set of goals and policies.

[29] Thompson, *The Regulatory Process in OPA Rationing, op.cit.,* pp. 27-30.

Standards and goals of regulation are never permanently fixed and usually outlive their usefulness and timeliness. Once they are established, they tend to become accepted as basic elements of public regulation. Efforts to modify the standards and objectives of social control are usually resisted by groups that have made a satisfactory adjustment to existing ones. Continuous redefinition of goals and standards is necessary to enable the agency to keep abreast of rapid changes in industrial development and economic organization. Even if an agency takes the initiative in modifying its goals and standards, it must still face the task of securing legislative revision. Because regulation tends to develop by fits and starts, its goals and standards are rarely appropriate to current economic, industrial, financial, and technological conditions.

The task of securing continuing revision of goals and standards points up the vital function of planning the regulatory program. No agency finds a regulatory recipe or formula ready-made for its use. There is no escaping the task of developing basic policy goals, devising appropriate methods and techniques of regulation, and identifying the public interest in the maze of private interests which clamor for favorable attention and legitimacy. To develop intiative in these matters, an agency must maximize its foresight and its grasp of the social and political setting of regulation. It must undertake immediately the job of winning the consent of the regulated and of the general public to its program. According to William O. Douglas, "The battle will be won only by constantly progressive administrative standards quickly and surely applied and delicately adjusted to requirements of particular cases."[30]

The planning capacity of a commission is closely related to its ability to maintain a spirit of initiative and an aggressive search for the public interest. But to note the significance of these factors is also to note the great obstacle

[30] Douglas, *op.cit.*, p. 252.

to satisfactory achievement. Administrative regulation developed partly in response to the demand for timely, speedy, and responsible public action, but these advantages are frequently lacking. One of the features of American political experience has been the relative ease with which the regulatory mold becomes firmly fixed in the early stages of regulation and the universal tendency of regulatory agencies to glorify the judicial pattern of operation. Initiative gives way to passivity. Aggressive search for the public interest is replaced by cold neutrality toward the public purposes of regulation. Planning is a vital necessity, but at the same time it is apt to be conspicuous by its absence.

The tools of regulation are paper, forms, and procedures.[31] They must be carefully designed to aid in the constructive handling of business. The policy-making task of an agency is tied directly to the available methods for accumulating and analyzing data, for giving due consideration to the views of the parties in interest, and for weighing the factors which bear on the public interest. A regulatory agency cannot rise above the level of development of its methods. In this sense, housekeeping and management become essential ingredients in the process of policy formulation.

Given the controversial character of regulatory policy, the determination of relevant facts also becomes highly controversial. Facts must be deduced from evidence which is often conflicting and possibly obscure. They are frequently in dispute, especially when they are likely to be key elements in the policy decision. Private parties may be reluctant to submit evidence to the agency, and they often become adept at concealing or distorting the data. The fact-finding process, moreover, is delicate and tedious. It involves such things as examination, analysis, and auditing of reports; inspection of property and other tangible items; receipt and study of applications, petitions, and other docu-

[31] See Charles S. Hyneman, *Bureaucracy in a Democracy*, Harper and Brothers, New York, 1950, pp. 507-508.

ments; and conduct of hearings and cross-examination of witnesses.

The fact-finding process may be accompanied by attempts of the regulated to soften up the agency in order to make it more responsive to their wishes. At the worst extreme, regulated groups may attempt to bribe experts to make their evidence suit the demands of the private parties. Unlike a regulatory agency, regulated groups do not necessarily restrict themselves to methods permitted by law. For example, they may resort to subterfuge, distortion, and concealment to color the evidence. They may stimulate a campaign of propaganda to make the environment of the regulatory agency as hostile as possible to the careful examination of the evidence. The point is that fact finding is a complex rather than a simple process. It does not permit an agency to rely on the untested data submitted in evidence by the private parties. It is a process which requires alertness and vigilance as well as ingenuity and technical competence. Above all, it requires integrity, fairness, sound judgment, and courage.

The actual processes by which decisions are made have only recently been subject to analysis. Nevertheless, we know enough about decision making to recognize that the traditional picture of a board or commission determining policy in judicial detachment by applying a rule of law or public policy to the facts leaves out of consideration the most influential factors in the process. The values which individuals bring to the job, their sense of identification with the purposes for which their agency or office stands, the symbols of status and prestige which surround their position, their estimate of the balance of forces among the conflicting interests in regulation—all have their part to play in the making of decisions.

### Regulation as a Two-Way Process

Regulation is usually considered to be an effort of a government agency to control the behavior of private parties. However, it is best conceived as a two-way process in which the regulatory agency and the regulated group try to control each other's behavior. To understand the process of regulation, one must examine the activities of the government and the private parties subject to regulation. One of the most useful concepts in this connection is "private government," in the study of which the concepts which have hitherto been reserved for governments are applied to private organizations. Groups which seek to influence the course of regulation need to be studied in terms of their structure of authority, the power which they wield, systems of security designed to maintain their survival, the assignment of duties and responsibilities to various parts of the group, and the development of an organization to administer the program of the group.[32] In the light of the concept of private government, regulation becomes a struggle between public and private governments to write the rules of conduct for regulated industries and industrial practices.

## Conclusion

To sum up: An adequate approach to the regulatory process must be based on the following considerations: (1) Regulation cannot be understood apart from its social and political context. (2) Regulation is not a narrow, self-contained process which can be separated from the main drift of national economic policies. (3) Regulation is an intensely political process. (4) From the point of view of regulated groups, regulation is a process of interaction in which each group interested in regulation attempts to secure for its interest the protection and sanction of public policy. (5) The adjustment which a regulatory agency makes to the demands and activities of the parties in interest is roughly a balance of the forces which affect its political environment, its internal operations, and prevailing attitudes toward public issues. (6) Regulation is an

[32] This concept of private government is applied in a highly suggestive and enlightening manner to the Cement Institute in Earl G. Latham, *The Group Basis of Politics*, Cornell University Press, Ithaca, 1952.

effort to direct the behavior of parties in interest in accordance with prescribed rules of conduct deemed to be in the public interest. (7) Regulation can be viewed functionally as a process of formulating and determining public policy. (8) Finally, regulation can be viewed as a two-way process in which the regulatory agency and the regulated interest attempt to control each other.

There need be no apology for attempting to formulate a realistic approach to the regulatory process. The United States is likely to widen and deepen its experience in regulatory affairs in the future, and further study is required to make regulation a more effective tool in behalf of the public welfare. The study of regulation focuses attention on aspects of the political process which need further investigation, namely, the operation of private government, factors that influence the making of decisions, the maintenance of responsible government, the molding of human behavior according to a democratically determined pattern, the dynamics of group organization and operation, and the character of the political process itself.

There is value, finally, in recalling the judgment of one student of regulatory administration who has found it a fascinating subject: "The processes of government come to a focus under the lens, and it is possible to get a glimpse of the atomic structure of society. Regulation is a social process. It has legal, administrative, and political questions that can be so labeled; but the problems are invariably related to others that form a continuous chain, perhaps an endless chain. Society is not a pyramid with a cap stone of rulers and a mass of ruled, nor is it a layer cake with the governors on top and the governed below. The differences in power, position, wealth, and influence are obvious, but all are governed, regulated, and controlled, even those who govern most. None stands outside the process of social control."[33]

[33] Graham, "Regulatory Administration," *op.cit.*, p. 20.

# CHAPTER 10

# An Appraisal of Regulation
# by Commission

## *The Nature of the Regulatory Process*

REGULATION of business, as has been suggested, is an intensely political process which arouses pervasive antagonisms and bitter disputes. The economic stakes are sufficiently significant to render the control of regulatory practice an important, and sometimes crucial, political objective of regulated groups. Regulatory activities of the government are part and parcel of the political process and are affected by the over-all political environment. Regulatory policies may modify the concept of private property and affect the relative status of organized groups in the American economy. Regulation, in turn, is affected by the formulation of national economic policies and the administration of economic programs by other government agencies, including the programs which aim to promote selected forms of economic enterprise. Regulation, in short, has a relation of interdependence with national economic policies and with promotional programs. It cannot be isolated from the web of economic and political relationships.

Groups whose activities are affected by regulatory programs attempt continuously to influence the course of regulation. Various parties vie with one another in pressing their private interests as worthy of acceptance as the interest of the community at large. A regulatory agency is forced to play a role, either passively or creatively, in the struggle of groups for political and economic advantage, and the regulatory process is a significant area for study of the behavior of organized groups in American politics. Regulatory policies and programs affect the balance of political forces, while the adjustment of relations among rival groups in an industry in turn modifies the course of regulatory developments.

Because of the concern of regulated parties with the process of regulation and their skill in devising methods to influence its evolution, the achievement of regulatory goals, as outlined in enabling legislation by Congress, cannot be taken for granted. The search for the public interest in regulatory matters must be carried on against formidable obstacles. Not only must the agency prevent the use of public power to benefit private interests exclusively, but it must forge a creative role in defining the nature of the public interest.

Regulation is a form of public action which is neither automatic in execution nor simple with respect to technique and procedure. It seeks to influence the behavior of the regulated by indicating certain lines of conduct as being desirable or required and other lines as being undesirable or prohibited. Compliance with regulations must be induced by rational persuasion, economic incentive, fear of punishment for noncompliance, and the formulation of a program which convincingly establishes the nature of the public interest.

Above all, regulation is a process which is neither isolated in its relation to the general political and economic environment nor self-contained in its evolution. The public interest is served best when regulation is conceived as a vital element in the comprehensive relationship between government and the economy. It is served worst when regulation is treated as a phenomenon which is separable from the context of society and therefore unrelated to general notions about the proper relations between government and economic life.

Complexity rather than simplicity marks the regulatory process. The greater the impact of regulation on the regulated groups, the more subtle and complicated the regulatory process becomes. The line between public regulation and private management becomes more difficult to define, and the government's involvement in the affairs of a regulated industry raises increasingly difficult questions of public policy and private right. Whether regulation serves the public interest or enhances private interests, it cannot escape from politics. In a democratic society, policies of regulation are inescapably political.

## Concept of Regulation as Expressed in the Commission Movement

The concept of regulation which emerges from an analysis of the commission movement contrasts strikingly with the concept outlined above. Implicit in the development of the commission movement is the notion that the political process is peculiarly susceptible to fraud and corruption and hence that regulation must repudiate and avoid involvement with politics. Escape from politics is regarded as both desirable and essential to the development of effective regulation. The goal of getting out of politics can be achieved presumably by maintaining the freedom of the regulatory commission from control by the president. Congress regards the independent commission as a government agency which exercises discretionary authority without increasing the power of the executive branch of the government.

The independent commission is considered as an agency with an expert staff, continuing leadership, and freedom from executive domination equipping it to chart regulatory policy with proper regard for the general welfare. Analysis of technical problems and impartial application of reasonable regulatory rules to uncontroverted facts are considered tasks for experts and for commissioners who remain independent of the president. On the one hand, regulation is considered to be so complex that the commission's success hinges on the recruitment of qualified technical experts and direction by commissioners whose manner of appointment assures stability and continuity of policy. On the other hand, relevant facts presumably are readily available. Hence methods and techniques are regarded as simple rather than complex. The experts are expected to function satisfactorily so long as they remain free from partisan influence and presidential domination.

While the commission has been supported as a device for overcoming the deficiencies of courts and legislative bodies as agents of regulation, its chief backing has come from those who hope to convert the commission into an administrative tribunal conceived in the image of the courts. The independence of the courts, so highly cherished in the American political experience, became a model for the commission to emulate, and judicial procedure was adopted by commissions as the only satisfactory means of achieving impartiality and objectivity in deciding regulatory controversies.

The commission movement rejects the idea of the interdependence of economic policies and regulatory and promotional programs affecting the economy. While broadly conceived economic policies and promotional programs are regarded as necessarily having to be administered by executive agencies, regulatory policies, it is held, must be administered by agencies that remain uninfluenced by other governmental activities. Independence, in practice, means that the commissions are enjoined not to consider the impact of their decisions on other industries and industrial practices or the economy as a whole, nor are the commissions supposed to give much consideration to national economic policies in the exercise of their regulatory authority. Regulation, therefore, is narrow in scope, self-contained, and separable both from the political process and from the political and economic framework of society.

In the traditional concept of regulation by commission, the achievement of impartiality seems to be incompatible with the development of political responsibility. While commission theory acknowledges the responsibility of the commission to Congress, almost no consideration is given to strengthening that responsibility. Congress, in practice, has been more skillful in investigating details of commission regulation than it has been in clarifying regulatory goals and policies and holding commissions accountable for achieving results. Consequently, a commission's responsibility to Congress is ephemeral and inadequate. According to the concept of regulation by commission, salvation lies not in democratic accountability of the commission to the president and Congress but rather in unfettered and impartial administration by experts under the stable and continuing direction of judgelike commissioners.

There is little or no room in the concept of regulation by commission for consideration of psychological factors concerning the control of human behavior or the role of the commission in the process of adjustment among the various regulated groups. The ability of the expert staff of commissions, as well as the commissioners, to avoid favoritism to private parties and to remain aloof from the regulated interests is taken for granted. The notion of regulation as a two-way process in which the regulatory commission and the regulated group try to control each other is alien to the commission movement. With its emphasis on impartial adjudication and settlement of regulatory controversies, the commission movement has betrayed almost no recognition of the dynamic activity of organized groups in the political process.

### Requirements of Effective Regulation of Business

Given the nature of the regulatory process and the controversial character of governmental regulation, the requirements of effective regulation of business in the public interest are formidable and difficult to achieve. All of the requirements cannot be met by a regulatory agency all or even most of the time. Nevertheless, some approximate achievement of most of the requirements is a necessary prerequisite to satisfactory regulatory performance. The requirements may be summarized briefly.

POLITICAL LEADERSHIP

Strong political leadership is basic to regulatory success. Without the backing of political leaders in the legislative and executive branches of the government, a regulatory agency will be unable to make significant headway against the opposition of the regulated interests. The failure of political leaders to formulate regulatory goals and give support to regulatory policies paves the way for acceptance by the agency of the philosophy and values as well as specific regulatory proposals of the affected groups. It is sentimental and useless to deplore the alleged lack of public spirit and concern for the public welfare on the part of regulated interests. Unless the public interest has alert and politically powerful spokesmen who promote and protect it, regulated groups cannot be expected to give precedence in their own affairs to vaguely defined policies supposedly in that interest. Given the unorganized state of the general public, only effective political leadership can mobilize democratically the consensus of the community in behalf of regulation in the public interest.

POPULAR SUPPORT

The corollary of political leadership is popular political support. Political leadership is indispensable to public understanding of issues concerning the proper relations between government and business, the elimination of abusive economic practices, the mobilization of national economic strength for national security, recovery from depression, and maintenance of a viable, prosperous economy. As governmental regulation becomes more interdependent with national economic policies and with policies of promoting business enterprise, the task of educating the citizen on public economic questions becomes increasingly complex. Overcoming popular apathy and lack of understanding concerning such matters is an essential factor in constructing a suitable framework for governmental regulation of business. Without the sustained interest of a majority of voters, the public interest is neglected and a regulatory agency is ripe for capture by the regulated groups.

## CLEAR LEGISLATIVE MANDATE

A closely related requirement is the formulation of a clear legislative mandate reflecting the consensus of the community and supported and nourished by strong legislative backing. Such a mandate is needed not only to illumine the broad outlines of the public interest in governmental regulation of business but also to provide the necessary guides for administrative regulation. In the absence of legislative declaration of goals which regulatory policy should follow, a regulatory agency will function without benefit of political compass and without adequate intelligence or supply lines. Unfortunately, the clarity of the legislative mandate can never be more than approximate. So long as regulation of business remains one of the most controversial issues of public policy in American political life, legislative decisions on regulatory issues will inevitably represent compromises among major forces in society and will be stated in terms which are likely to be internally inconsistent and misleading. And it is too much to expect that the staff of a regulatory agency, no matter how expert it may become, will chart the evolution of regulatory policy along lines which will promote the public interest unless it is provided with a public policy sanctioned by Congress, actively promoted by the president, and affirmatively supported and sustained by an organized public.

## POLICY INTEGRATION

In view of the intertwining relations among regulatory programs, promotional programs, and national economic policies, integration is essential. Integration makes it possible to relate regulatory and other economic policies so that regulation can contribute to national economic objectives. Regulation of any industry or industrial practice may have the effect of promoting other kinds of economic activity, and promotion of one industry may have regulatory effects on other industries. Consequently, no regulatory agency can afford to regard its economic environment as insulated against outside influences, such as the activities of other government agencies dealing with economic matters.

The Presidency is not necessarily a secure source of political strength and superior wisdom on regulatory matters. A regulatory agency needs the support of the chief executive, but it also needs to bolster the political leadership of the president on behalf of effective regulation. Each must draw support and encouragement from the other and help to broaden the perspective and technical competence of the government. Through a closer association with other government bodies, a regulatory agency may risk loss of prestige and destruction of continuity and stability of policy as a result of national political changes. But it will also have an opportunity to secure the benefits of political leadership, popular support, and policy integration, and at the same time increase its usefulness and significance in the area of economic policy.

ACCEPTANCE OF REGULATION AS LEGITIMATE
GOVERNMENTAL ACTIVITY

The close relationship between governmental regulation and private management and the detailed nature of modern regulatory practice make for constant and intimate contact between a regulatory agency and the regulated industry. While an agency may be able to make its way for some time against the opposition of regulated groups, it cannot in the long run expect to develop an effective program unless those groups agree that social control of industry is a legitimate area of governmental activity in a democratic society. If public demand for regulation is rejected by private parties, the public is likely to demand governmental ownership and operation as the only practical alternative.

OFFERING INCENTIVES FOR COMPLIANCE

The seemingly adverse impact of regulation on regulated enterprises can be offset by offering them some positive incentive to promote acceptability of a regulatory program and compliance with it. Cooperation with government agencies that administer programs of financial and other governmental assistance to private business may provide appropriate opportunities to couple promotional programs with regulation and provide inducements to regulated industries to comply voluntarily with government regulations. The association of regulatory administration with governmental powers to promote economic stability, raise revenue, assist industrial development, purchase goods and services, and provide for national security may place regulatory programs in a broader perspective and make government appear less as a policeman and more as a guardian of the public interest in a productive economy.

### MAINTENANCE OF POLITICAL RESPONSIBILITY

The political goal of a democracy is not good government but self-government. It is not sufficient that public institutions operate well in the sense that the material results of their activity are valuable and praiseworhy and contribute to the public welfare. They must also act responsibly and be accountable for their activities and policies to the political branches of the government and through them to the citizens. A benevolent paternalism or an "efficient" dictatorship cannot be accepted by the theory of democracy as a substitute for the political responsibility of elected public officials. Ultimate responsibility for major regulatory policies must be asserted by the legislative and executive branches on behalf of the electorate.

### ECONOMY OF COERCION

A regulatory program should reduce the element of coercion in regulation to the minimum consistent with public goals. Unnecessary burdens should not be placed upon the regulated parties, and compliance with regulations should be expedited as much as possible. Regulation for its own sake must be avoided at all costs, and individuals who like to impose controls over business as a pleasurable manner of influencing human behavior should not be employed in regulatory agencies.

In order to reduce the administrative burden undertaken by a regulatory agency, its supervisory and restrictive activities should be minimized. In a democratic society governmental institutions can scarcely rise above the general level of morality, ethics, and values of the community at large, and governmental administration rarely surpasses prevailing levels of private business efficiency. Regulation is so complex and difficult that the burden assumed by the government should be as limited as the achievement of the public interest permits.

ABLE ADMINISTRATIVE DIRECTION

The need for competent, imaginative, and courageous administrative direction is so obvious that extended comment is gratuitous. The commission movement tends to disparage the aggressive search for the public interest and to prefer a neutral and rather passive type of direction. The heads of administrative agencies should be fair-minded and independent in judgment, but they should not be neutral concerning the legislative mandate of the agency. They should be able to match the officials of regulated businesses in ingenuity, drive, and imagination without sacrificing devotion to the public interest.

EFFECTIVE ORGANIZATION AND MANAGEMENT

The organization of a regulatory agency should be appropriate not only to the work of adjudicating individual cases but also to planning and providing adequate direction for the program. The debilitating effects of professionalism should be avoided in arranging the structure of organization and controlling the flow of work in an agency. The unfortunate distinction between so-called executive-type work and regulatory activity should not be carried to the point of understating the need for effective direction of the day-to-day activities of the agency, for delegation of adequate authority to major officials, for development of appropriate methods and techniques of regulation, and for the progressive improvement of the staff. Analogies to judicial proceedings in courts should not be accepted as realistic indications of the nature of the regulatory process.

### FAIRNESS AND JUSTICE IN ADMINISTRATIVE ADJUDICATION

In order to command respect, win the support of the judiciary, and deal equitably with regulated persons and groups, a regulatory agency must adopt acceptable standards of fair procedure for rule making and adjudication. A reasonable separation of the functions of judge and prosecutor is essential, although such separation cannot be counted upon to forestall criticism of regulatory methods and policies. There must be adequate legal safeguards against arbitrary, capricious, and unreasonable action. In the American environment the court of law has been the required model for administrative adjudication and will undoubtedly remain so. A judicialized process of adjudication is not incompatible with effective regulation provided adjudication is treated as only one aspect of regulatory administration.

### COMPLIANCE AND ENFORCEMENT

Voluntary compliance with regulations cannot be taken for granted. The agency must use all of its resources to publicize its regulations, explain their meaning, teach regulated groups how to comply, and win the consent of the parties affected by regulatory controls. The agency must also be prepared to discover instances of violation and to dispose of these cases by the application of appropriate sanctions. Habits of noncompliance must be forestalled and corrected and the fringe of flagrant violators punished. The agency will have to work closely with the Department of Justice and the United States attorneys in order to promote understanding of its program and to secure adequate service in litigating appropriate cases of violation in the courts. Sanctions should be appropriate to the types of violations, and an agency should have some authority to apply sanctions administratively in certain cases of violation.

REGULATORY REVISION

There must be progressive revision of regulatory goals, policies, and methods in order to keep pace with technological and industrial developments and changes in democratic political goals. Regulatory agencies must work closely with Congressional committees and with the Executive Office of the President in order to capitalize on opportunities for legislative action to improve regulatory statutes by plugging loopholes in the regulatory process, by strengthening administrative resources, or by adding statutory amendments to take account of new developments.

## The Commission and the Requirements of Effective Regulation

To what extent does the independent regulatory commission meet the requirements of effective regulation of business in the public interest? And to what extent does the commission exhibit the qualities and characteristics which its advocates claim for it?

Given the nonpolitical approach of those advocates, the commission tends to insulate itself from the government as a whole. It tends to deplore presidential support and interest even though its political survival and regulatory effectiveness are heavily dependent upon the president's leadership. The commission tends to rely upon the presumed expertness of its staff rather than political leadership and widespread popular support for effective regulation. The commission's activity does not have an educative effect upon the public, which scarcely comprehends the detail of regulatory administration. Nor is the public encouraged to maintain interest and concern in regulatory problems. The fear of control by the executive usually leaves a commission without the political strength and stamina needed to balance the advice and counsel of the regulated groups. Insulation from sources of popular political strength is matched by close relations with the regulated groups.

A commission's capacity for securing clarification of its legislative mandate normally is severely limited. Periods of regulatory advance are those in which a strong president is able to command the support of a legislative majority in Congress and an aroused public demands regulatory reform. While commissions frequently recommend legislative amendments to the appropriate Congressional committees, they have had little success in obtaining progressive revision of their statutes. They have been unable to mobilize the necessary political support for the enactment of legislation in controversial areas of public policy. It has not been sufficient that a proposed amendment is firmly rooted in the regulatory experience of a commission and in the expert judgment of its staff. Congress is more apt to be impressed with popular clamor for action than with expert recommendations.

The emphasis upon independence of commissions from presidential control establishes major obstacles to the integration of regulatory policy into the total content of governmental economic policy. Indeed, commissions take pride in the development of a high degree of specialism and expertness in a narrow field of regulation and regard suggestions to relate regulatory policies to other economic programs of the government as destructive of the objectivity and impartiality of regulation by commission. The implicit denial of the interdependence of economic activity leads to the fragmentation of the regulatory process. The effectiveness of regulation becomes restricted by its lack of consistency and integration with the broad outlines of economic policy, and the efficiency of a commission in its own specialized area of regulation declines. Its regulatory program does not benefit from the experience of other agencies, and its own experience is not made available to them. The political insularity of the commission may make it hazardous for the president to give it much support.

The commissions' record of political responsibility is unsatisfactory. While it is an exaggeration to describe commissions as a "headless fourth branch of the government," their political accountability is seriously deficient. In theory the president assumes no responsibility for the activities and policies of commissions, which are supposed to look to Congress for policy direction and control. However, the lack of clarity in the legislative mandate, the divisive nature of regulatory policy, and the inadequate development of responsible legislative practices nullify accountability to Congress to a considerable extent. A commission tends to be responsible more to the chairmen of the applicable committees in the Senate and the House of Representatives than to Congress as a whole.

Apart from the relations between commissions and Congress, the theory upon which the independence of the commission is based represents a serious danger to the growth of political democracy in the United States. The dogma of independence encourages support of the naïve notion of escape from politics and substitution of the voice of the expert for the voice of the people. Expertness is made to appear incompatible with the democratic political process instead of as a necessary complement to the development of political democracy. Because it is based upon a mistaken concept of the political process which undermines the political theory of democracy, the commission has significant antidemocratic implications.

Commissions have shown little understanding of the need for promotion of voluntary compliance with, and for vigorous enforcement of, their regulations. The growth of passivity in the process of regulation by commission tends to dilute and eventually destroy the assertion of regulatory initiative by the commissions. The comforts afforded by judicialized procedure and the role of administrative tribunal are more highly regarded by commissions than searching for the public interest in regulatory policies, winning the consent of the regulated to a vigorous program of regulation, and enforcing regulations in a manner which deters violations and maintains the integrity of the program.

Administratively, commissions leave much to be desired. Plural direction by a board of commissioners tends to stress adjudicatory functions rather than continuing administrative direction and control. The lack of adequate management in turn becomes reflected in declining appropriations, mounting backlogs of work, inability to keep abreast of technological and industrial trends, and the development of a type of professionalism which jealously seeks to promote the position of particular professional staff groups instead of devising more effective and efficient methods of transacting regulatory business. There is some indication that the designation of the chairman of the commission by the president and the vesting of considerable administrative responsibility in the chairman may improve the administrative performance of the commissions, but it is not possible to generalize about this development until further experience is available.

With respect to the achievement of fairness and equity in administrative adjudication the record of commissions is good. The major problems in this area deal not with fairness to the private parties but with the tendency to overjudicialize procedures. Commissions have generally attained a satisfactory internal separation of the functions of judge and prosecutor, although they and the Civil Service Commission are still faced with difficulties in administering the hearing examiner provisions of the Administrative Procedure Act.

For the reasons noted above, the commissions have not been satisfactory instruments of governmental regulation of business. They have been founded on a basically undemocratic concept of the political process and have helped to perpetuate naïve notions about regulation of business, the virtues of group decision, and the uses of expertness.

By insulating themselves from popular political forces, the commissions have subjected themselves to undue influence from the regulated groups and tend to become protective spokesmen for the industries which they regulate. By virtue of their emphasis upon formal procedures of adjudication, commissions gradually forsake the vigorous search for the public interest for the role of administrative tribunal.

Not only do the commissions fail to fulfill the requirements of effective regulation, but they also have been unable to develop the advantages claimed for regulation by commission. As stated most recently by the Task Force on Regulatory Commissions of the Hoover Commission, the independent regulatory agency is deemed useful and desirable when the following conditions are required for effective regulation: constant adaptation to changing conditions; delegation of wide discretion in administration; a means for insulation from partisan influence or favoritism; deliberation, expertness, and continuity of attention to regulatory matters; and combining adaptability with consistency of policy. The record of the commissions does not substantiate these sweeping generalizations. They have been singularly uninventive and unadaptable. The commission form tends to enthrone not adaptability and consistency of policy, but apathy and passiveness. It increases opportunities for the exercise of influence by regulated groups and minimizes the impact of the democratic political process upon regulation. Where continuity of attention and stability of policy have prevailed, they have tended to reflect inability to adapt to changing conditions. Commissions appear to have no unique qualities which enable their staffs to rise above the general level of competence in government agencies. While commissions exercise broad discretion in regulatory matters, the devices and institutions available for maintaining their political accountability are unsatisfactory. Consequently, their wide scope of discretion is not controlled by firm lines of responsibility.

Regulation of business is one of the most distinctive activities of American government. No other nation has attempted to control economic activities and business operations through independent commissions on a comparable scale. No other country has placed as much confidence in governmental regulation as opposed to public ownership and management, viewing such regulation as a means of promoting the public interest and maintaining an economy in which the major decisions continue to be made by private persons and firms instead of public officials. Despite prolonged political agitation over regulation and the controversial nature of such activity, regulation by commission has not been able to match the ingenuity, imagination, and inventiveness of American business. It has been conventional in method, passive in attitude, and orthodox in the evolution of policy.

The persistence of myths about the qualities of independent commissions endangers the achievement of effective regulation of business in the public interest. Commissions have proved to be more susceptible to private pressures, to manipulation for private purposes, and to administrative and public apathy than other types of governmental organizations. They have lacked an affirmative concept of the public interest; they have failed to meet the test of political responsibility in a democratic society; and they tend to define the interests of the regulated groups as the public interest. The effectiveness of regulation of business by commission hangs by a thin thread. As a method for ordering economic relations in society short of governmental ownership and operation, it has not proved itself.

For the immediate future there appears to be little likelihood that the United States will turn to public ownership and operation of utilities and other industries as a basic alternative to governmental regulation of private economic affairs. In view of the American reliance upon governmental regulation as a major process for adjusting human relations in a capitalist economy, it is essential to develop new forms, techniques, and ideas which are adapted to a more realistic concept of the regulatory process. Governmental regulation cannot in the long run remain an effective alternative to other ways of controlling economic life unless the nature of the regulatory process is more fully grasped.

# INDEX

Addams, Jane: 43-44
Adjudication (see also Procedural due process; Litigation and legal functions): fairness and justice in, 290; general discussion, 188-216; incompatible with executive functions? 212-216; separable from management? 256-257
Administration of regulatory statutes: essential requirements of, 288-290; internal management problems, 172-175; lack of concern with, 83; multiple direction of commissions, 172-174; obsolescence of procedures and objectives, 100; organizational responsibility for enforcement, 235-238; problems of, 58, 89-90, 93-94, 276
"Administrative absolutism": 54, 72, 209
Administrative Procedure Act: 69, 98, 192-211
Administrative regulation: see Government regulation of economic life; Independent regulatory commission
American Bar Association: administrative law committee of, 57; attitude toward government regulation, 16, 32; campaign in 1930's to check growth of administrative discretion, 53-54; reform of administrative adjudication, 188-195, 197, 211
Appleby, Paul: 73, 115, 124, 129, 160-161, 162
Appointment of commissioners: 51-52, 106-107, 109-113, 148
Attorney General of the United States: 199
Attorney General's Committee on Administrative Procedure: 65

Barkley, Alben W.: 136
Bauer, John: 182-183
Bazelon, Judge: 203
Bias: 169-171, 185

Bipartisanship in membership of commissions: argument during debate on Interstate Commerce Act of 1887, 25; general experience, 104; legal requirement of, 9-11
Blue-sky laws: 78
Board of Examiners: 196-199
Board of Investigation and Research: 103, 106-107, 129, 142-143, 165-166, 178-182
Brandeis, Louis: 39, 50, 52, 78
Brewer, J. David: 30-32
Brownlow, Louis: 23, 92, 132-133, 157-158
Buck, Solon: 20
Bureau of the Budget: 68, 90, 93, 137, 144-145, 147-148, 175
Business community: attitude toward commissions, 56-57
Byrd Committee: 128-129

Canadian Wartime Prices and Trade Board: 227-228
Carey, William D.: 115, 119, 138-139, 173
Chairmen of commissions, appointed by president: 131, 132, 134-137, 172-174
Charlesworth, James C.: 84, 193
Civil Aeronautics Board: 8, 11, 53, 105, 131, 210-211, 214-215, 222, 225, 230, 237-238, 243
Civil Service: 8, 26, 131, 196-209
Clark, John Maurice: 128
Clientalism, clientele influence: 146, 177, 217-219, 270-271
Clinard, Marshall B.: 230
Commissions: see Independent regulatory commissions
Commissioners (see also Appointment of commissioners): age of, 104-105; characteristics of, 104-109; charged with bias, 169-171; influenced by regulated groups, 82, 83, 98; procedures used in making decisions, 211-212; qualifications analyzed, 38, 103-109; rec-

299

ord of state commissioners, 69; relations with staff, 174-176; removal by president, 9, 11; salaries of, compared with those of other officials, 9, 11; Securities and Exchange Commission, 79; staggered terms of, 107-109; tenure, 105-106, 107

Committee on Ministers' Powers: 168

Communications Act Amendments, 1952: 203-204

Community participation in regulatory administration: 234-235

Compliance (see also Enforcement): activities to promote, 231-235; Croly's views, 43; encouraged by coordination of government economic policy, 221-223; incentives for, 218-220, 272, 287-288; inducement of, 271-274; promoting voluntary, 223-224, 274; relation to enforcement, 223-224; requirements of effective, 290-291; as test of effectiveness of a commission, 217-249

Congress: action on Interstate Commerce Act, 21-25, 77-78; appropriations for commissions, 68, 90, 93; attitude on hearing examiners, 188-216; attitude toward commissions, 4, 35, 53, 56-57, 83, 89, 90, 101, 130-131, 133-134, 136, 165-166; Byrd Committee, 128-129; Cullom Committee, 22-23, 77; Eastman's view of commission's relation to, 51; enactment of regulatory statutes by, 77, 96; investigations of FCC, 86; Joint Committee on the Economic Report, 68-69; obstacles to rational action by, 261-262; opposed to policy integration, 165-168; refusal to reorganize the ICC, 134-137; resolving conflicts in regulatory policy, 260; responsibility of commissions to, 79, 150-154; Senate Committee on Labor and Public Welfare, 92, 94; vague standards in regulatory statutes enacted by, 56, 263-264, 286; views of Speaker Rayburn, 67

Continuity in regulatory policy: see Stability in regulatory policy

Cooley, Thomas M., first chairman of the ICC: 29, 32-35, 134

Coolidge, President Calvin: 110, 132

Cooper, Robert M.: 259

Coordination of economic policy: general comments, 54-55, 143; interdependence of regulatory controls, 221-223; need for, 163; OPA-ICC conflict during World War II, 68; policy integration, 164-168; recommendations of President's Committee on Administrative Management, 58; regulatory and promotional policies, 55, 254-255; relation of expertness to, 117-118; relation to compliance and enforcement, 219-220; Roosevelt-Eastman exchange, 63-64

Council of Economic Advisers: 68-69

Coy, Wayne: 159-160

Crawford, Finla G.: 58, 254

Croly, Herbert: attitude on expertness, 113-114, 115; criticism of commissions, 41-43, 75, 253; views on role of lawyers in American politics, 15

Cross sanctions: 244-247

Cullom Committee: 22-23, 77

Cushman, Robert M.: 22-23, 24-25, 110-111, 116, 177-178

Davis, Kenneth C.: 69-70, 80, 88, 95, 101, 171, 174

Department of Justice: 240-243

Deportation proceedings: 206

Depression of the 1930's: 53, 57, 78, 164

Dickinson, John: 195

Dooley, Mr.: 46-47

Douglas, Senator Paul: 92, 158-160

Douglas, William O.: 65, 251, 261, 267, 275

Drafting regulations: 226-230

Dunn, Samuel: 37-39

Dunne, Finley Peter: 46-47

Eastman, Joseph B.: attitude toward commissions in 1920's, 51-52; ca-

Interstate Commerce Commission: appointment of commissioners, 106; arguments favoring its creation, 24; arguments opposing its creation, 24-25; Brownlow's story, 132-133; characteristics of ICC operation, 1887-1906, 26-35; conflict with OPA, 68; development of, 1887 to 1906, 21-35, 264-265; Eastman's views on, 61-64, 116; enforcement record of, 222, 225, 226, 230, 237-238, 239, 242-243, 248; established in 1887, 17; expanded authority under Transportation Act of 1920, 49; as expression of *laissez faire*, 84; hearing examiners in, 198, 206-207; Hoover's attitude toward, 110-111; as model of independence from executive control, 134-135; multiple direction of, 173-174; Olney-Perkins correspondence, 264-265; originally in Department of the Interior, 8, 23; as part of structure of railroad industry, 254; pattern of regulation in, 74, 254; period of gestation of, 77-78; planning by, 178; quality of commissioners in 1920's, 52, 106; Reorganization Plan No. 7 of 1950, 134-137; as referee of disputes between railroads and shippers, 83-84; report of National Transportation Committee, 58-59; revocation of motor carrier certificates, 210; Roosevelt-Eastman exchange, 63-64; safety regulation by, 214-215; Sharfman's study, 64; in stage of maturity, 90-91; tenure of commissioners of, 105, 108; views of Justice Holmes, 40; views of Speaker Rayburn, 67

ICC v. Alabama Midland Ry. Co.: 28

Investigations of alleged violations of regulations: 223, 229, 235-238

Investment Trust Bill: 56

Jackson, Robert H.: 194
Jaffe, Louis: 169
Jennings, W. Ivor: 170
Johnson, Senator Edwin C.: 135-137

Joint Committee on the Economic Report: 68-69

Judicial pattern of regulation by commission: 28-29, 34-35, 72, 89, 101, 134, 170-171, 174, 179-182, 188-195, 209-210, 242, 261-262, 270, 290

Judicial review of administrative decisions: attitude of American Bar Association, 54; by special administrative court, 54; widening scope of, 96-97

"Keeping regulation out of politics" see "Taking regulation out of politics"

Kerr, William D.: 81

*Laissez faire*: as bias in American political thinking, 13, 126-127; as doctrine of limited state intervention in economic affairs, 20-21, 84

Landis, James: 64-65, 119, 140-141, 149-150, 166, 244

Laski, Harold: 120-122

Latham, Earl G.: 76, 278

Laws, Judge Bolitha: 202, 204

Lawyers in American politics: American Bar Association, 16; ascendancy in regulatory administration, 115; bias toward regulation, 127; drive for uniform procedures, 188-195; hostility toward administrative adjudication, 194; as professional group, 118-120; views of Herbert Croly, 15

Leiserson, Avery: 233, 262

Lilienthal, David: 122-123

Lindsay, A. D. (Lord Lindsay of Birker): 120

Litigation and legal functions of commissions: 81-82, 83, 116-117, 127, 240-242

Loyalty program: 204-205

Lyon, L. S., Watkins, M. W., and Abramson, V.: 65

McCarran, Senator Pat: 192, 200
McKeough, Raymond S.: 255-256
Mansfield, Harvey: 52, 104, 106